Floods
Upon the
Dry
Ground

**Giving Foundation and Understanding to the
Progressive Move of the Holy Spirit in the Earth**

Floods
Upon the
Dry
Ground

Giving Foundation and Understanding to the
Progressive Move of the Holy Spirit in the Earth

Charles P. Schmitt

Revival Press

An Imprint of
Destiny Image® **Publishers, Inc.**
P.O. Box 310
Shippensburg, PA 17257-0310

ISBN 0-7684-2012-1

For Worldwide Distribution
Printed in the U.S.A.

First Printing: 1998   Second Printing: 1999

This book and all other Destiny Image, Revival Press,
and Treasure House books are available
at Christian bookstores and distributors worldwide.

For a U.S. bookstore nearest you, call **1-800-722-6774**.
For more information on foreign distributors, call **717-532-3040**.
Or reach us on the Internet: **http://www.reapernet.com**

Cover photo by Charles P. Schmitt, August 1997
Banff National Park, Alberta, Canada

Dedication

*This book is dedicated to those who
hunger and thirst after righteousness.
They shall be filled!*

*"For I will pour water upon him that is thirsty,
and floods upon the dry ground:
I **will** pour* [out] *My spirit....*
[promises the Lord]" (Isaiah 44:3 KJV).

Discussion Questions for each chapter are available for classroom or study group use. They may be obtained from Immanuel's Church website (www.immanuels.org) or by writing Immanuel's Church—16819 New Hampshire Ave., Silver Spring, MD 20905.

Acknowledgments

The psalmist admonished, "Let this be written for a future generation, that a people not yet created may praise the Lord" (Ps. 102:18 NIV). This shows that we do have some scriptural encouragement to write down the history of God's dealings with His people—that we and future generations might praise the Lord.

In this present updating and rewriting of my earlier book, *Root Out of a Dry Ground,* I have again found myself grateful for those who had written before me. In my own sense of deep indebtedness I felt somewhat like the historian Luke:

> *Many have undertaken to draw up an account of the things that have been fulfilled among us, just as they were handed down to us by those who from the first were eyewitnesses and servants of the word. Therefore...it seemed good also to me to write an orderly account...* (Luke 1:1-3 NIV).

I have, consequently, borrowed from those who have written before me, even as they, in turn, borrowed from those who wrote before them, who, in turn, borrowed from those who wrote before them, and so on, right back to the very eyewitnesses from whom we now all draw and quote.

My understandings and writings have been greatly influenced by five writers of history—two from past days and three from contemporary times.

A History of the Christian Church by Lars P. Qualben of St. Olaf College was the first Church history book I studied. Qualben's text was the one used at Prairie Bible College in Alberta, Canada. Consequently, you will find Qualben's influence all over this book. Through my wife, Dotty, I was then later introduced to *A History of the Christian Church* by Williston Walker of Yale University. Walker's was the text from which Dotty had studied at Biblical Seminary in New York, and his fresh and honest approach, particularly on difficult historical issues, was a delight to my inquiring mind. Thus, these two books became the main footings for my original work, *Root Out of a Dry Ground.*

When Destiny Image Publishers first contacted me in the Spring of 1997 about updating the original book, I felt I needed good resource material, especially for the latter part of the twentieth century. Three volumes then came across my desk by the sovereign providence of our Lord. I have spoken personally with all three of these authors, and each were pleased to have me quote from them and utilize their scholarship in this current volume. I am deeply indebted to Richard M. Riss and the excellent insights gleaned from his book, *A Survey of 20th-Century Revival Movements in North America.* It is excellent! *The Holiness-Pentecostal Tradition* by Vinson Synan of Regent University became my second invaluable resource. (I think his volume is worth its weight in gold!) Then, *2000 Years of Charismatic Christianity* by Eddie L. Hyatt inspired me to rethink, not only my original treatment of the twentieth century, but my original treatment of the whole of Church history. Hyatt opened my eyes to the amazing fact that even when the spiritual tide was at its lowest, our Lord was pleased to pour out His Spirit upon the dry ground in answer to the cries of His believing people. Out of the insights gained from Hyatt's book, *Root Out of a Dry Ground* was soon re-christened *Floods Upon the Dry Ground.*

I owe much to the excellent scholarship of Hyatt, Synan, and Riss, as well as to that of other historians and authors, including Philip Schaff, Lewis Drummond, Brian H. Edwards, Bishop Ithiel C. Clemmons, William E. Allen, Arthur Wallis, Cheryl J. Sanders, co-authors Timothy K. Beougher and Lyle W. Dorsett, John W. Kennedy, John Greenfield, Colin C. Whittaker, Winkie Pratney, and John White. (A bibliography appears at the end of this volume.)

My final acknowledgments and my sincerest thanks also go to those members of our church staff who made this book a reality. Foremost has been my patient and diligent secretary, Fran Ladson. She entered and reentered these pages so many times that I think she must have memorized the whole book in the process! Without her, there simply would be no book. The computer skills of Dr. Warren Palmer were also an essential ingredient to this volume. And the editing skills of Dr. Aija Ozolins, Linda Walker, and the staff at Destiny Image have contributed to it all coming out correctly. I am grateful to all of these.

A final thanks goes to James Mannarino, whose spiritual roots are in the Mother of God Catholic Charismatic Community, for his help in addressing sensitive issues involving the Catholic Church. One of my concerns has been that my handling of the various sides of the history of the Church would not be viewed as an attack on any religious body. Church history is the history of the Church—my Church, your Church, our Church. As Christians, we share in all the Church's failures as well as in all its triumphs. I trust that spirit comes across in these pages. The sins of the Church confessed herein are our sins, but the glories are ours as well. This is *our* history. In reality this is also *His* story—the history of how He revived His inheritance when it was weary and how He poured out *Floods Upon the Dry Ground*! I praise our Lord Jesus Christ!

Gratefully, in His Name,
Charles P. Schmitt
Immanuel's Church

Endorsements

Charles Schmitt's *Floods Upon the Dry Ground* represents a new generation of Pentecostal/Charismatic historians who now re-interpret all of Church history in light of the Pentecostal and Charismatic movements of the present century. It is a helpful and well-written book that can serve as a textbook for Pentecostal colleges as well as a historical resource for the general reader.

—Vinson Synan
Dean
Regent University School of Divinity

In *Floods Upon the Dry Ground*, Charles Schmitt has produced an excellent survey of Church history from a charismatic/revival perspective. It is a valuable historical resource and will make an excellent text for Church history courses in a variety of settings. It is both scholarly and readable, qualities not often found together, which make it accessible to both academia and the general public.

—Eddie Hyatt
Bible Teacher and Author
2000 Years of
Charismatic Christianity

In *Floods Upon the Dry Ground*, Charles P. Schmitt provides an excellent overview of some of the most important events of Church history. This book is suitable for use as a text in the history of Christianity, but it is far more than that. Because of his appreciation for the various outpourings of the Holy Spirit, both past and present, he has brought Church history to life.

—Richard M. Riss
Author
A Survey of 20th-Century Revival Movements
in North America

Why This Book?

The history of the Christian faith is the most important and intriguing study that one can undertake next to the study of the Holy Scriptures themselves. As with Alex Haley and his novel *Roots,* something within Christians also longs to know the simple facts of their origins. This longing, coupled with the realization that we are presently seeing a most unusual world-wide outpouring of the Holy Spirit in which an understanding of the *Church* has come to be of utmost importance, makes this study expedient indeed!

The definition we are giving to the Church in this study is simple. Biblically, the *Church* is that people of God in whose midst is found *the manifest presence and dynamic activity of Jesus Christ.*

In this light, we shall study the history of the Christian Church with the underlying intent of giving understanding and historical validity for the ongoing move of the Holy Spirit as the most genuine expression of the true life of Christ in His people—that holy, apostolic, catholic Church of our Lord Jesus Christ in all the earth.

This study was originally inspired, under the title *Root Out of a Dry Ground,* by a hearty band who first studied this material in our intense discipleship training sessions in the Fellowship of

Believers in Grand Rapids, Minnesota, in the mid-1970's. My own dear wife was among this band, and her scholarship and inquiring heart continue to be a real inspiration to me.

Some 20 years later, it is now my joy to present to the Body of Christ this new and updated version of the original study under a new and more relevant title: *Floods Upon the Dry Ground.*

Charles P. Schmitt

Contents

Prologue

Where Are We Going?

At the very outset of our study, it is important for us to know that blest end to which our study will take us.

Initially, we will trace the tide of vibrant first-century Christianity. We will then watch as the life of God's people begins to ebb and become a stagnant pool in the Dark Ages, offset only by those sovereign outpourings of the Holy Spirit that the God of all grace was pleased to pour from time to time upon the dry, thirsty ground.

We shall then trace the gradual rise of a fresh tide of God's Holy Spirit in the 600 years of reformation and restoration that follow the Middle Ages. We will ride the crest of those great waves of revival and recovery that were so evident in the 1700's, the 1800's, and the 1900's and that bring us up to the year 2000 and the expectancy of the vast flood tide of God's promised end-time outpouring of the Holy Spirit and the resulting worldwide evangelism and harvest that are to come. We anticipate the restoration of the people of God to a new virgin simplicity and the return of our glorious heavenly Bridegroom to take up His universal reign.

This is where we are going in our study. Actually, to this end we are *compelled* to go, for this is where our Lord Himself is going in His culmination of all human history!

"In the last days, God says, *I will pour out My Spirit* on all people...before the coming of the great and glorious day of the Lord" (Acts 2:17,20 NIV; see Joel 2:28,31).

"And this gospel of the kingdom will be preached in *the whole world* as a testimony to *all nations*, and then the end will come" (Matthew 24:14 NIV).

"Look, *He is coming* with the clouds, and every eye will see Him.... So shall it be! Amen" (Revelation 1:7 NIV).

"... there before me was a great multitude that no one could count, *from every nation, tribe, people and language*, standing before the throne and in front of the Lamb..." (Revelation 7:9 NIV).

"...The kingdom of the world has become *the kingdom of our Lord and of his Christ*, and he will reign for ever and ever" (Revelation 11:15 NIV).

Amen and amen! So be it!

Now let us begin!

Chapter 1

The Rich Root of the Vine

The Foundations of the Early Church

In order to understand the new covenant Body of Christ, one must first of all understand the work of the Holy Spirit in the Old Testament. To the early apostles, the Messianic community was very much alive and well throughout the Old Testament, even in the hours of Israel's deepest apostasy. Although the day of Pentecost ushered in a new, end-time move of the Spirit of God[1] that was especially to include the Gentiles on a wide scale, we must remember that the Gentiles were simply added to the existing "commonwealth of Israel" and made "fellow members of the body" that included the patriarchs and saints of all ages.[2]

In another figure of speech, the Gentiles were grafted in to become partakers with Israel of their rich root.[3] The apostolic church indeed was rooted in Abraham, Isaac, and Jacob. Both

---

1. Joel 2:28-31.
2. Ephesians 2:12-19; 3:4-6.
3. Romans 11:17.

Abraham and David knew the blessing of Paul's justification by faith, and Abraham stands as the patriarchal head of the whole family of God.[4] The prophets of old had likewise experienced "the Spirit of Christ *within* them."[5] As a matter of fact, nearly all the New Testament charismatic gifts of the Holy Spirit were drawn from the life experiences of the saints of old. These saints are viewed by the author of Hebrews as "elders,"[6] joint members of a Body without which they could not be made perfect.[7]

Paul's glorious vision of the Church as the many-membered Body of Christ was likewise drawn from the insights and experiences of the inspired prophets of ancient Israel. Moses had seen the Israel of God as a corporate man in Deuteronomy 32:9-10. David had spoken of Israel as that corporate "son whom Thou hast strengthened for Thyself...the man of Thy right hand...the son of man whom Thou didst make strong for Thyself."[8] Isaiah had viewed the suffering exalted servant as both the single man, the Messiah, and also the corporate man, the true Israel of God. To the prophet's vision, the Messianic community was the very embodiment of that suffering, exalted Christ Himself.[9] Daniel, in his vision of chapter 7, had also seen the coming Son of man as a corporate man.[10]

In every sense of the word, the apostolic church had its roots in the richness of the corporate Israel of God of the Old Testament. The notion that the Church was "born on the day of Pentecost" as a Kingdom different from the Israel of God is without apostolic, New Testament warrant and mars the continuity of God's dealings throughout the old and new covenants.

---

4. Romans 4.
5. 1 Peter 1:11.
6. Hebrews 11:2 KJV.
7. Hebrews 11:40.
8. Psalm 80:15,17.
9. Isaiah 49:1-7.
10. Daniel 7:13-14 with 7:18,22,27.

The Pentecostal Church of the Book of Acts was simply the end-time greening of the corporate vine planted by the God of Israel millennia before. The apostolic church was deeply rooted in Noah, in Abraham, in Joseph, in Moses, in David, in Daniel, and in Isaiah; for the same Spirit of Christ that was in them fell in a fuller, fresher way on *Shevuos,* the day of Pentecost, A.D. 30.

The World Into Which Christianity Came

Paul had written to the Galatian churches that *"when the fulness of the time* came, God sent forth His Son."[11] In that single statement, *"the fulness of the time,"* Paul had summarized those long centuries of God's sovereign activity in the nations of men that had been necessary to prepare the world for the coming of Jesus the Messiah.

Interestingly enough, the inscription placed on the cross of Jesus was "written in Hebrew, Latin, and in Greek."[12] And these three cultures, more than any others, prepared the soil for the rich greening of the Messianic vine in the first century. First of all, the *Hebrews,* in their dispersion,[13] had carried with them into every place the understanding of the one true God, Jehovah. Also, rooted deep in their understanding was the expectation of the end-time Kingdom of the Messiah. The Messiah was indeed the hope of Israel and the light of the Gentiles!

Second, the *Greek* culture contributed to the world its matchless language, the common tongue of the whole known world of that time. It was initially the medium of the spoken apostolic proclamation, the *kerygma,* and later the medium of the written apostolic instruction, the *didache.* Also, the then morally bankrupt Greek culture in its exploitation of the very best of all human abilities in art and literature, philosophy and science, had only served to prove the wisdom of the poet Bonar, "All that my soul has tried, left but a dismal void." The

---

11. Galatians 4:4.

12. John 19:20.

13. Acts 2:5-11; 1 Peter 1:1; James 1:1.

way was clearly paved for the bold declaration of the gospel: "There is *only Christ: He is everything* and He is in everything."[14]

Third, the contribution of the *Roman* culture to "the fulness of the time" lay in its *unification* of the whole disjointed empire inherited from the Greeks. By its network of transportation, its postal and communications system, and by its culture, laws, and military government, Rome had consolidated and compacted together the "meal" of the whole mass of humanity so that it could be more easily "leavened" by the gospel of Christ. Jesus was clearly born "in the fulness of the time." A decadent, morally bankrupt world was indeed *prepared* to hear the anointed declaration of Christ's exalted Lordship from the lips of that small group of men whom Jesus had personally discipled and then sent forth into all the world as the spokesmen of His universal redemption.

---

14. Colossians 3:11b NJB.

Chapter 2

The Falling of the Early Rains

The First-Century Apostolic Church

The most outstanding characteristics of the Church have always been the manifest presence and dynamic activity of Jesus Christ in its midst. This is the true catholic and apostolic Church. And in the first century, Christ was manifestly present in His people! On the day of Pentecost He again came to them from His ascended glory in the power of His outpoured Spirit.[1] By that Spirit He was active in them, spontaneously continuing to do His works and continuing to unfold His teachings through them as His Body.[2]

In our considerations of the early church, we are impressed with three of its most outstanding characteristics—its message, its experience, and its unity in worship and life.

The Apostolic Message

The apostolic message, as we have already noted, may be divided into the apostolic *kerygma,* the proclamation, and the

---

1. John 14:18,20.
2. Acts 1:1-2.

apostolic *didache,* the teaching. Apostolic preaching was not a sterile mental religious formula; it was simply the proclamation of *the resurrected Christ Himself*! One burning theme can be traced through all apostolic preaching, whether by Peter or by Paul, whether to Jews or to Gentiles, and that is simply that "God raised Him up again..."![3] The fact of Christ's literal resurrection transformed the cowering disciples into flaming witnesses. The single fact that Christ was alive had transformed the ardent persecutor, Saul of Tarsus, into a devout defender of the cause of the Nazarene, making Paul the most powerful human personality in the history of the Church. Thus, the *resurrection* of Jesus became the basic apostolic appeal to the world. Jesus was alive and well in the earth!

The apostolic teaching that founded and established the new believers was likewise simple and practical: "...wholesome words, even the words of our Lord Jesus Christ, and to the doctrine which is according to godliness."[4] Foundational apostolic teaching was the teaching of Jesus, which focused on a living relationship with God as Father, of husbands with their wives, fathers with their children, employers with their employees. Jesus' *didache,* the New Torah, centered in mercy and forgiveness and kindness.[5] The teaching of Peter, Paul, James, and John—the apostolic writers—likewise concerned itself with moral issues, issues of practical living. There was little of the technical, rigid, well-defined theological (and often divisive) "orthodoxy" that became so highly prized in the Church in the following centuries. The era of doctrinal systematization had not yet come. This systematization would, however, become the outstanding characteristic of a church on the decline—as we shall shortly see.

---

3. Acts 2:24,32,36; 3:13,15,26; 4:10; 5:30-31; 10:40; 13:30; 17:31; etc.

4. 1 Timothy 6:3 KJV.

5. Matthew 5–7.

The Apostolic Experience

In the Church of the Book of Acts, God had no "grandchildren." There were no second or third generations of people *assumed* to be Christian, absorbed into the Church by some form of spiritual osmosis. Every member of Christ's Body—whether man, woman, or child—was such because of a fresh, dynamic experience with the resurrected Christ. Christ being born within men by the power of His outpoured, indwelling Spirit was the only definition given to becoming a Christian in the Book of Acts.[6]

One of the peculiar characteristics of this age of the outpoured Spirit was its eschatological, or *end-time* dimension. Because the outpoured Spirit was "the Spirit of prophecy," there was a sense in which the early Christians were caught up in the Spirit into the day of the Lord.[7] From that perspective they could say, "The end of all things is at hand...."[8] To them, as living in the Spirit, Christ was truly "coming quickly,"[9] and this hope spoiled them for anything other than His heavenly Kingdom! They were indeed, like Abraham their father, "strangers and pilgrims on the earth."[10]

Apostolic Worship and Life

In one of his surveys, Rufus M. Jones, Christian historian and philosopher, describes apostolic worship and life in the following words—contrasting them with the subsequent more structured life of the second-century Church.

> "While this mystical stage of primitive Christianity lasted, the fellowship was an organism rather than an organization. The members had a common experience. They were fused. They were baptized into one Spirit. They ate a community meal, all partaking together of one loaf, and

6. Acts 2:1-4,38-41; 4:4,31; 8:14-17; 10:44-48; 19:1-6.

7. See Revelation 1:10, literally in the Greek: "on the imperial day."

8. 1 Peter 4:7.

9. Revelation 22:20.

10. Hebrews 11:13 KJV.

all together drinking of one cup....There was no rigid system. 'Custom' laid no heavy hand on anyone. Routine and sacred order had not come yet. There was large scope for spontaneity and personal initiative. Persons and gifts counted for everything. Procedure was fluid and not yet pattern-stamped and standardized. There was a place for the independent variable. The fellowship was more like a family group than like the Church as we call it. Love, rather than rules, guided it. Everything was unique, and nothing repeatable....No leader dominated the group meetings. No program was essential. The little body met as a community of the Spirit; and as Paul said, where the Spirit is, there is liberty—not bondage or routine. The exercises were charismatic, that is, due to the display of 'spiritual gifts' possessed by those who were present. The leading gift was prophecy, which consisted of the spontaneous utterance of a message believed to be inspired by the Spirit by those who had formed a well-stored subconscious life to draw from; it was often illuminating and constructive, 'edifying' as Paul would say....There was also a strain of another type persistently present. There was a greatly heightened moral power. They walked in the Spirit and they bore the fruit of the Spirit: love, joy, peace, long-suffering, kindness, goodness, faithfulness, meekness, self-control...which, as an inward working constructive force, would make them a single body, a unified fellowship."[11]

Truly, the key characteristic of apostolic worship and life was its spontaneity. The resurrected Christ, by the power of His Holy Spirit, was simply free to be Himself in His Church! In His Body He freely lived and moved and had His being.

Community Life

Some historians refer to what is called the "Jerusalem experiment" in which "all those who had believed were

---

11. Jones, as quoted by Charles P. Schmitt, *New Wine in New Wineskins* (Grand Rapids, MI: Fellowship of Believers, 1965), 4-5.

together, and had all things in common."[12] This phenomenon was neither peculiar to Jerusalem, nor was it an experiment.[13] Although apostolic community was not everybody living together under one roof with one purse,[14] neither was it merely a passing fancy or an "experiment." Apostolic community was simply the permanent, abiding outgrowth of the love of God shed abroad in the hearts of men and women by the Holy Spirit that caused those who believed to be of "one heart and soul" so that "...not one of them claimed that anything belonging to him was his own; but all things were common property to them."[15] Thus it was that "...there was not a needy person among them..."![16] And this was in simple obedience to the pointed teachings of Jesus, "So therefore, no one of you can be My disciple who does not give up all his own possessions."[17]

Historical Outline of the First Century

Acts 1:8 contains a historical outline of the growth and advance of the apostolic church of the Book of Acts. Chapters 1 and 2 of Acts concern themselves with the promise, "You shall receive power when the Holy Spirit has come upon you...." The rest of the Book of Acts concerns itself with the historical unfolding of that promise: "...and you shall be My witnesses both in *Jerusalem* [Acts 2–7] and in *all Judea and Samaria* [Acts 8–12], and even to *the remotest part of the earth"* [Acts 13–28]."

In the orderly process of the unfolding of this expansion to the very ends of the earth, we notice the rise of certain geographical centers of influence out of which the truth of God emanates. The first such center of apostolic influence

---

12. Acts 2:44.

13. See Romans 12:13.

14. See Acts 2:46; 5:4; 11:29; 1 Corinthians 16:2.

15. Acts 4:32. The statement *"belonging* to him" evidences *individual owner-ship of* the things mentioned. The rest of the statement evidences that the practice was one of *common sharing, or use,* rather than common *owner-ship:* "all things were common property to them."

16. Acts 4:34.

17. Luke 14:33.

was Jerusalem, home of the apostolic team of Peter and John. These men were two of the three "pillars"[18] whom Jesus intimately discipled and were probably the apostles of the "churches of Judea."[19] The influence of the church in Jerusalem, whose members grew into the many thousands,[20] was powerful and became far spread,[21] but not always for the good. Out of Jerusalem came the whole Judaistic emphasis that threatened to limit the newborn churches into being just another Jewish sect steeped in damaging legalism.[22] These abuses necessitated the disciplinary action recorded in Acts 15 (which is overzealously termed by some the "First General Council of the Church").

Out of Jerusalem, likewise, undoubtedly came those troubling "super-apostles"[23] whom Paul later castigates as "false apostles, deceitful workers,"[24] who dogged his steps and subverted whole fellowships with their legalistic teachings. The widespread and powerful influence of Jerusalem as a center was finally diminished by Titus' destruction of Jerusalem in the fall of A.D. 70.

The basic subtle error of legalistic Judaism, however, survived the fall of Jerusalem and clearly reappeared in the ongoing teaching of the early Fathers. This basic error produced its full harvest of bitter fruit in the Dark Ages and ultimately became the burning issue in the Reformation and the cause for the irreconcilable difference between the Reformed and Catholic theologians. To Paul, and to Luther, justification rested solely on the unmerited and free grace of God given to men *objectively in Christ Jesus* through the merits of His all-atoning Blood. To the Christian Judaizers and to the later Church theologians, justification rested on the grace of God that was

---

18. Galatians 2:9.
19. Galatians 1:22.
20. Acts 4:4; 21:20.
21. Acts 8:1; 11:19.
22. Acts 15:1.
23. 2 Corinthians 11:5 NIV; see also Galatians 5:12.
24. 2 Corinthians 11:13.

subjectively operative within men, inducing them to do good works—namely, the deeds of the law!

In the first century, Antioch of Syria became the second center of apostolic influence, existing concurrently with Jerusalem for a season. It was from here, according to Acts 13 and 14, that Paul, a teacher, and Barnabas, a prophet, were sent forth on their first apostolic journey into Asia Minor, where they established the four Galatian churches—Antioch of Pisidia, Lystra, Iconium, and Derbe. In these they ordained elders[25] for each fellowship—the simplest form of early church government under the headship of Christ Himself.

From Antioch of Syria, Paul, the teacher, was then sent with Silas, a prophet, on a second apostolic journey into eastern Europe[26] during which the churches of Philippi (in Macedonia), Thessalonica, and Corinth were established.

Originating again from Antioch of Syria[27] was Paul's third apostolic journey during which the church at Ephesus was founded, which, in turn, became a third dynamic center of influence in the earth. From Ephesus "...all who lived in Asia heard the word of the Lord...,"[28] resulting undoubtedly in the founding of the three small Christian communities in the Lycus Valley—Colossae, Laodicea, and Hierapolis—as well as the founding of the other historic churches of Asia for which John bore such godly care and concern as evidenced in the Revelation.[29]

These were indeed years of the falling of the early rains! This was the holy, catholic, apostolic church, "...built upon the foundation of the apostles and prophets, Jesus Christ Himself being the chief corner stone"![30] Jesus was manifestly present and dynamically active among His people!

---

25. Presbyters; Acts 14:23.

26. See Acts 15–18.

27. See Acts 18:22-23; 19:1.

28. Acts 19:10. "Asia" here signifies the west coast province of Asia Minor.

29. See Revelation 1:4; 2–3.

30. Ephesians 2:20 KJV.

A Concluding Note on New Testament Realism

Down through the succeeding ages, many have tended to look back on the first-century Church through those proverbial "rose-colored glasses," seeing only the ideal, the positive, and the good. But New Testament realism reveals a first-century Church beset by serious sins, doctrinal errors, and hurtful extremes. By approximately A.D. 55, the Galatian churches were steeped in doctrinal error.[31] The Ephesians struggled with issues of racism.[32] Even the Philippians, the fruit of Paul's most successful labors, were marred by selfish ambition and disunity.[33] The Colossian church was overrun with false doctrine and legalism.[34] The Thessalonians, as stunning as their conversions were, still wrestled with issues of immorality and apocalyptic fanaticism.[35] The Corinthians had also experienced a most unusual manifestation of the revival presence of God, bringing many out of their sin and shame into the Kingdom of God. Notwithstanding this, the Corinthians wrestled with severe moral and doctrinal problems and a rash of unproductive fanatical extremes in the arena of the manifestations of the Holy Spirit.[36]

Consequently, from the very outset of the history of the Christian Church, wise students of history will learn that even though the mighty work of the Holy Spirit is always *perfect* in its origins, the vessels through whom and upon whom the Spirit moves are often *flawed* and *broken* and capable of the most grievous of sins and errors and extremes. For this reason there would never be a genuine move of the Holy Spirit in the earth from the first-century onward that would not gender justifiable criticism, opposition, and even rejection.

---

31. Galatians 1:6-7.
32. Ephesians 2:11-20; 4:3.
33. Philippians 2:1-4; 4:2.
34. Colossians 2:2-4,8-10,16-23.
35. 1 Thessalonians 4:3-8; 2 Thessalonians 2:1-3; 3:6.
36. 1 Corinthians 1:10-12; 5:1-2; 6:1; 11:29-32; 14:23-40; 15:12,33-34.

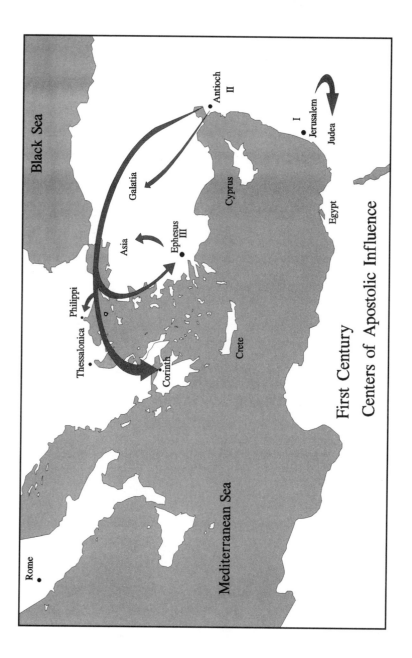

First Century

Centers of Apostolic Influence

Chapter 3

The Rain Is Well-Nigh Over and Gone

The Transition From First- to Second-Century Christianity

Historian J.L. Hurlburt aptly comments, "For fifty years after St. Paul's life a curtain hangs over the Church, through which we strive vainly to look, and when at last it rises...we find a Church in many aspects very different from that in the days of St. Peter and St. Paul."[1]

It is apparent to most historians that a dramatic change took place in the decades of transition from first- to second-century Christianity. Though some may choose to see in these changes a maturing, a developing, and an evolving of the life of the Church from one degree of glory to another, unfortunately, the *facts* reveal quite the opposite.

The internal facts from John's Revelation, the final apostolic writing, show a movement on the decline by the end of the first century. The rain is well-nigh over and gone. John's description of the churches of Asia shows communities hopelessly

---

1. J.L. Hurlburt, *Story of the Christian Church* (Grand Rapids, MI: Zondervan, 1967), 41.

entangled in webs of deception and decay.[2] Ephesus, which 40 years before had been the scene of a mighty Pentecostal visitation by God,[3] is now enjoined to "remember therefore from where you have fallen, and repent, and do the deeds you did at first; or else I am coming to you, *and will remove your lampstand out of its place*—unless you repent."[4]

The decline of second-century Christianity from its original purity in precept and practice is seen to be in direct proportion to the decline of the presence and power of the Holy Spirit in the midst of the Church. Lutheran historian Lars P. Qualben describes this spiritual decline as follows: "...the enthusiastic prophetic element in early Christian life was gradually being replaced by a growing formalism in teaching and in worship.... The specially 'gifted' became fewer and their prophecies perhaps less reliable; the expectation of the speedy return of the Lord was no longer so general; a new generation had grown up that had not been won directly for the Church from heathenism, but had been born and educated in Christian homes. Instead of the immediate gifts of the Spirit, Christians rather relied on organizations and outward religious authority."[5]

Church Structure

It is likewise apparent to all Church historians that a shift takes place in the *government* of the churches. In the churches of the apostles spontaneity is the rule of the day. The church is an organism, carried along by the buoyant life of the Holy Spirit. In the second century we notice a change. The church becomes less an organism and more an organization. Structure begins to replace spontaneity. The churches of the apostles, such as the Ephesian church, were originally headed up by a college of presbyters, or elders.[6] These were the bishops, or overseers,

---

2. Revelation 2–3.

3. Acts 19:17-20.

4. Revelation 2:5.

5. Lars P. Qualben, *A History of the Christian Church* (New York: Thomas Nelson & Sons, 1933), 86, 96.

6. Acts 20:17.

of the church. And these were to shepherd, or pastor, the flock of God.[7] Though men within this college would differ in their maturity, authority, and their abilities to serve, official distinctions were not made between them as they later would be in the Church when bishops were distinguished from presbyters. Philip Schaff describes apostolic church government in contrast to that of the second century in this way:

> "The terms Presbyter (or Elder) and Bishop (or overseer, superintendent) denote in the New Testament one and the same office....They appear always as a plurality or as a college in one and the same congregation, even in smaller cities, as Philippi....The office of the presbyter-bishops was to teach and to rule the particular congregation committed to their charge. They were the regular 'pastors and teachers' (Eph. 4:11)....The presbyters always formed a college or corporation, a presbytery....They no doubt maintained a relation of fraternal equality....The nearest approach to the idea of the ancient catholic episcopate may be found in the unique position of James, the brother of the Lord....But in fact he was only 'primus inter pares,' or first among equals. In his last visit to Jerusalem, Paul was received by the body of the presbyters, and to them he gave an account of his missionary labors (Acts 21:18). Moreover, this authority of James was exceptional and due chiefly to his close relationship with the Lord and his personal sanctity, which won the respect even of the unconverted Jews.

> "The institution of episcopacy proper [the single bishop] cannot be traced to the apostolic age, so far as documentary evidence goes, but is very apparent and well-nigh universal about the middle of the second century."[8]

---

7. Acts 20:28.

8. Philip Schaff, *History of the Christian Church*, Vol. 1 (New York: Charles Scribner's Sons, 1882), 491-498.

Historian Williston Walker calls attention to the problems inherent in the first-century simplicity of the collegiality of elders in his observation that "leadership...by a committee of equals is unworkable for any protracted time...,"[9] and indeed it is. Actually, it is *virtually impossible* in the decline of the presence of the Holy Spirit. A college of men can only be induced to be "of the same mind, maintaining the same love, united in spirit, intent on one purpose"[10] as long as Christ's manifest presence and dynamic activity is strong among them!

The Gnostic Heresy

Apart from the legalistic teachings of the Jerusalem Judaizers, the other major first-century error was Gnosticism in its beginning forms, a peculiar hybrid heresy of half Judaism and half oriental mysticism. The inroads made by Gnosticism plainly affected the Colossian church, which caused Paul to write using the strongest of language. The basic errors in Gnostic thinking are addressed by Paul in his letter. First, Paul combats the heretical notion that God was only to be approached through a long list of intermediaries, of whom Jesus was only one, and that those hierarchies were to be adored. Paul's insistence is that "there is *only* Christ: He is everything...."[11] In Him *alone* dwells all of God's fullness, and in Him *alone* we are complete.[12] Some Church historians are naive enough to believe that the Church eventually uprooted Gnosticism and overcame it. But this was not true. The whole later notion of the adoration of the heavenly host with its long graduation of celestial intermediaries, including the mother of our Lord, was simply declining Christianity's way of accommodating Gnosticism into Christian theology.

---

9. Williston Walker, *A History of the Christian Church* (New York: Charles Scribner's Sons, 1959), 42.

10. Philippians 2:2.

11. Colossians 3:11b NJB.

12. Colossians 2:9-10.

The ascetic, legalistic tendencies of Gnosticism, born out of its understanding that the body and all other matter is intrinsically evil, consequently taught, "Do not handle, do not taste, do not touch!"[13] These understandings, unsuccessfully uprooted, became the seeds for the later extreme notions concerning physically inherited sin and for the extremes of legalistic asceticism and its "severe treatment of the body,"[14] which by the fourth century would become fairly well crystallized in austere monastic and celibate practices within the Church.

For our present treatment of the subject, we need principally to see how Gnosticism became one of the chief causes of the more formal structuring of the Church. The height of Gnostic influence was from about A.D. 135 to 160, although it continued on in strength for centuries following. Lest we underestimate how subtle the error of Gnosticism was and yet how orthodox its followers appeared, I have quoted one of their hymns in Appendix I of this book as evidence of their "orthodoxy." It is of importance, however, to note the absence of the name of *Jesus* in this hymn. The decline of the Spirit's antiseptic presence seemed to allow this heresy to break forth as a plague in the second century, and it threatened, as Williston Walker states, "to overwhelm the historic Christian faith, and by so doing brought upon the Christian church its gravest crisis since the Pauline battle for freedom from law."[15] The Church in its attempt to counteract Gnosticism "developed a closely knit organization and a clearly defined creed, which contrasted with the more spontaneous and charismatic nature of primitive Christianity."[16]

Undoubtedly second-century Christianity appeared to have no other alternative, for the tide of the Lord's manifest presence was ebbing. The rain was well-nigh over and gone!

---

13. Colossians 2:21.
14. Colossians 2:23.
15. Walker, *op. cit.,* 51.
16. *Ibid.*

Chapter 4

Green Leaves in Drought

The Second-Century Church
(A.D. 100–175)

Our source material for the history of apostolic Christianity is primarily the corrective, instructive correspondence of the first-century apostolic company. This included the three Jerusalem "pillars"[1]—*Peter, James,* the Lord's half-brother,[2] and *John.* Then there was *Paul,* apostle to the Gentiles and author of some 13 letters. Apart from these four main apostolic writers, we also have the correspondence of *Jude,* the brother of the above mentioned James,[3] as well as that of *Mark,* Peter's disciple.[4] Finally we have also the writings of *Matthew* of the original 12, and the historical compilations of *Luke,* who traveled with Paul himself as part of his apostolic company. This

---

1. Galatians 2:9.
2. Galatians 1:19.
3. Jude 1.
4. 1 Peter 5:13. Mark is termed by Papias, in a fragment dating back to A.D. 125, as "the interpreter of Peter...."

apostolic correspondence of the apostles and of men closely associated with them comes down to us in the form of our New Testament.

The Post-Apostolic Writings

Our source material for the history of second-century Christianity is primarily the correspondence and writings of men called "the post-apostolic fathers." Among these are *Clement of Rome* (A.D. 96), *Barnabas* (A.D. 132),[5] *Hermas of Rome* (A.D. 140), *Ignatius*—"bishop" of Antioch (A.D. 110–115), and *Polycarp of Smyrna*, a disciple of John the apostle (A.D. 110–117). To the writings of these may be added also the *Didache,* or the *Teaching of the Twelve Apostles,*[6] dating from A.D. 130–160.

One of the more interesting prophetic thoughts to appear in this era was the following, found in the writings of the above mentioned Barnabas:

"God made in six days the works of his hands; and he finished them on the seventh day and he rested...Consider, my children what that signifies...that in six thousand years the Lord God will bring all things to an end.[7] For with him one day is as a thousand years...Therefore, children, in six days, that is, in six thousand years, shall all things be accomplished. And what is that he saith, and he rested the seventh day: he meaneth this; that when his Son shall come, and abolish the season of the Wicked one, and judge the ungody...then he shall gloriously rest in that seventh day...[and] shall begin the eighth day, that is, the beginning of the other world. For which cause we observe

---

5. Some historians date the letter by Barnabas at a much earlier time, believing him to be the Barnabas of Acts 13 and 14 who traveled with Paul; the majority do not.

6. It is almost certain that these writings were not written by the 12 apostles, but come to us rather through their disciples as an attempted summary of their instruction.

7. Many Christian students place the beginning of biblical human history at 4000 B.C. That would make Barnabas' "six thousand years" end at approximately A.D. 2000!

the eighth day with gladness, in which Jesus rose from the dead...."[8]

Around various of the above men, generally reputed to be personal disciples or "pupils" of the original apostles, clustered the leadership and authority of early second-century Christianity. These were green leaves in drought; in their writings we can trace the significant earmarks of second-century Christianity and, sadly enough, its subtle deviations from original apostolic life and teaching.

Clement of Rome (A.D. 96), a disciple of Peter, is probably the earliest of the post-apostolic writers. Clemens Alexandrinus calls him an apostle. Clement's evangelical letter to the Corinthian church, in which he pleads for their continuing in unity, was publicly read in the assemblies of the primitive church according to the historian Eusebius, and it is included in one of the ancient collections of the canon of Scripture. In Clement's understanding the church is still ruled by a college of elders. He writes, "only let the flock of Christ be in peace, with *the elders* that are set over it."[9] He further acknowledges only two basic offices in the church, "bishops and deacons."[10] He terms these leaders of the church "priests."[11] He became, thereby, one of the first to distinguish between "clergy" and "laity," a clear departure from the apostolic understanding of the priesthood of the whole Church.[12] The two most significant contributions of Clement's letter are his fervent appeal to the authority of the writings of Paul in his pleas for unity, which marks the beginnings of a formulation of the canon of New Testament Scripture, and also his tracing of the existence of church officers to the apostles, which later became misconstrued as

---

8. *General Epistle of Barnabas* 13:4-6,9-10.
9. *Epistle of Clement to the Corinthians* 22:14.
10. *Ibid.* 19:5-6; Clement uses *bishops* and *elders* interchangeably, as did Paul and Peter.
11. *Ibid.* 20:24.
12. 1 Peter 2:5.

"apostolic succession." On this issue, Clement simply wrote, "So likewise our Apostles knew by our Lord Jesus Christ that there should arise contentions on account of the ministry. And therefore having a perfect foreknowledge of this, they appointed persons, as we have before said, and then gave direction how, when they should die, other chosen and approved men should succeed in their ministry."[13]

As we shall continue to see, in the absence of the Holy Spirit's strong antiseptic presence, these two weapons—the canon of apostolic writings as the embodiment of the final truth, and the recognition of the true Church as the Church of the original apostles—were destined to become the chief battle weapons against the threatening Gnostic heretics with their heretical "revelations" and their self-styled claims to authority.

Polycarp (A.D. 110–117), the sainted martyr and personal disciple of John, writes to the Philippians, addressing them as from "Polycarp and the presbyters that are with him."[14] His understanding of Church government is the same as Clement's. Like Clement, he appeals to the writings and "wisdom of the blessed and renowned Paul," an appeal that became a further foundation for the formulation of a canon of New Testament writings. Polycarp, like Clement, acknowledges only "deacons and elders" in the Church. However, he also calls the latter "priests,"[15] thereby indicating a subtle distinction between "clergy" and "laity."

As Polycarp was being led to his execution, he was implored to recant and save his life. His noble response was: "Eighty-six years have I served Him, and He has done me no wrong; how then can I blaspheme my Savior and King?"[16]

---

13. Clement, *op. cit.*, 19:16-17.

14. Polycarp, *Philippians* 1:1.

15. *Ibid.* 2:13.

16. John W. Kennedy, *The Torch of the Testimony* (Gospel Literature Service, 1965; Goleta, CA: Christian Books, reprint), 57.

Ignatius (A.D. 110–117), the "bishop" of Antioch, allegedly writing seven letters to various churches en route to Rome to his martyr's death, differs widely in thrust from Clement and Polycarp. Ignatius rather appeals to the episcopate, the office of the bishop, and to one principal brother within each church whom he calls *"the* bishop," as the best means of maintaining soundness and unity in the face of the onslaught of the divisive heretics. Ignatius "wanted to have the *episcopos* [bishop] in undisputed control, and *because he did not see this in any church other than his own* he emphasized the virtues of monarchical episcopacy[17] as strongly as possible."[18] To the Ephesians, Ignatius writes "that *being subject to your bishop,*[19] and the presbytery, ye may be wholly and thoroughly sanctified";[20] and "it will become you to run together according to *the will of your bishop ...*";[21] and "it is therefore evident that we ought to look upon *the bishop, even as* we would do upon the Lord himself."[22] He further exhorts the Magnesians to regard their "bishop (as) presiding *in the place of God....*"[23] Here Ignatius singles out Damas among the other leaders as their sole bishop.[24] The Trallians he enjoins to "reverence the deacons as Jesus Christ; and *the bishop as the Father*; and the presbyters as...the Apostles. Without these there is no Church....."[25]

---

17. The single bishop.
18. A.M. Renwick, *The Story of the Church* (London: InterVarsity Fellowship, 1958), 26.
19. Onesimus, whom Ignatius singles out from among the other elders and to whom he ascribes supremacy as bishop over the other elders—a very grave departure from the original apostolic understanding of Acts 20:17,28.
20. *Epistle of Ignatius to the Ephesians* 1:9; see also 1:4-5.
21. *Ibid.* 1:13.
22. *Ibid.* 2:4.
23. *Epistle of Ignatius to the Magnesians* 2:5.
24. *Ibid.* 1:4.
25. *Epistle of Ignatius to the Trallians* 1:8-9.

On yet other matters, Ignatius writes to the Ephesians revealing his strong convictions concerning the sacraments of "our God Jesus Christ...born and baptized, that through his passion he might purify water, to the washing away of sin."[26] He further enjoins the Ephesians to obey their "...bishop and the presbytery with an entire affection; breaking one and the same bread, which is the medicine of immortality; our antidote that we should not die, but live forever in Christ Jesus."[27] On the matter of Christology, Ignatius views Jesus as God's "inseparable spirit,"[28] "who proceeded from one Father, and exists in one, and is returned to one,"[29] Himself "the Father before all ages, and (who) appeared in the end to us."[30] In his Christology, Ignatius is almost modalistic (see Chapter 5). Ignatius, as also Barnabas, recognizes Christianity as "no longer observing sabbaths, but keeping the Lord's day in which also our life is sprung up by Him...."[31]

Ignatius, writing to Smyrna, is the first to call the Church "the Catholic church,"[32] meaning by that "the universal church." He further enjoins the Smyrnaeans that "it is not lawful without the bishop, neither to baptize, nor to celebrate the Holy Communion...." Thus he becomes one of the first to make such a wide distinction between "the clergy" (the chosen ones) and "the laity" (the masses). Ignatius' emphasis on the "single bishop" stands so blatantly out of character with the apostolic writings of the first century and with the other post-apostolic writings of the early second century that some Church historians actually question the authenticity of "Ignatius'" writings as his, or as actually belonging to the *early* second century, but

---

26. Ignatius, *Ephesians* 4:9; concerning the second-century Church's understanding of baptism, see Appendix II.
27. *Ibid.* 4:16.
28. Ignatius, *Magnesians* 4:12.
29. *Ibid.* 2:11.
30. *Ibid.* 2:5.
31. *Ibid.* 3:3; see also *The General Epistle of Barnabas* 13:9-10.
32. *Epistle of Ignatius to the Smyrnaeans* 3:4.

rather see them as *later* writings. Lars P. Qualben describes the more gradual rise of this distinction between clergy and laity as it takes place between the first and the second centuries. Commenting on the first century, he notes:

"The local churches had elders and deacons, who supervised and directed the work of the congregation....But *the early church organization was not centered in office and in law, but in the special gifts of the Spirit.* The teaching, the preaching, and the administration of the Sacraments were conducted by the 'gifted men' in the congregation. An elder might also teach, preach, and administer the Sacraments, but he did not do so because he was an elder, but because he was known to have 'the gift'...

"*Toward the close of the first Christian century a change took place.* A general lack of confidence in the special gifts of the Spirit, a desire for more specific order, and *a pressing demand for proper safeguard against heresy* resulted in a gradual transfer of the preaching, the teaching, and the administration of the Sacraments from the 'gifted men' to the local elders.... The official functions were now performed by elders only. The ministry of the Word and the Sacraments became *official, which marked the beginning of the division of the Christians into 'clergy' (chosen ones) and 'laity' (the masses).* During the second and third centuries another important change took place. Instead of government by a group of elders, the local churches were headed by single officials for whom the name 'bishop' was exclusively reserved....The presence of 'the bishop'...was now essential to every valid act of the congregation. In fact, without the bishop there was no church; and any person desiring to be a Christian must be subject to a bishop. Outside of this Church, the Church of the bishops, there was no salvation."[33]

---

33. Lars P. Qualben, *A History of the Christian Church* (New York: Thomas Nelson & Sons, 1933), 94-96; emphasis added.

To men like Ignatius, who in his own words did personally love and "enjoy Jesus Christ," can be traced some unfortunate and devastating seeds of error, which although sown in an honest attempt to counteract the Gnostic heretics, nevertheless grew up in following centuries to produce some very bitter fruit. In the absence of the manifest outpouring of the Holy Spirit, these post-apostolic fathers believed these measures to be the best that could be done under the circumstances and with what was available to them. These men sought to maintain green leaves in a time of drought.

Attempts at Reformation

Marcion is termed by historians as "the first church reformer." He was excommunicated from the Church at Rome in A.D. 144 because of his strong heretical Gnostic and Docetic teachings that declared that Christ came in a phantom body. He formed churches of his own that spread throughout the empire and continued into the fifth century. Marcion, a preacher of grace, rejected all those forms of legalism and Judaism that he felt were prevalent in the structured Church. He attempted to compile a canon of authoritative New Testament writings—the first of its kind—but included only Paul's writings to the churches and Luke's Gospel as the true apostolic interpretation of the gospel of grace. Marcion's Gnostic schism could not but help drive second-century Christianity into a more structured system of doctrine and organization, as we have already noted.

Montanus led a movement called after his name that is regarded by historian Williston Walker and other historians as "distinctly of Christian origin." It was a charismatic reformation dating around A.D. 156 in Mysia, complete with *glossolalia* (tongues-speaking), prophecies, visions, and an eschatological expectation. Unfortunately, as with many Pentecostal outpourings, it also had its share of excesses and fanaticism. Eusebius comments how the Montanists introduced a new type of prophecy "contrary to the traditional and constant custom of the Church." Nonetheless, unlike Marcion, Montanus and his two female prophetesses, Priscilla and Maximilla, stood for a genuinely *orthodox* reformation in the midst of the stagnating, formalistic, worldly Christianity of the second century.

British author and missionary to India John W. Kennedy aptly notes that the "crystallization of Christianity is…the prime reason for the emergence of fresh expressions of the life of the Gospel. Where the vitality of spiritual life could not be contained within the increasingly restricted limits of a humanly imposed organization and rule, it burst the bounds and found its fuller expression in an atmosphere of direct and free communion with God."[34]

Because Montanism posed such a threat to the authority of established Christianity, it was formally condemned by the synods of the various threatened bishops of Asia Minor who then swung, in reaction, even further away from the spontaneous movings of the Holy Spirit into a yet more structured formalism. Well might we wonder what the results could have been had second-century Christianity rather received this genuine Pentecostal outpouring and thereby helped to balance and steady it, as well as allow itself to be revived and renewed by it!

The Persecutions

Christianity, as a Jewish sect, enjoyed initial protection under Rome's policy of freedom for local religions. However, because the early believers came declaring "that there is another king, Jesus,"[35] it did not take long for the Church to be viewed as a serious threat in the emperor-worshiping Roman Empire. Christianity was totally incompatible to Rome's world system— politically, socially, and religiously. As a result, persecution began in the first century under Nero (A.D. 54–68), who falsely accused the Christians of setting fire to Rome. Persecution

---

34. Kennedy, *op. cit.,* 37-38.
35. Acts 17:7.

also ensued under Domitian A.D. 81–96. Under Emperor Trajan (A.D. 98–117), Ignatius of Antioch was thrown to the wild beasts in the Colosseum at Rome in A.D. 115, and Symeon of Jerusalem, successor of James and a relative of our Lord, was tortured for many days and finally crucified in A.D. 107. The saintly Polycarp of Smyrna, disciple of John, as previously mentioned, was burned at the stake in A.D. 155 under Emperor Antonius Pius because, by his own testimony, he would not blaspheme the King who had saved him. Under Marcus Aurelius (A.D. 161–180), the persecution continued for years, and included the beheading of Justin Martyr the apologist in Rome in A.D. 166. But it seems, as always, that "the blood of the martyrs is the seed of the Church," for by A.D. 180, the Church was established in all parts of the Roman Empire and far beyond its borders to the south and to the west. Special note must here be made of the extensive growth of the Church throughout Persia, especially in the first three centuries after Pentecost.

During the middle of the second century an anonymous writer wrote to a Roman citizen, Diognetius, giving a description of Christians. He wrote, "Christians display to us their wonderful and confessedly striking method of life…Every foreign land is to them as home, yet their every homeland is foreign. They pass their days on earth, but they are citizens of heaven. They obey the laws of the land, and at the same time surpass the law by their lives. They love all and are reviled by all."[36]

The Apologists

The second-century apologists were Christian writers who defended the Christian faith against the false accusations and slander of the antagonists of the Church. The Lord's Supper had been misinterpreted as cannibalism, and the affection and love of the believers for each other had been misconstrued as immorality and indecency. The true Church was always destined to be

---

36. Kennedy, *op. cit.,* 59.

misunderstood and slandered. When it was applauded and popular, it was usually on the decline.

The greatest of the early apologists to defend the Church was Justin Martyr (A.D. 100–165). He writes of the then current move of God: "There is not a nation either Greek or Barbarian or of any other name, even those who wander in tribes or live in tents, among whom prayers and thanksgiving are not offered to the Father and Creator of the universe in the Name of the crucified Jesus." Justin Martyr's *First Apology* was addressed to the Emperor Antonius Pius and the Senate and to all the Roman people in its defense of Christianity. His longest apology is his *Dialogue with Trypho the Jew,* an explanation of the Christian faith to the Jews.

It is especially important for us to note Justin Martyr's statements in *Trypho* concerning the continuation of the gifts of the Holy Spirit into the second century, lest we assume that these passed away with the first-century apostles. He comments, "the prophetical gifts remain with us even to the present time...it is possible to see among us women and men who possess gifts of the Spirit of God."[37]

Other apologists were Quadratus of Athens (A.D. 125), Athenagoras (A.D. 177), and Melito, bishop of Sardis (A.D. 169–180). It was the latter who wrote so impressively concerning Jesus: "Jesus is all. When He judges, He is Law; when He teaches, He is Word; when He saves, He is Grace; when He begets, He is Father; when begotten He is Son; when He suffers, He is Lamb; when buried, He is Man; when risen, He is God. Such is Jesus Christ! To Him be glory forever, amen!" Such men were indeed green leaves in a time of drought!

---

37. Justin Martyr, *Dialogue with Trypho,* in Vol. 1 of *The Ante-Nicene Christian Fathers,* eds. Alexander Roberts and James Donaldson (Peabody, MA: Hendrickson Publishers, Inc., 1994), 240, 243.

Chapter 5

The Autumn
of the Year

The Early Catholic Fathers
(A.D. 175–325)

The "ante-Nicene" era is that century and a half *before* Emperor Constantine convened the First General Council of the Church at Nicea in A.D. 325. The prominent men of this era are called "the early Catholic fathers." Of these, five stand out as the most brilliant and devoted—Irenaeus, Tertullian, Cyprian, Clement, and Origen.

Irenaeus, with his disciple Hippolytus, stands out as the *earliest* theological leader of the rising Catholic[1] Church. Born in Asia Minor around A.D. 130, he was discipled by Polycarp of Smyrna, who himself was discipled by John, the disciple of Jesus. From the eastern branch of the Church in Asia Minor, he went as a missionary to the western branch of the Church

---

1. We are still using this word to denote the universal Church, except that now in a more formal sense the word is capitalized to reflect the increasingly institutional character of the Church during this period. As yet there was no division between East and West, between Greek and Roman Catholics. There were only Catholics and schismatics (such as the Gnostics and the Montanists).

at Lyons in Gaul,[2] where he served as bishop until his death, around A.D. 200. His chief contribution was his five-volume work, *Against Heresies,* written primarily to refute Gnosticism. His principal concern was our great salvation through "the only true and steadfast Teacher, the Word of God, our Lord Jesus Christ, who did through His transcendent love become what we are, that He might bring us to be even what He is Himself."[3]

Also, in *Against Heresies,* Irenaeus, as did Justin Martyr a century before, testified to the ongoing gifts and manifestations of the Holy Spirit in the Church—"For some do certainly and truly drive out devils, so that those who have been thus cleansed from evil spirits frequently both believe and join themselves to the Church. Others...see visions and utter prophetic expressions. Others heal the sick by laying their hands upon them, and they are made whole...the dead even have been raised up, and remained among us for many years...we do also hear many brethren in the Church who possess prophetic gifts and who through the Spirit speak all kinds of languages....It is not possible to name the number of gifts which the Church throughout the whole world has received from God in the name of Jesus Christ."[4]

Irenaeus, in *Against Heresies*, also sounds the same prophetic note as did Barnabas before him: "For in as many days as this world was made, in so many thousand years shall it be concluded...and God brought to a conclusion upon the sixth day the works that had he made...This is...also...a prophecy of what is to come...in six days created things were completed: it is

---

2. France.

3. Preface to *Against Heresies*, in Book V of *The Ante-Nicene Christian Fathers,* eds. Alexander Roberts and James Donaldson (Peabody, MA: Hendrickson Publishers, Inc., 1994), 526.

4. Irenaeus, *Against Heresies,* in Vol. 1 of *The Ante-Nicene Christian Fathers,* eds. Alexander Roberts and James Donaldson (Edinburgh: T & T Clark, 1874), 409, 531, as quoted in Eddie Hyatt, *2000 Years of Charismatic Christianity* (Tulsa: Hyatt International Ministries, Inc., 1996), 4.

evident, therefore, that they will come to an end at the sixth thousand year."[5] (This prophecy is of significant interest to those alive and awaiting the turning of the year A.D. 2000!)

The Two Theologies

Within the Church of the second and third centuries there began to appear a difference in theological thought between the Greek mentality and the Roman or Latin mentality, a subtle prelude to the ultimate division between the Greek churches and the Latin churches. Latin theology, principally represented by Tertullian and his successor Cyprian, both of Carthage in North Africa, tended to be more realistic and practical, dealing with the Church and salvation, as well as more pointedly hostile to Gnosticism and all philosophy. On the other hand, Greek theology, principally represented by the Alexandrian school of Clement and Origen, was more philosophic and idealistic, dealing more with the doctrines of Christology and the Incarnation, and sought to reinterpret Gnosticism in the light of Christian orthodoxy.

The Latin Theologians of the West

Tertullian of Carthage (A.D. 155–255), with his brilliant mind, is aptly called "the Father of Latin theology." Converted from paganism in his thirties, he rose to the level of presbyter in the Catholic Church at Carthage. Partially because of his resentment of the morally lax Church at Rome, which was by this time rising in prominence over all Christendom, and partially because of his own personal ascetic convictions, he broke with the Catholic Church and joined the puritanical but orthodox charismatic sect of the Montanists at the turn of the century. At the same time he began his extensive literary career of apologetic defense and definition of orthodox Christianity. In his 30 treatises, he wrote in an orderly, authoritative, and vivid manner.

---

5. Irenaeus, *Against Heresies,* Book V, 28:3, in *The Ante-Nicene Christian Fathers, op. cit.*

Tertullian wrote apologetically against the heathens, the Jews, and the injustices of the Empire against Christianity. Tertullian wrote sarcastically and viciously against the Gnostic heretics, among them Marcion,[6] defending the Church of the apostles as the only true Church, alone containing the valid deposit of apostolic truth. In his challenge to Marcion, Tertullian, as did Irenaeus before him, described the miraculous gifts of the Holy Spirit as present evidence of the true Church of the apostles—"Let Marcion then exhibit, as gifts of his god, some prophets...let him produce a psalm, a vision, a prayer—only let it be by the Spirit...whenever an interpretation of tongues has occurred to him. Now *all these signs are forthcoming from my side without any difficulty.*"[7] From his Montanist viewpoint, Tertullian attacked the lukewarm Catholics as well. On the positive side, he wrote on prayer, on penance, on patience, on baptism, and also on Trinitarian Christology, the positives and negatives of which shall be discussed later. He likewise majored on Paul's great themes of sin and grace, laying the foundations for the later theology of the great North African thinker, Augustine, Bishop of Hippo.

Cyprian of Carthage was born in A.D. 200 and martyred by beheading on September 14, A.D. 258. He was converted to Christ at age 46, 12 years before his death. In literal obedience to the teachings of the gospel, he sold his luxurious estates, giving the money to the poor. Two years after his Christian baptism, he became a Catholic presbyter and soon thereafter was elected Bishop of Carthage. On his baptism Cyprian wrote: "...by the aid of the regenerating water, the stain of my former life was washed away; as soon as I drank the Spirit from above I was transformed by a second birth into a new man...." Cyprian viewed the Montanist Tertullian as his teacher

---

6. "Nothing in Pontus is so barbarous and sad as the fact that Marcion was born there, fouler than any Scythian..." etc.

7. Tertullian, *Against Marcion*, in Vol. 3 of *The Ante-Nicene Christian Fathers, op. cit.,* 447; emphasis added.

(by reading his writings), though it is possible the two men never personally met. Cyprian's main contribution to third century thought was in the development of episcopal Catholicism. This belief that everyone must be subject to an *episkopos* (bishop) in order to be in the one universal Church he advocated in reaction against the schismatics of his day, although he would never attack by name his venerated teacher, the Montanist Tertullian.

In stark contrast to the apostolic mentality of the first century, Cyprian wrote: "Whosoever he is, and whatsoever his character, he is not a Christian who is not in the Church of Christ....There is no salvation outside the Church...; it is not possible that he should have God for his Father, who would not have the Church for his mother....*The Church is constituted of bishops, and every act of the Church is controlled by these leaders...; he who is not with the bishop, is not in the Church....*"[8] Though Cyprian highly regarded the Roman bishop as *primus inter pares* (first among equals), and the Roman Church as the highest Church in dignity, he resisted the attempt of Bishop Steven of Rome to bring all the churches under his authority on the controversial subject of the baptism of heretics. The Roman bishop had yet the long road of centuries of struggle ahead of him before he was able to declare himself the unchallenged head of the Catholic Church in the West.

The Greek Theologians of the East

Clement of Alexandria (A.D. 150–220) and Origen, his pupil, were principal leaders in the catechetical school at Alexandria in Egypt, seat of the second mainstream of theological thought, the Greek school. The catechetical school at Alexandria was originally designed for the practical purpose of preparing converted heathen and Jews for baptism, and it was conducted by Christian teachers in their homes.

---

8. *The Epistles of Cyprian*, 265-409; also *The Treatise of Cyprian on the Unity of the Church* in Vol. 5 of *The Ante-Nicene Christian Fathers*, *op. cit.*, 421-429; emphasis added.

Unlike Tertullian with his adamant distrust of philosophy, and unlike Cyprian with his strenuous Church organizationalism, the Greek school sought rather to interpret God and Christ by blending the philosophies of their day with the message of Christianity, thereby producing a "Christian Gnosticism." Clement was no systematic theologian; this was to be left to his pupil and successor Origen, one of the most brilliant teachers and writers in the emerging Christian Church.

Origen (A.D. 185–254), the son of the Christian martyr Leonides, was born in a Christian home and ascended to the leadership of the Alexandrian catechetical school as a young man of 18, and over the next 28 years, he developed it to its highest degree of fame until he was excommunicated from Alexandria by Bishop Demetrius, his superior, because of his jealousy of Origen. Origen then built another school of learning in Caesarea, where he was received by the Church and where he taught and wrote for the next 20 years. According to Jerome, the ascetic Origen (who had castrated himself) "produced more books than any other man could read in a lifetime." Among these were his *Hexapla,* a Hebrew and Greek translation of the Old Testament, and his voluminous *Commentaries* on the Scriptures. His most celebrated work is probably his four-volume *De Principiis,* the first great systematic presentation of the doctrines of Christianity, believed by historians to be the greatest intellectual achievement of the ante-Nicene Church.

Origen's weakness in scholarship was his almost Gnostic allegorical method of interpreting the Bible, which enabled him to bring forth from the Scripture almost anything he wished. One of Origen's principal doctrinal contributions to third-century theology, as with Tertullian, was his Christology, the strengths and weaknesses of which shall be discussed presently. Perhaps Origen's most controversial teaching, which was finally condemned by the Fifth General Council of the Catholic Church in A.D. 553, was his "universalism," which held that all men, including the fallen spirits, would ultimately be saved—viewed as an extreme of the apostolic understanding of Christ's total and universal triumph over all sin and evil.[9]

Out of fairness to this issue, I would be remiss not to call attention to other revered men of God of this time who shared—whether in part or wholly—Origen's convictions. Origen himself writes on this subject: "But he that despises the purification of the word of God, and the doctrine of the gospel, only keeps himself for dreadful and penal purifications afterwards; that so the fire of hell may purge him in torments whom neither apostolic doctrine nor gospel preaching has cleansed, according to that which is written of being 'purified by fire.' But how long this purification which is wrought out by penal fire shall endure, or for how many periods or ages it shall torment sinners, He only knows to whom all judgment is committed by the Father."

Clement of Alexandria similarly penned these words: "The Lord, says John in his First Epistle, is a propitiation, 'not for our sins only,' that is, of the faithful, 'but also for the whole world.' Therefore He indeed saves all universally; but some as converted by punishments, others by voluntary submission, thus obtaining the honour and dignity, that 'to Him every knee shall bow, of things in heaven, and things in earth, and things under the earth,' that is, to say, angels, and men, and souls who departed this life before His coming into the world."

Gregory of Nazianzus (A.D. 330–390), in a passage that alluded to the sect of the Novatians, said of them: "These, if they will, may go our way, which indeed is Christ's; but if not, let them go their own way. In another place perhaps they shall be baptized with fire, that last baptism, which is not only very painful, but enduring also; which eats up, as if it were hay, all defiled matter, and consumes all vanity and vice."

---

9. See Paul's understanding in Romans 11:36; 1 Corinthians 15:22-28; Ephesians 1:10; Philippians 2:9-11; Colossians 1:19-20; Hebrews 2:8-10; see also John's understanding in John 12:32 and Revelation 5:13.

Gregory of Nyssa (A.D. 332–394) declared in a similar vein: "Wherefore that at the same time liberty of free-will should be left to nature and yet the evil be purged away, the wisdom of God discovered this plan...either being purged in this life through prayer and discipline, or after his departure hence through the furnace of cleansing fire." (Thus we also can detect some of the origins of the doctrine of *purgatory* in these statements.)

So far spread were these universalistic views, not only in the East but also in the West, that the respected German Church historian Johann Gieseler (1792–1854), in his five-volume *Ecclesiastical History,* wrote: "The opinion of the indestructible capacity for reformation in all rational creatures, and the finiteness of the torments of hell, was so common even in the West, and so widely diffused among *opponents* of Origen, that though it might not have sprung up without the influence of his school, yet it had become quite independent of it."[10]

In all, these five men—Irenaeus, Tertullian, Cyprian, Clement, and Origen—were the principal shapers of Christian thought in the later second and early third centuries, spiritually "the autumn of the year," just before the coming of those cold blasts of doctrinal controversy that would further herald the coming of that bleak and dark spiritual winter, the Dark Ages.

Significant Changes in the Ante-Nicene Era

Five significant changes take place in the ante-Nicene era of Irenaeus, Tertullian, Cyprian, Clement, and Origen. All these are a direct result of the growing struggle of fragile Catholic Christianity against the schismatic heretics, particularly the Gnostics. These five changes are the emerging rule of faith, the consolidation of the canon of New Testament writings, the strengthening of the episcopacy, the rising supremacy of the Roman Church, and the formation of a defined Christology (an

---

10. Johann Gieseler, Vol. 1, *Ecclesiastical History*, section 82.

interpretation of exactly who Jesus was and is). These we will examine in order.

The Developing Rule of Faith

The Gnostic threat, carrying with it its own Gnostic scriptures and Gnostic revelations and allegorical Gnostic methods of interpreting even the original apostolic writings, necessitated the gradual formulating of some sort of basic creed within the Catholic Church by means of which the Spirit of truth could be more easily discerned from the spirit of error.

In connection with baptism, the earliest baptismal confession to be used was simply "Jesus is Lord."[11] With the complexity of the Gnostic threat, however, a more complex and comprehensive creed gradually developed by the second century, called the *Apostles' Creed,*[12] consisting of 12 apostolic statements of faith, the confession of which was required by each baptismal candidate:

1. I believe in God the Father Almighty;
2. I also believe in Jesus Christ His only Son, our Lord,
3. conceived of the Holy Spirit, born of the Virgin Mary,
4. suffered under Pontius Pilate, crucified, dead and buried; He descended into hell,
5. rose again the third day,
6. ascended into heaven,
7. sat down at the right hand of the Father,
8. thence He is to come to judge the living and the dead.
9. I believe in the Holy Ghost,
10. the Holy Catholic Church, the communion of saints,
11. the remission of sins,
12. the resurrection of the flesh and life eternal.[13]

Herein is the simplest definition of orthodoxy to arise out of the post-apostolic era—succinct, comprehensive, and clear.

---

11. See Romans 10:9 and 1 Corinthians 12:3.

12. See Appendix III for the currently used text of the Apostles' Creed.

13. Henry Bettenson, ed., *Documents of the Christian Church* (London: Oxford University Press, 1943), 35.

The Emerging Canon of Apostolic Writings

The word *canon* comes from the Greek word *kanon,* meaning "a measuring rod" or "a rule." It is the word given by the early Church fathers to those first apostolic writings that alone could be that "measuring rod" or "rule" by which to evaluate all other revelations and writings, especially those of the schismatic Gnostics. In the face of certain circulating Gnostic gospels and epistles, Irenaeus insisted that the test of the validity of any *inspired* writing was whether it was written by the apostles or by men closely connected with them. These writings Irenaeus called "scripture." Tertullian refers to these writings as the New Testament, which he considered as equal to the Old Testament in regard to divine inspiration. By about A.D. 200, according to the Muratorian fragment, western Christendom had recognized a New Testament canon basically including Matthew, Mark, Luke, John, Acts, First and Second Corinthians, Ephesians, Philippians, Colossians, Galatians, First and Second Thessalonians, Romans, Philemon, Titus, First and Second Timothy, Jude, First and Second John, Revelation, and the Apocalypse of Peter.[14] The development of the New Testament canon into its final form (as we know it today), however, continued until about A.D. 400 in the Latin branch of the Church and until even later in the Greek branch of the Church.

The Strengthening of the Episcopacy

It is not difficult for us to see how the declining charismatic activity of the Holy Spirit in the Church by the end of the first century made the full-orbed ministry of the local Body[15] a difficulty. It is further possible for us to see how the presence of heretics in local meetings of the Church[16] further made the "open" ministry of the Body undesirable, causing the public ministry rather to be shifted from the whole Body

---

14. *Ibid.*, 40-41.

15. 1 Corinthians 14:26.

16. Jude 10-12.

to the recognized presbyters of the Church alone. In this shift we have noticed the first subtle distinctions between the clergy (the "priests") and the laity of the Church.

We have also already noted the strong alleged emphasis of Ignatius of Antioch (A.D. 110) on obedience to the "singular bishop" as the best safeguard, in his understanding, against the inroads of the Gnostic heresy. It was apparently felt that allegiance to a single man was more possible and effective than allegiance to a plurality of men, especially if those men were not of one mind, with one heart. For the same reason the ante-Nicene era of the second and third centuries saw a further strengthening of that monarchical episcopate, the singular bishop, and further emphasized the validity of only that episcopacy that was in direct succession to the apostles themselves. Irenaeus, Clement, Tertullian, and especially Cyprian, in their battle against the Gnostics, greatly strengthened these concepts of the monarchical episcopate as the successors of the apostles. It should perhaps be a wonder as to why, in all this decline and the resultant outgrowths of heresy, there was not more of an emphasis on the apostolic warning: "Remember therefore from whence thou art fallen, and repent, and do the first works...."[17] Well may we ponder why these saintly men placed more emphasis on apologetics and structure as a remedy than on a renewed outpouring of the Holy Spirit as in the days of the apostles!

In his excellent book, *2000 Years of Charismatic Christianity,* Eddie L. Hyatt traces and explains the decline of spiritual gifts in the post-apostolic Church. Hyatt comments:

> "Spiritual gifts continued to be manifest after the first century. As institutionalism increasingly dominated the life and ministry of the Church, however, their prevalence and influence gradually diminished. *Institutionalism* is an emphasis on organization at the expense of other factors. In the Church such an emphasis, or over-emphasis, on

---

17. Revelation 2:5 KJV.

ways comes at the expense of the life and
Spirit.

...e move toward institutionalism in the early Church
arose as a means of defense against persecution from the
state and imposition of error from heretical sects such as
Gnosticism and Marcionism. Reacting to these threats, the
Church formalized worship and centralized power in the
bishop....

"For those who embraced this emphasis on organizational structure, spiritual authority was no longer seen as
residing in the person with the spiritual gift. That authority now resided, instead, in the one occupying the ecclesiastical office. This generated mounting tensions between
those who continued to embrace spiritual gifts and those
who preferred the emerging organizational structure.

"Those who desired the freedom and spontaneity of the
Spirit felt squelched by the growing ritual and formality. On
the other hand, church leaders, who by now might occupy
the office without the spiritual gift, felt uncomfortable with
the charismatics' claim of direct communion with God."[18]

The Rising Supremacy of the Church of Rome

Historian Qualben makes an interesting observation at this
juncture in the history of Christendom: "Although the Church
had not yet become a hierarchy, it developed rapidly in that
direction...the bishops of Rome, Constantinople, Antioch,
Jerusalem, and Alexandria naturally secured special prominence because of their location, and the unusual influence of
their churches."[19]

Specific significance is particularly attached to the influence of the Church at Rome, initial seat of the Roman Empire.
By A.D. 100 the Roman Church stands as the largest single

---

18. Hyatt, *op. cit.*, 22, 25.
19. Lars P. Qualben, *A History of the Christian Church* (New York: Thomas Nel-
    son & Sons, 1933), 98.

congregation in Christendom. By 251, it had continued on to be the strongest, most vibrant Church of its day, having some 30,000 adherents under the single Bishop, Cornelius, with 46 presbyters, 7 deacons, 7 subdeacons, 42 acolytes, and 52 exorcists, readers, and janitors. It had stood successfully in the defense of the Christian faith against the Gnostics, the Montanists, and other schismatics. With this in mind, Irenaeus, writing at the close of the second century, declares of Rome that "it is a matter of necessity that every church should agree with this church." According to Eusebius, the influence of Rome was further enhanced by its famed generosity. By A.D. 251 more than 1,500 dependents were supported by the Church. Ignatius addressed the Romans, in his epistle to them, as "having the presidency of love." Rome, the congregation of charity, the place where the creed was formulated and the canon consolidated, foremost in defense of the apostolic faith, had naturally risen in the ante-Nicene era to a position of importance that its later bishops would use to advantage in their struggle for the official supremacy of the Roman See (seat of power) over the whole of Christendom.

The Forming of a Defined Christology

The New Testament definition of God[20] is simple. Paul writes, "For even if there are so-called gods whether in heaven or on earth...yet for us there is but *one God,* the Father, from whom are all things, and we exist for Him...." To the apostolic mind there is but "one God...and one Lord, Jesus Christ...."[21] To the apostolic mind there is also the simple insight that somehow one God is revealed and expressed to men as "the Father and the Son and the Holy Spirit."[22] Beyond this simplicity there are no elaborate or expanded definitions of God in the New Testament.

New Testament Christology is also quite simple. The apostle John, a close personal friend of Jesus, is probably the most

---

20. This is basically what theology is.

21. 1 Corinthians 8:5-6.

22. Matthew 28:19; see also 2 Corinthians 13:14; 1 Peter 1:2; Revelation 1:4-5.

definitive of any of the New Testament writers as to the person of our Lord Jesus Christ. In the clearest of terms Jesus is presented by John as the great "*I AM*"[23] He is "the only begotten God, who is in the bosom of the Father...."[24] He is the Word, and as such He is "*God.*"[25] He is the full revelation of the Father, for He declares, "He who has seen Me has seen *the Father....*"[26] To Thomas, Jesus is "My Lord and *my God!*"[27] To John, Jesus is indeed "*the true God and eternal life.*"[28] As to Jesus' true and real humanity, John is equally emphatic: "...Every spirit that confesses that Jesus Christ has come in *the flesh* is from God."[29] Only the deceiver and the antichrist does not "acknowledge Jesus Christ as coming *in the flesh.*"[30] This, in a nutshell, is apostolic Christology. Jesus Christ is true God and true man.

The theology and Christology of the ensuing centuries is unfortunately more technical and complicated and therefore more divisive. It is true that there were grievous theological and Christological errors present in this period, errors that chipped away at the solidarity of the original apostolic simplicity. There were false teachings that detracted from Jesus' true humanity, such as Gnostic docetism—the belief that Jesus only appeared in a phantomlike body. Other teachings detracted from His true deity, such as Arianism (to be discussed later in more detail). But it is also true that much controversy arose among orthodox Christian believers of this era simply over the hybrid additions and elaborations added by their theologians to the original simple apostolic definitions of the first century.

Tertullian, the Montanist, is one of the first to elaborate on the word *Trinity* to define the Godhead. The Montanists, with

---

23. John 8:58.
24. John 1:18.
25. John 1:1.
26. John 14:9b.
27. John 20:28.
28. 1 John 5:20; See also 1 John 1:2.
29. 1 John 4:2.
30. 2 John 7.

their strong emphasis on the distinct Person and work of the Holy Spirit, seem to be among the first to so strongly define the Trinitarian understanding of God. The first-century apostolic mentality, rooted in strong old covenant monotheism, tended to treat warily *excessive* distinctions between Father, Son, and Holy Spirit, because it feared a tritheism. The Montanists, with their Trinitarian "Logos" theology, as it was called, were less fearful. Tertullian wrote rather obscurely concerning the Trinity in *Against Praxeas,* who was a heretic in Tertullian's eyes: "All are of one, by unity of substance; while the mystery of the dispensation is still guarded which distributes the unity into a Trinity, placing in their order the three, the Father, the Son, and the Holy Spirit; three, however...not in substance but in form; not in power but in appearance, for they are of one substance and one essence and one power, inasmuch as He is one God from whom these degrees and forms and aspects are reckoned under the name of the Father, and of the Son, and of the Holy Spirit."

Tertullian further described these distinctions of the Godhead as "persons," and frankly admitted in *Against Praxeas* the problem that his more elaborate and expanded definition of the Godhead caused: "The simple—I will not call them unwise or unlearned—who always constitute the majority of believers, are startled at the dispensation of the three in one, on the ground that their very rule of faith withdraws them from the world's plurality of gods to the one only true God." Historian Williston Walker comments on this objection: "It was difficult for them [the majority of believers] to see in Trinitarian conceptions aught else but an assertion of tritheism"[31] (i.e., three gods).

In reaction to these so-called *tri*theistic tendencies of the Trinitarians, the Monarchians (so dubbed by Tertullian because of their strong monotheistic stand) strongly declared their faith in the absolute unity or oneness of God. The most widespread form of Monarchianism was "Modalistic Monarchianism" (the ancient

---

31. Williston Walker, *A History of the Christian Church* (New York: Charles Scribner's Sons, 1959), 68.

counterpart of twentieth-century "oneness" Pentecostal theology). To the Monarchians, God was one God, revealing Himself in three *modes* or ways—Father, Son, and Holy Spirit. Along with Praxeas, the outstanding proponent of this Christology was Sabellius, who was eventually excommunicated at Rome (A.D. 215), but who nonetheless exerted great influence over the emerging Christology of the Church. Epiphanius of Salanius (c. 375) defined Sabellianism in these words: "Their doctrine is that Father, Son and Holy Spirit are one and the same being, in the sense that three names are attached to one substance. A close analogy may be found in the body, soul and spirit of man. The body is as it were the Father, the soul is the Son; while the Spirit is to the Godhead as the spirit is to a man...."[32] This latter observation regarding the Spirit is actually very much like Paul's own statements of First Corinthians 2:11! Had Paul lived in the third or fourth century even *he* might have been suspected as a modalist! Surely both Ignatius of Antioch and Melito of Sardis during the second century would have been so condemned. (See Chapter 4.) Sabellius' absolute identification of Father, Son, and Spirit implied an *equality* that eventually won out, theologically, over the "subordination" theory that characterized the Trinitarian Christology of Tertullian and especially Origen. This "subordination" theory, declaring the emanation of the Son from the Father, and the emanation of the Spirit from the Father and the Son, actually became one of the foundations of the later Arian heresy, the fourth-century version of our modern Jehovah's Witnesses, who subordinate Jesus Christ to the Father as a "lesser god."

Well may we reckon at this juncture in our study of Church history that the apostolic era of doctrinal simplicity is over. Technical definitions and expanded explanations are now the order of the day. And with this new "hybrid" orthodoxy will come untold controversy and schism and a continued authoritarian struggle to define and control the borders of the "true, apostolic, catholic faith." Historically, this was the autumn of the year.

---

32. *Adversus haeresus* (62:1), in Bettenson, *op.cit.,* 54.

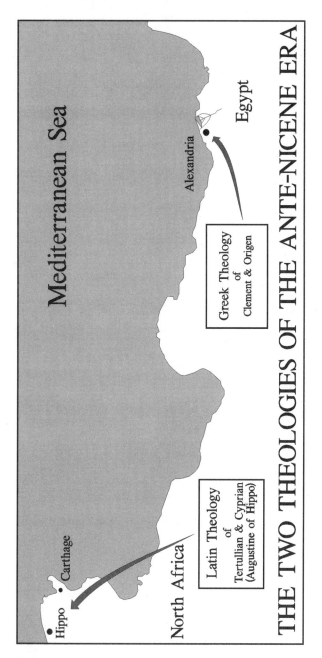

THE TWO THEOLOGIES OF THE ANTE-NICENE ERA

Chapter 6

Cold Blasts of Controversy

The Seven Councils of the Catholic Church[1]
(A.D. 325-787)

The Great Persecution

For 75 years, just prior to the famed first Council of Nicea in A.D. 325, the Christian Church suffered its gravest and severest persecution under the Roman emperors. Among its martyrs were notable women such as Catherine of Alexandria, tortured to death by Maxentius, the son of the Roman Emperor Maximian, and Dorothy of Caesarea, martyred in Cappadoria in 313. Christianity had become a grave threat to the collapsing Roman Empire. By the early 300's it was estimated that half of Asia Minor alone was Christian. Under Decius, the Christians and their leaders were imprisoned and tortured and

---

1. From this juncture in history, we shall use the word "Church" to denote the ongoing structure of organized Christianity. The degree to which this "Church" as a whole represents the true, catholic, apostolic Body of Christ must be left in God's hands to judge. For sure, there always will be found within structured Christianity, even in the Dark Ages, those true members of Christ's Body, made such by the indwelling presence of Christ Himself.

slain. Christian places of worship, which by now had sprung up in various places, were pillaged and destroyed.[2] Christians met for worship in caves, in desert places, and in catacombs—underground tunnels two to four feet wide where the bodies of deceased believers were entombed within the walls. Great pressure, even the threat of death, was exerted to induce believers to defect to the pagan worship of the State.

During these persecutions not a small number "lapsed" under that pressure into their old pagan practices. When these scourges finally ended, many of the defectors sought reinstatement into the Church; and the issue of reinstatement became but another source of bitter controversy and schism in Rome.

Novatian (A.D. 210–280), a presbyter of the Church in Rome, opposed Cornelius, Bishop of Rome, because of the laxity Cornelius had shown toward those Christians who had lapsed during the persecution. Novatian, consequently, spawned a separate movement, spreading from Asia Minor to Spain, of those seeking purity. They were called the *Cathari* (the "pure ones"), the Puritans or the Holiness movement of their day. In his valued work, *The Trinity*, Novatian gives us an important insight into the ongoing supernatural work of the Holy Spirit in the authentic Church. He writes that the Holy Spirit "places prophets in the church, instructs teachers, directs tongues, gives powers and healings, does wonderful works, offers discrimination of spirits, affords powers of government, suggests counsels, and orders and arranges whatever other gifts there are of charismata; and thus making the Lord's Church everywhere, and in all, perfected and completed." These Novatians, in their pursuit of purity, were not unlike the Donatists who arose in North Africa some 50 years later.

In the fall of 312, Emperor Constantine the Great allegedly experienced an unusual conversion. In the sky, he supposedly

---

2. "There is no clear example of a separate building set apart for Christian worship within the limits of the Roman Empire before the third century, though apartments in private houses might be specially devoted to this purpose" (Bishop Lightfoot).

saw a flaming cross and the words "By this sign conquer." By the following spring an epoch-making decree was issued from Milan that granted full toleration to Christianity within the Roman Empire. This decree was destined to produce both good and evil fruit within the Church, as Christianity would soon become the acceptable and popular religion of the changing Empire.

The First General Council of the Church at Nicea

In the face of internal dissension within the Empire and outward pressure by the barbarians, Emperor Constantine recognized the Catholic Church as the one main hope for unity and stability within the Roman Empire. But the Church itself was also being torn by strife and dissension, especially over the Christology controversy. In the hope of healing that breach, Constantine convened the first general council of the Church in May of 325 at Nicea in Bithynia, northwest Asia Minor. In attendance were 318 bishops, about one-sixth of the total bishops of the whole Church, summoned all the way from Spain to Persia to appear in Nicea at government expense.

The issue at hand was the controversy between the Alexandrian presbyter, Arius, and his bishop, Alexander, on the divine nature of the Lord Jesus Christ. Also present to oppose Arius was Bishop Alexander's young secretary, Athanasius. Both sides clung to the teachings of the Alexandrian, Origen; but Arius deduced from Origen's subordinationism that "the Son has a beginning, but God is without beginning."[3]

The final decision of the council was to anathematize Arius and his followers and rightly to declare in the language of the creed of Nicea: "We believe...in one Lord Jesus Christ...begotten, not made, of one substance with the Father...."[4]

As a result, Arius was banished with two others to Illyria. Two years later, however, the strife erupted again when the erratic Constantine received Arius back into favor and banished

---

3. Arius to Eusebius (c. 321), in *Documents of the Christian Church*, ed., Henry Bettenson (London: Oxford University Press, 1943), 55.
4. The full text of the Nicene Creed appears in Appendix IV.

Athanasius, now Bishop of Alexandria, for refusing to rein-state Arius. No less than five times was Athanasius exiled; and the unstable Constantine himself was finally baptized on his deathbed by an Arian! Athanasius, however, was long to be remembered in the church as "the Father of Orthodoxy," from whom the Athanasian Creed derives its name. The Athanasian Creed declares: "Whosoever will be saved, before all things it is necessary that he hold the true Christian faith...that we wor-ship one God in Trinity, and Trinity in Unity; neither con-founding the persons, nor dividing the substance...." It should be noted that salvation, by apostolic standards, was dependent upon a much simpler faith.[5]

Shortly before his death in 337, Constantine had moved the capital of his empire to Byzantium, modern-day Istanbul, renaming it Constantinople after himself. This decision would profoundly affect the course of future Church history. One result would be to further encourage the already growing rival-ry between the Greek churches and the Latin churches by ele-vating the Bishop of Constantinople to a position equal to that of the Bishop of Rome.

The Council of Constantinople, May A.D. 381

Attended by 186 bishops, mostly Greek, and convened by Emperor Theodosius the Great, this second council of the Church was held in the city of Constantine to further and final-ly deal with the Arian[6] controversy and to enlarge the Nicene confession by affirming the person and deity of the Holy Spir-it, "...who is the Lord and Giver of life, who proceedeth from the Father, who with the Father and the Son together is wor-shipped and glorified...."

This council, composed of mostly Greek clergy, also affirmed the rising supremacy of the Bishop of Constantinople,

---

5. See 1 Corinthians 15:1-8. Note: The full text of the Athanasian Creed appears in Appendix IV.
6. See previous page.

an affirmation that would eventually prove problematic to the future bishops of the Church at Rome.

The Third Council of the Church at Ephesus

Initially convened by Emperor Theodosius II on Pentecost Sunday in 431, and lasting through the end of October of that year, this council was a virtual battleground between the ambitious and violent Cyril, Bishop of Alexandria, and Nestorius, the eloquent Patriarch of Constantinople. Nestorius had made such a distinction between the divine and human natures in Christ that He was almost separated into two persons. Nestorius had opposed calling Mary the "mother of God," a practice present in the Church by now, insisting that she was the mother only of the man Jesus Christ and not of His divine nature. Certain acts of our Lord were also ascribed to His divine nature and certain others to His human nature by Nestorius. Nestorius was unjustly banished to the desert, and his followers formed the Nestorian Church, which grew with great vigor in Syria and Persia and Armenia, and even as far as China as a result of its missionary outreach. In answer to the imbalances of Nestorianism the council accurately defined itself thus: "We, therefore, acknowledge our Lord Jesus Christ...complete God and complete man...for a union of the two natures has taken place; wherefore we confess one Christ, one Son, one Lord...." Though we may wonder at the carnal, violent actions of the council, we may still honor their honest attempt at truth.

A second issue decided at Ephesus was the formal condemnation of the teachings of Pelagius, a British monk, in favor of the teachings of Augustine, Bishop of Hippo in North Africa, the outstanding churchman and author of *Confessions* and *The City of God*. Pelagius (like the American revivalist Charles G. Finney who in the mid-1800's followed some degree of Pelagius' thinking) attacked the growing view that original sin was inherited from Adam. Sin, to Pelagius (and to Finney), was a matter of will, not of inheritance. Consequently, infant baptism would be useless because infants have no hereditary, or original, sin. Also consequently, a man would be morally free to choose God and obey His laws. (Ideally, under these terms it could even be possible for a person to be saved by perfect obedience to the law.) Augustine opposed these teachings, affirming the growing Catholic belief in original sin by birth, the necessity of infant baptism, the inability of a person to truly choose God, and hence the necessity of the sovereign, irresistible grace of God in one's salvation (a view later adopted in the Protestant Reformation especially by John Calvin).

Though Pelagianism was here formally condemned by the Church, it lived on in the form of a semi-Pelagianism, which then increased and subverted medieval Catholicism theologically into believing in a form of justification by human works. Semi-Pelagianism was vigorously opposed by the Reformers, who denounced it as heresy.

Amidst his personal and spiritual virtues, Augustine nonetheless espoused certain other ideas that would later also bring forth much confusion in the Church. Of particular concern to Augustine were the Donatists of his native North Africa. Their insistence on a separate and pure communion (like the Novations before them) eventually elicited from Augustine his consent for the use of force against them. Augustine believed and taught that there was no salvation outside of the visible Catholic Church; he viewed it as the City of God, the true Christian Society, and thus Augustine laid the foundation for future claims and oppressive actions by the medieval papacy.

Other Outstanding Catholic Leaders

To this time also belong other outstanding Catholic leaders such as Ambrose (340–397), Bishop of Milan, probably the greatest pulpit orator of the western Church and a great, unbending champion of Catholicism against Arianism. It was through Ambrose that Augustine himself was converted from sensuality to Christ at Milan, in answer to the prayers of his godly mother Monica. Augustine was baptized by Ambrose in A.D. 387, at age 33.

In his treatise, *Of the Holy Spirit,* Ambrose describes the work of the Trinity in gracing the Church with spiritual gifts.

This was an evidence that even though Ambrose lived in a time of spiritual decline, he yet remained open to these charismatic manifestations. "You see," he writes, "the Father and Christ also set teachers in the churches; and as the Father gives the gift of healings, so too does the Son give; as the Father gives the gift of tongues, so too has the Son also granted it. In like manner…the Holy Spirit…grants the same kind of graces. So, then the Spirit gives the same gifts as the Father, and the Son also gives them."[7]

Another outstanding leader in this era was John Chrysostom, patriarch of Constantinople (347–407), the "Golden Mouth," so called because of his unrivaled eloquence in defense of Catholic orthodoxy and his fearless appeals for repentance. These appeals gained him banishment by the worldly empress. Also there was Jerome (343–420), the monastic celibate, known for his famous compilation of the Old and New Testament Scriptures into a Latin version known as the *Vulgate.* Following in the train of Athanasius, and yet outstanding in their own merits in the Eastern Church for their defense of the Nicene Creed against Arianism, were also the three committed Cappadocians: Basil, Bishop of Caesarea in Cappadocia (329–379); his younger brother Gregory, Bishop of Nyssa (332–394); and their common friend, Gregory of Nazianzus (330–390). A pioneer in the Monastic life was Macrina the Younger (328–380) sister of Basil and Gregory of Nyssa. Richard Riss describes her in the following way: "She healed, prophesied, and actively spread the Faith."[8]

To this era also belongs the godly martyr, Priscillian, Bishop of Avila. Condemned in A.D. 384 at the Synod of Bordeaux on trumped-up charges of heresy, immorality, and sorcery, Priscillian and six of his followers were beheaded. Priscillian had declared the Scriptures as the sole rule of faith and practice. He had also preached the need for a living faith through which

7. Ambrose, *Of the Spirit,* in Vol. 10 of *Nicene and Post-Nicene Fathers of the Christian Church,* 2nd series, eds., Philip Schaff and Henry Wace (Grand Rapids, MI: William B. Eerdmans, 1978), 134.

8. "Who's Who Among Women of the Word," *Spread the Fire*, October 1997, 9.

seekers become partakers of Christ, rather than through the sacraments of the Church. Priscillian also recognized no distinction between laity and clergy, declaring the ministry of the Word of God to be open to all according to the Spirit's pleasure, thus undercutting the Church's doctrine of apostolic succession and clerical domination. Two of the most noted churchmen of that day, Martin of Tours and Ambrose, Bishop of Milan, strongly opposed the unjust condemnation of the Priscillians, a movement that continued on for some two centuries after its founder's death.

The Fourth Council of the Church
at Chalcedon in Bithynia

Summoned on October 8, 451, by the Emperor Marcian at the insistence of the Roman bishop Leo, this turbulent council was convened with some 500-600 bishops, again almost all Greeks and Orientals, for the condemnation of Eutyches, abbot of a monastery near Constantinople. Eutyches had been the original unyielding opponent of Nestorius, the proponent of the two natures, at the council of Ephesus some 20 years before! Eutyches himself was now accused of teaching that Christ had only one nature—the human absorbed into the divine, an error called *monophysitism.* Eutyches declared, "As a drop of milk let fall into the ocean is quickly absorbed, so also was the human nature of Christ entirely absorbed by the Divinity." To this the creed of Chalcedon correctly answered: "We, then...all with one consent, teach men to confess one and the same Son, our Lord Jesus Christ...truly God and truly man...in two natures: unconfusedly, unchangeably, indivisibly, inseparably; the distinction of natures being by no means taken away by the union, but rather the property of each nature being preserved, and concurring in one person...the Lord Jesus Christ...."

History records, however, unchristian behavior by various bishops present at this turbulent council, including their insults, jeers, mob frenzy, and violence. As one messianic leader rose to address the council yet others cried out, "Cast

out the Jew, the enemy of God, the blasphemer of Christ!"[9]
Well might we wonder at the state that fifth-century Catholic
orthodoxy had fallen into, a state in which Jesus Christ was
now carnally argued about and bitterly fought over; and well
might we long for a return to that anointed apostolic simplicity of the first century in which our Lord Jesus Christ was simply worshiped and loved and adored in the power of the
outpoured Holy Spirit as true God and true man.

The Rise of Anti-Semitism

Unfortunately, one of the most ungodly notes sounded in the
era of post-apostolic Christianity was that of anti-Semitism. A
number of Church fathers held very bitter views concerning the
Jews. Chrysostom, for example, in one of his homilies given at
Antioch, unjustly preached: "The Jews sacrifice their children to
Satan...they are worse than wild beasts. The synagogue is a
brothel, a den of scoundrels, the temple of demons devoted to
idolatrous cults, a criminal assembly of Jews, a place of meeting for the assassins of Christ, a house of ill fame, a dwelling of
iniquity, a gulf and abyss of perdition....The Jews have fallen
into a condition lower than the vilest animal...." Then speaking
of the crucifixion, Chrysostom spewed out this invective against
the Jews: "[the] odious assassination of Christ for which crime
there is no expiation possible, no indulgence, no pardon, and for
which they will always be a people without a nation, enduring a
servitude without end." Chrysostom's final conclusion was, "I
hate the Jews....I hate the synagogue....It is the duty of all
Christians to hate the Jews."[10] (*Chrysostom would have been
amazed at how God Himself would restore Israel to nationhood
in the twentieth century, bring about one of the greatest ingathering of Jews into the Kingdom of the Messiah since the first*

---

9. Philip Schaff, Vol. 3, *History of the Christian Church* (New York: Charles Scribner's Sons, 1882), 742-743.

10. "Homilies Against the Jews," *Patrologia Graeca* (Paris: Garnier, 1857–1866),
843-902.

century, and begin the process of genuine reconciliation between Israel and the Church!)

Sorrowfully, similar rhetoric against the Jews is to be found in statements by Ambrose, Gregory of Nyssa, Augustine, Origen, and others. Origen referred to the Jews as "a most wicked nation" for their crimes "committed against our Jesus." One modern student of Jewish studies, Sandra S. Williams, observes, "The Church Fathers had sown the seeds of intolerance and Jews were to become the object of hatred and persecution all over Europe for centuries to come."[11] It was likewise true that Jews would even more reject this Jesus whom they had not known, in reaction to the hatred of those whom they had known and who claimed to be His.

Paul the apostle could have wished *himself* "cursed" for their sake,[12] while any number of the Church fathers could have wished *the Jews* cursed for Christ's sake. But Paul's was a generation of the fresh outpouring of the Holy Spirit of Jesus; theirs was a generation of the cold blasts of bitter controversy.

Leo the Great

No man of this time stands as a greater enigma than the Roman bishop and theologian, Leo the Great (440–461). In his Holy Week sermons, Leo declared, "The cross is our glory; by means of it the world is dead to us and we are dead to the world (Galatians 6:14)....Anyone who has nailed his sinful desires to the cross, who has laid down at his Savior's feet any resentments or bitterness that may have been in his heart, who has learned to forgive his enemies and to prefer God's will to his own, who refuses to give in to the urges of his lower nature and who walks in the way of God's Holy Spirit, has no need either to dread the evil one or to try to appease him...." And yet this very same Leo bent all his strength toward gaining recognition in the Church as "Universal Bishop." He it was who gave

---

11. Sandra S. Williams, *The Origins of Christian Anti-Semitism*, Judaic Studies Program, University of Central Florida, 1993.
12. Romans 9:3.

the theory of papal power a more final form. Though finally widely received as supreme pontiff (bishop) in the Western Church, Leo's claims were emphatically repudiated by the Eastern Church, a stand that contributed to the ultimate split between the Roman and the Greek Churches centuries later. The Council of Chalcedon had voted the patriarch of Constantinople to be the chief bishop of the entire Church, but had refused Leo's strenuous request to be recognized as Universal Bishop of the Church (though it did agree to reserve the title "pope" for the Roman bishop). And so Leo stands as an enigma—a man of deep spiritual conviction and yet a man of great personal ambition. This apparent contradiction of spirituality and carnality is unfortunately all too characteristic of most of what occurred among councils and bishops and churches in this waning era of Christianity.

The Fifth Council, Constantinople II, May 553

A full century after the council at Chalcedon, Emperor Justinian, without the consent of the Roman pope, convened the fifth Catholic council of the Church with 164 bishops for the correction of the continuing monophysite (single nature) controversy. Notwithstanding this attempt at correction, this doctrine still finds expression in the Coptic churches of Egypt and Ethiopia. The fifth council also, in a very confusing move, condemned as a heretic Origen, who had been previously received as "the greatest ante-Nicene theologian of the Eastern Church" and one whose thoughts had already helped frame and fashion more than a little of the thinking of the Church!

The Sixth Council, Constantinople III, November 680

More than a century after the preceding council, the sixth Catholic council was convened at which monotheletism, the teaching that Christ had but a single will, was condemned. The council proclaimed "that Christ has two volitions or wills, and two natural operations without division or change, without partition or co-mingling...." J. Oliver Buswell, professor of Systematic Theology at Covenant Theological Seminary in

St. Louis, aptly commented on the doctrinal problem caused by the theory of two wills: "The decision of the third council of Constantinople, 680, declaring that Jesus Christ has two 'wills'...is perhaps the most disturbing to our modern consciousness...I cannot deny that the wording of the decision of the council seems to imply that a 'will' is a substantive entity, like a hand or a foot. Yet I do not believe that such an opinion can be dogmatically asserted as the actual meaning of the decision of the council....In any case we are not dealing with the infallible word of God, but with the decisions of the venerable council generally held to have been true."[13] (Actually, Jesus Christ has but one will—truly human, yet truly divine.)

In the process of its decisions, Constantinople III also condemned Pope Honorius (638) as a heretic. Historian Philip Schaff comments on the further problem that this action created: "The condemnation of a departed pope as a heretic by an ecumenical council is so inconsistent with the claims of papal infallibility, that Romish historians have tried their utmost to dispute the fact, or to weaken its force by sophistical pleading."[14] These centuries of increasing controversy and confusion demonstrate the waning of the life of the Spirit of Christ within the churches of Christendom.

The Seventh Council, Nicea II

Convened by Empress Irene in 787, this final council of the splintering Catholic Church did not do much more than make the unscriptural decree, "If any bishop from this time forward is found consecrating a temple without holy relics, he shall be deposed as a transgressor of the ecclesiastical traditions!"

At this time the Greek and the Roman Churches parted, and truly ecumenical councils, those representing the entire Church, ceased to exist. Later on, after 336 years, the Roman Church—

---

13. J. Oliver Buswell, Vol. 1, *A Systematic Theology of the Christian Religion* (Grand Rapids, MI: Zondervan, 1962), 53-54.

14. Schaff, *History of the Christian Church* (New York: Charles Scribner's Sons, 1882), *op. cit.,* 352.

in pursuance of her claims to universality—convened the first Roman ecumenical council of the medieval Church at Lateran (1123). By then the Greek Church was officially severed from its Roman sister in an irreconcilable division that began in 1054 and continues to this very day.

These were centuries full of cold blasts of bitter controversy and ambition, heralding the coming of that dead winter known as the Dark Ages of Church history—an era in which the dimly flickering light of the glory of God was all but extinguished from the face of the earth.

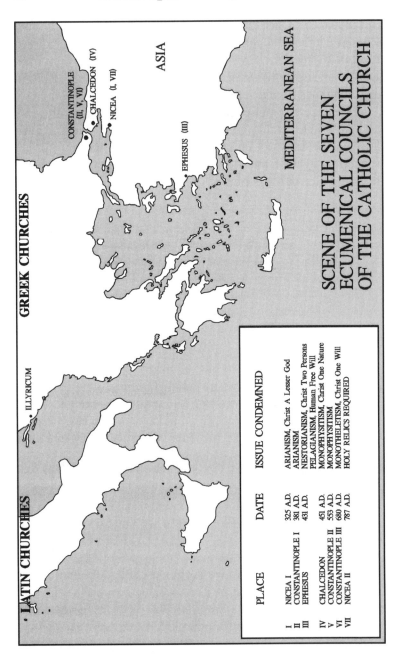

LATIN CHURCHES

GREEK CHURCHES

ILLYRICUM

ASIA

CONSTANTINOPLE (II, V, VI)
CHALCEDON (IV)
NICEA (I, VII)

EPHESUS (III)

MEDITERRANEAN SEA

SCENE OF THE SEVEN
ECUMENICAL COUNCILS
OF THE CATHOLIC CHURCH

	PLACE	DATE	ISSUE CONDEMNED
I	NICEA I	325 A.D.	ARIANISM, Christ A Lesser God
II	CONSTANTINOPLE I	381 A.D.	ARIANISM
III	EPHESUS	431 A.D.	NESTORIANISM, Christ Two Persons
IV	CHALCEDON	451 A.D.	PELAGIANISM, Human Free Will
			MONOPHYSITISM, Christ One Nature
V	CONSTANTINOPLE II	553 A.D.	MONOPHYSITISM
VI	CONSTANTINOPLE III	680 A.D.	MONOTHELEITISM, Christ One Will
VII	NICEA II	787 A.D.	HOLY RELICS REQUIRED

Chapter 7

The Bleakness and Deadness of Winter

The Dark Ages (A.D. 590–1294)

Author's note: We have now come to those chapters in Church history which, unfortunately, will be of grief to any sincere Catholic reading them. I have sought to be honest and straightforward in both my statement of the facts and in my evaluations of those facts. I do sincerely trust, however, that neither the facts nor my evaluations will in any way impugn those many thousands of sincere, believing Catholic brothers and sisters who are part of the present outpouring of the Holy Spirit.

*These chapters of history are necessary if we are to understand the sixteenth-century quest for reformation and restoration, both from within and from without the Catholic Church. No personal offense to anyone's conscience has been intended, but rather, simply an open investigation of the facts of history. And bright spots **do** exist within this era—especially among the Irish, and among the Monastics—as God poured out His Spirit on the ones who were thirsty like "floods upon the dry ground"!*

This fascinating era of medieval (or "Middle Age") Church history can be divided into two main periods: the rise of the papacy, from Gregory I to Gregory VII (590–1050), and the era of absolute papacy, from Gregory VII to Boniface VIII (1050–1294).

The Rise of the Roman Catholic Church

Two principal reasons have been advanced by historians for the supremacy of Roman Christianity over Greek Christianity and for the consequent rise of the Roman papacy: (1) the fall of the West to the barbarian hordes and (2) the fall of the East to Islam.[1]

In the East, in Syria alone, 10,000 Greek Catholic Church buildings were destroyed or became Moslem mosques during this time. The North African churches of Tertullian, Cyprian, and Augustine were virtually obliterated by Islam. Only the miraculous salvaging of Europe by the triumph of the Frankish Charles Martel at Tours in 732 preserved the Western Latin churches from the same fate as the Eastern Greek churches that were crushed by the crescent of Islam. And the crippling of Eastern Greek Catholicism could not but enhance the unrivaled rise of Roman Catholicism in the West.

In the West, the eventual fall of the Roman Empire in 476 to the Teutonic barbarians actually infused the effete, decaying Roman Empire with a new strength and vitality. Many of the invading barbarians were already Arian[2] Christians, and not a

---

1. Islam, the Moslem religion, is a monotheistic religion, whose deity is Allah and whose chief prophet and founder is the Arabian Mohammed (A.D. 570?–632). The Islamic scriptures are the Holy Koran. Islam is a religion with no priesthood, no hierarchy, no sacraments, no complicated theology, and no unattainable ideals (*Encyclopedia Americana*). Islam holds to five major beliefs—in Allah, in his prophet Mohammed, in the Koran, in the angels, and in the day of judgment. Islam also rests on "5 pillars": declaring "Allah is God and Mohammed is his prophet"; prayer; almsgiving; fasting (in the month of Ramadan); and the holy pilgrimage. One sect adds a sixth pillar, the Holy War.

2. See pages 53-54.

few, in the course of time, became Catholics, a fact that ultimately would greatly enhance the power of the defender of Western Catholicism, the Bishop of Rome.

Patrick and the Conversion of the Irish

One of the brightest spots of the fifth century was the apostolic work of Patrick among the Irish. Patrick was born around 387 in Britain of Celtic Christian parents. At age 16 he was kidnapped by Irish bandits and taken to Ireland, where he was sold as a slave to Miliucc, a regional king in the northeast of Ireland.

During his six years of captivity, Patrick gave himself wholly to Christ, who then spoke to him in a dream instructing him to escape, which he did. He returned home to his parents in Britain via France. There at home the Lord spoke again to him clearly by revelation that he was to return to the Irish as a missionary-evangelist. At age 45, after some 20 years of training and preparation, Patrick embarked on his Irish apostolic mission. He labored in Ireland, winning thousands to Jesus over 30 years. Some estimate that over 100,000 came to Christ through his labors! He died, it is believed, on March 17, 461, at nearly 75 years of age. One biographer comments on his death: "Thirty years before, he had come to a race that was almost entirely heathen; he left it almost completely Christian!"

The secret of Patrick's revival-filled life was that he was a Spirit-filled man. In his *Confession*, an authentic, brief personal biography, Patrick refers to his experiences in the Holy Spirit no fewer than ten times. He writes: "He poured out abundantly on us the Holy Spirit, the gift and pledge of immortality...." In describing his intense devotion to Jesus just after his conversion, Patrick writes: "I was praying up to a hundred times every day—and in the night nearly as often...because, as I now realize, the Spirit was fervent within me."

Of his labors, Patrick writes: "I felt all the more His great power within me...His Spirit is within me and works in me to the present day...nor will I conceal the signs and wonders which the Lord has shown to me...The Lord also foretells through the prophet, saying: 'and in the last days...I will pour out My Spirit over all flesh and your sons and daughters will prophesy...indeed in those days I will pour out My Spirit....' "

After his death, Patrick's works lived on. Irish missionaries "swarmed like bees into the dark places of heathen Europe." Ireland itself was called "the Isle of Saints," the "University of the West." Copies of the Bible marked with commentaries to the Teutonic, Scandinavian, and Italian peoples are still extant. Thirteen monasteries were founded in Scotland by the godly Columba, 12 in England, and over 75 on the continent.

We call special attention to Columba's anointed work at Iona, just off the west coast of Scotland. Columba viewed himself as but "a first among equals" in a community that was governed by presbyters or elders. It was the Holy Spirit, he held, not the ordinations of men, who made servants and ministers of God. The Scriptures were the rule of faith; rituals and traditions were discounted. From Iona, men were set apart and sent forth to take the gospel of Jesus Christ to other regions of the world.

Of the other Irish who were recognized as founders of churches, there were 150 in Germany, 45 in Gaul, 30 in Belgium, 13 in Italy, and 8 in Norway and Iceland. Surprisingly, all these Celtic works *remained officially unconnected to the emerging papacy and the developing Roman hierarchy* until 1172, when the Synod of Cashel bound them to the Roman Church in England.

Mixed Gains for the Catholic Church

In 496, Clovis, King of the Franks, was baptized along with 3,000 of his soldiers into the Catholic Church. In 587, Recared, the Visigoth King of Spain, was converted from Arianism to the Catholic faith. The 700's saw the conversion of the Germanic tribes to Catholicism, with the Frankish kings Pepin and Charlemagne giving large land grants—the papal states—to the Bishop of Rome. Needless to say, in many places this boon for the Catholic Church was little gain for the Kingdom of God. It was merely another step in the secularization of the Catholic Church that had begun centuries before under Constantine. Catholicism was now to be further glutted with large numbers of unconverted and heathenish people who would actually bring with them into Catholicism a dark cloud of demonic oppression and demonic spirit activity, which would speed its decline into the Dark Ages.

These masses of nominal "converts" simply transferred their paganism onto Christian symbols. In the place of their pagan gods they now venerated images, relics, angels, martyrs, Mary "the mother of God," and the saints. The apostolic practice of praying *for* the saints degenerated into praying *to* the saints. Pagan fetishism was replaced by the veneration of relics: the bones of martyrs, their clothes, and the instruments of their martyrdom. Principal among the sacred relics was the cross of Christ, which Helena, Constantine's mother, is said to have discovered in Jerusalem in A.D. 326. Pious pilgrims carried splinters of the cross from Jerusalem all across the Roman Empire until eventually there were sufficient splinters for several crosses.[3]

Pagan idolatry found its counterpart in the veneration of images and pictures of Christ, Mary, the apostles, and the saints. So great and alarming was this abuse that it eventually became the source of sore controversy between the Church and the Emperor—the iconoclastic controversy—as images and pictures were kissed, candles were lit before them, and people prostrated themselves before them, seemingly worshiping not the divine and abstract reality, as they had been instructed, but the very image itself. To the "Christianized" pagan mentality, the Lord's Supper was to be viewed no longer as merely a sacrament but now as a "sacrifice." Souls were believed to be purged by fire in a place under the earth. Elaborate basilicas, in

---

3. Lars P. Qualben, *A History of the Christian Church* (New York: Thomas Nelson & Sons, 1933), 131-132.

replacement of pagan temples, flourished. In opposition to the apostolic mentality, God no longer dwelt in the hearts of men alone but also in buildings of stone and wood. Robed Christian priests replaced the orders of robed pagan priests in the keeping of these temples. And so it was not difficult for a pagan, whether Roman or Greek or barbarian, to make the transfer from paganism to Christianity. Often nothing changed but the semantics. To many, the practices were virtually the same.

Monasticism: A Light in the Dark

Both the adoption of Christianity as the state religion under Constantine in the fourth century and the fall of the Roman Empire before the invading paganistic barbarian hordes in the fifth century glutted the ranks of Christendom with impurity and worldliness from which honest and godly souls sought relief and retreat in the seclusion of monasticism and the monastic orders that were ultimately birthed in the Middle Ages.

In his book, *2000 Years of Charismatic Christianity,* historian Eddie L. Hyatt observes how the structures and the secularization of the Church "had devastating ramifications for the ministry of the Holy Spirit through the people of God. The gifts that once had flowed spontaneously among the whole congregation were now bound to the ecclesiastical office and transmitted by a sacramental act. In the New Testament Church, the people had been participants in spontaneous worship, but they now became passive spectators in a highly developed sacramental ritual presided over by ecclesiastical officials."[4] Hyatt quotes A.J. Gordon, founder of Boston's Gordon College: "It is not altogether strange that when the Church forgot her citizenship in heaven and began to establish herself in luxury and splendor on earth she should cease to exhibit the supernatural gifts of heaven."[5]

---

4. Eddie L. Hyatt, *2000 Years of Charismatic Christianity* (Tulsa: Hyatt International Ministries, Inc., 1996), 35.

5. A.J. Gordon, *The Ministry of Healing* (Harrisburg: Christian Publications, 1961), 64, as quoted by Hyatt, *op cit.*, 38-39.

In a chapter entitled "Monasticism: The Rise of Another Charismatic Movement," Hyatt further states: "The miraculous gifts of the Holy Spirit which disappeared from the institutional Church now appeared among the monastics. Many monks gained notoriety for their power in prayer and their ability to produce healing, deliverance from demonic oppression, and other miraculous phenomena."[6] Hyatt then observes: "Cardinal Leon Joseph Suenens is correct in saying, 'In its beginnings, monasticism was, in fact, a charismatic movement.' "[7] From the Benedictines to Bernard of Clairvaux, to the Franciscans and the Dominicans, these monasteries with their monastic orders became centers of light and learning, art and music, and preeminently centers of spiritual renewal and revival. To a real degree, they preserved the true light of the Lord Jesus within a rapidly falling and benighted religious system.

Benedict of Nursia (480–547), in reaction to the fallenness of the city of Rome, retreated as a hermit for 30 years to the mountains east of Rome. In 529, he founded a monastary and bequeathed to it *The Rule of Benedict*, one of the most valued blueprints for monastic life in the Middle Ages. Benedict was a powerfully anointed man of God. "He cured [the] sick, relieved the distress[ed], and is said to have raised the dead on more than one occasion."[8]

Hildegard (1098–1179), leader of the Benedictine convent near Bingen on the Rhine who was considered a woman of great spiritual importance in her day, followed in Benedict's anointed footsteps. "Scarcely a sick person came to her without being healed," and apparently she sang in tongues, as "concerts in the Spirit" were attributed to her by her peers.[9] Unfortunately, her

6. Hyatt, *op cit.*, 39.

7. Cardinal Leon Joseph Suenens, *A New Pentecost?* (New York: Seabury, 1975), 38, as quoted by Hyatt, *op. cit.*, 41.

8. Michael Walsh, ed., *Butler's Lives of the Saints* (San Francisco: Harper, 1991), 212.

9. Philip Schaff, Vol. 5, *History of the Christian Church* (New York: Charles Scribner's Sons, 1882), 372.

"visions" were called into question, and she was put on trial by the Church in 1148. Hildegard had prophesied against the papacy: "God's justice is about to strike! His judgments shall be accomplished: the empire and the papacy have fallen and shall go down together. But from their ruins, the Holy Spirit will cause a new people to rise. All men shall be converted, and the angels shall return in confidence to dwell among the children of men."[10] In her visions, she undoubtedly saw the centuries of reformation now on the horizon.

Likewise Bernard (1090–1153), founder of the monastery at Clairvaux and author of the pristine hymn "Jesus, the very thought of Thee with sweetness fills my breast...," was a Spirit-anointed man. "From all quarters sick persons were conveyed to him by the friends who sought from him a cure."[11] Bernard's great weakness, however, was that he could not see any church beyond the organizational structure of the Roman Church and bitterly opposed those "groups of believers who refused to recognize any man as their founder."

Francis of Assisi (1182–1226), born Giovanni Bernadone, was the son of a cloth merchant in central Italy. At age 27, as he was listening to the reading of the gospel, Francis felt God's call to preach the Kingdom of God. As others were drawn to him (including Claire of *Brother Sun, Sister Moon* fame), Francis drew up a simple monastic "rule." In 1210, Francis gained the reluctant approval of Pope Innocent III to establish the Franciscan order, viewed as "perhaps the most thoroughly charismatic [order], in its primitive period, that the church has ever known."[12] Prophecy, miracles, healings, and speaking in tongues were evident, as well as a high degree of revival power.

10. Hildegard, as quoted by Omer Englebert, *St. Frances of Assisi, A Biography* (Ann Arbor, MI: Servant Books, 1979), 57.

11. Augustus Neander, Vol. 4, *General History of the Christian Church* (Boston: Crocker Brewster, 1853), 154.

12. F. Sullivan, *Charism and Charismatic Renewal: A Biblical and Theological Study* (Dublin: Gill and Macmillan, 1982), 48.

Historian Richard Riss calls attention to Anthony of Padua (1195–1231), a contemporary of Francis and a member of the Franciscans, who a year before his death devoted himself to the public preaching of repentance. Riss notes, "According to historian Mary E. Rogers, his extraordinary gifts as a preacher included, in addition to a clear voice and a compelling manner, prophetic powers and miracles. At his Lenten series in Padua in 1231, there were 30,000 in attendance at one time, and there were massive reconciliations and restitutions to such an extent that the number of clergy was insufficient for the needs of the people."[13]

Likewise, there was Dominic (1170–1221), a contemporary of Francis of Assisi and founder of the Dominican order. Dominic was himself a powerfully anointed man to whom signs and wonders were attributed, including speaking in tongues and raising the dead. (It should be noted, however, that often the "speaking in tongues" attributed to these saints was the instantaneous supernatural impartation of a *known* language—French in the case of Francis [for that reason he adopted the nickname *Francis*], and German in the case of Dominic, needed in the preaching of the Gospel to unconverted foreigners. Thomas of Celano recorded that "it was always in French that St. Francis expressed himself when he was filled with the Holy Ghost...."[14]) Omer Englebert also recorded how "the Office [Matins] was sometimes interrupted by the infectious gales of laughter that would sweep over" the early Franciscans.[15]

These passionate monastics sought for God, and He came to them, as "floods upon the dry ground"!

---

13. Richard Riss, *A Survey of 20th-Century Revival Movements in North America* (Peabody, MA: Hendrickson, 1988), 8-9.
14. Thomas as quoted by Englebert, *op. cit.*, 40.
15. Englebert, *op. cit.*, 168.

The Rise of the Roman Papacy

In stark contrast to anointed Monasticism, the rise of the medieval papacy is a study of political intrigue and human ingenuity.

In understanding the rise of the medieval papacy, we must understand something of the four great architects of the papal system—Leo the Great, Gregory I, Gregory VII, and Innocent III. We have already considered the enigmatic Leo the Great of the previous century (440–461) in his struggle for supremacy over the other ruling patriarchs of the Church and his vast claims to supreme leadership in the Catholic churches.

Gregory I, following in his train a century and a half later (590–604), has been aptly called "the last of the Roman bishops and the first of the Roman popes," and as such he marks the beginning of the rise of the medieval papacy in the earth. He, like Leo, is an enigma spiritually. He opposed the title "Universal Bishop" given to John, the Patriarch of Constantinople, assuming rather for himself the title "servant of servants of God." In the next breath he described himself as "the vicar of Christ on earth." Historian Philip Schaff summarizes Gregory as "monastic, ascetic, devout, and superstitious; hierarchical, haughty, and ambitious; yet humble before God"[16]— a true enigma.

Powerful preacher, able Augustinian theologian, shrewd political and ecclesiastical organizer, Gregory stands out foremost as a missionary organizer. The archbishopric of Canterbury with its famed cathedral was established during his pontificate, following the baptism of King Ethelbert of Kent and 10,000 of his people into the Catholic Church through the labors of a missionary team of 40 sponsored by Gregory and headed up by Gregory's fellow monk and personal friend, Augustine.[17] Author John W. Kennedy notes that "there was,

---

16. Philip Schaff, Vol. 1, *Medieval Christianity* (Grand Rapids, MI: William B. Eerdmans, 1978), 212.

17. Not Augustine of Hippo, who lived some hundreds of years before.

however, a fierce conflict between the old British churches and the system which Augustine introduced. He died having failed miserably to bring the Christians of Ireland and Scotland under the domination of the Pope."[18] Under Gregory, however, the influence of the Roman See would extend to France, Spain, and Africa, as well as to England.

Within a century after Gregory I the Germanic tribes were converted to Catholicism and to the obedience of the Bishop of Rome. The British monk Boniface, "apostle to the Germans" (672–755), labored faithfully in Thuringia, Bavaria, and Hesse to bring the German tribes under the authority of the Church of Rome. He founded dioceses, built church buildings and monasteries and schools according to the Roman pattern, and was consecrated Archbishop of Mainz in 732, faithfully serving the interests of Gregory III, Bishop of Rome.

Toward the end of the eighth century, all German Saxony was compelled to embrace Christianity by Charlemagne's decree to "convert the Saxons by the Word and the sword." In one day, 4,500 Saxons were beheaded for their resistance, which initiated 30 years of bloodshed and revolt.

The close of the eighth century saw a union between the papacy and the German Frankish kings, which would then pave the way for the eventual struggle for world political supremacy between the Holy Roman Empire and the Holy Roman Catholic Church. In 752, Pepin II, "the Short," was crowned king by the papal legate (representative). And on Christmas day, A.D. 800, in St. Peter's Church, Pope Leo III crowned Charlemagne Emperor of the Holy Roman Empire, an act that Roman pontiffs for many centuries to come would use as an argument for their claim to supreme authority over all kings and kingdoms on earth.

In the years following the death of Charlemagne, further vital missionary efforts were begun. Ansgar (801–865) labored

---

18. John W. Kennedy, *The Torch of the Testimony* (Gospel Literature Service, 1965; Goleta, CA: Christian Books, reprint), 106

in Scandinavian Denmark, Norway, and Sweden. The Balkan Bulgars under their king, Boris, who had been baptized in 864, adopted Christianity in the 800's. For some time undecided between Constantinople and Rome, Boris finally chose spiritual allegiance with the Patriarch of Constantinople, a definite gain for the Greek Church in Eastern Europe. (By the year 1000, all Russia would be Christianized under the umbrella of the Greek Church.)

Following Paul as He Followed Christ

In the mid-seventh century, in the region of Mesopotamia, a group of believers emerged, simply known as "Christians" or "brethren." They were dubbed "Paulicians" by others, perhaps because they sought to follow the apostle Paul as he followed Christ. The Catholic Church charged them with all sorts of heresies, including holding the Gnostic Manichaean doctrine of the essential evil of the whole material creation. Historian Williston Walker believes that the Paulicians *were* indeed influenced by Marcionite and Gnostic thinking, but other historians such as John W. Kennedy believe these were false charges and that the Paulicians represented a genuine move of the Holy Spirit.

Among other foundational "heresies" of the Paulicians were these: an unusual respect for the authority of the Holy Scriptures, baptizing only those who were repentant and believing, living a holy life consistent with God's Word, and accepting no central authority over their autonomous assemblies!

Of the Catholic persecution that mounted against the Paulicians, Kennedy writes: "The history of the Roman Church in its dealings with those who refused to bow to its dominion is a sordid tale of pillage and persecution. Not only did it seek to destroy the persons of those who opposed it, but also to bring the very memory of their names into ignominy by the most gross accusations, and to obliterate what they themselves wrote or anything written about them in their favor."[19] Kennedy then

19. *Ibid.*, 110.

describes the Paulician movement in these words: "The Paulicians attracted men who had a passionate devotion to
Christ...men of humility and apostolic spirit who poured out
their lives in the proclamation of the truth and died rather than
deny their Lord."[20]

Among these Paulicians, in A.D. 653, was a convert to
Christ named Constantine Silvanus. (Constantine was his
given name, which he changed to Silvanus, after the traveling
companion of the apostle Paul.) Silvanus was stoned to death
around 684 by the emperor for his faith and for his refusal to
submit to the Catholic Church. By the middle of the eighth
century Paulicians had preached the gospel and established
numerous churches in the Balkan area. There they were known
as "Bogomils," meaning "friends of God." So powerful was
their witness that by the end of the twelfth century the ruling
family of Bosnia and 10,000 Bosnians had become "Bogomils."
Catholicism had lost its hold on Bosnia. In its place were many
simple New Testament congregations. Threatened by this loss,
Pope Innocent III ordered the king of Hungary to invade
Bosnia. The country was ravaged by a war that continued for
years. Then, in 1291, an Inquisition was begun to exterminate
these followers of Christ. Only after the Muslims overran
Bosnia in the mid-fifteenth century did the "friends of God"
seem to die out. They were a truly great revival and renewal
movement in the midst of the Dark Ages!

The Struggle

The long history of the rise of the Roman bishops and their
claim to world supremacy is the story of two bitter struggles.
The first struggle was initially for supremacy within Christen-
dom over the patriarchs of the Greek Church, particularly
Constantinople. The second struggle was for supremacy in the
Holy Roman Empire over the rulers of the nations. This long
history reveals fairly clearly how far the leadership of the
Church had strayed from simple New Testament Christianity.

---

20. *Ibid.*, 112.

This discrepancy between the New Testament model and the actual one of the medieval period undermined, for many, the claims of the Roman Church of being the true apostolic Church and the transmitter of true, holy, apostolic authority through an unbroken line of bishops. Actually, the painful facts of history reveal that here were men whose actions and statements indicate that they had neither root nor branch in the Kingdom of God. Apart from the communities of those who were pure in heart, the apostolic church had virtually ceased to exist. This was the bleakness and deadness of winter, the Dark Ages.[21]

The ninth century saw the circulation of the infamous "Pseudo-Isidorian Decretals." *Decretals* was the term for papal decrees and official announcements; this particular collection, supposedly dating back to the first century, was ascribed to the celebrated prelate and writer, Isidore of Seville. The aim of these spurious decretals was to support the exaggerated claims then presently being made by the pope for supremacy in Church and state. On such a false foundation the power of the Roman papacy was very largely to be built. Since the Renaissance in the fifteenth century, scholars have realized that the documents were spurious, but this realization did not affect in the slightest degree the imposing edifice that was erected on these false foundations.

Likewise false were the *Donations of Constantine,* a document circulated a century before the *Decretals,* which claimed that the Emperor Constantine had received baptism from Pope Sylvester in 325. (Actually Constantine had been baptized on his deathbed in 337 by an Arian bishop.) In return, Constantine allegedly had given to Sylvester absolute supremacy over all the churches in Christendom and material supremacy over

---

21. The Catholic Church has openly admitted the corruption of various bishops, but it holds that, in spite of human failure, the Holy Spirit yet protects, guides, and keeps His Church in every generation. This redemptive work of the Holy Spirit is perhaps best seen in the revival-oriented monastic communities.

Rome, all of Italy, and Western Europe. The deceitful purpose of this forgery was obviously to bolster the eighth- and ninth-century notion of papal world supremacy. Pope Nicholas I (858–867) was the first pope to take full advantage of these false documents, proudly declaring, "That which the pope has decided is to be observed by *all*." He and his successors sought to interfere with not only ecclesiastical decisions but also political decisions within the Empire. Such behavior only served to spark a rage of political intrigue and disruption that sadly surrounded the papacy during this period.

The papacy itself was vitally affected, so much so that pope followed pope in rapid succession, and many of them were imprisoned and perished in violence. In this same dark hour a further tragedy occurred. Three aristocratic women—Theodora the elder and her two daughters, Morozia and Theodora—controlled the papacy, filling it with their lovers and, in turn, with their illegitimate children. The shocking accounts of their immoralities with the princes of Catholicism have frankly been admitted by honest Catholic historians and exist as a deep stain on the Roman papacy. Likewise, at one juncture, from 1044 to 1046, Catholicism had three rival pontiffs at the same time—Benedict IX, Sylvester III, and Gregory VI.

Although history sadly reveals the intrigue, immorality, violence, ambition, and fraud that reigned in the midst of the Church and the Roman bishopric, the claim would still be made of unbroken, apostolic succession, supremacy, and infallibility. This can be seen in the declaration of Gregory VII (Hildebrand), elected pope in 1073: "The Roman Church was founded by God alone; the Roman pope alone can with right be called universal; he alone may use the imperial insignia; his feet only shall be kissed by all princes; he may depose the emperors; he himself may be judged by no one; the Roman church has never erred, nor will it err in all eternity!"

The Great Divide

As we have already noticed, the deteriorating relationship between the Greek Catholic Church and the Roman Catholic Church had its roots in the second and third centuries, evidenced in the difference between the Greek theology of Origen and the Latin theology of Tertullian and Cyprian. And we have also already observed the increasing rivalry between the two most powerful and ambitious men in all Christendom, the pope of Rome and the patriarch of Constantinople.

The middle of the ninth century further witnessed Photius, Patriarch of Constantinople, and Nicholas I, Pope of Rome, each excommunicating the other. This schism was temporarily healed by the Synod of Constantinople in 869.

But on July 16, 1054, the final break came in which the Roman legates to Constantinople, on behalf of the Roman pope, Leo IX, placed on the high altar of the Church of Sophia a final decree of excommunication, shaking the dust off their feet as they left the building. The Patriarch of Constantinople, Michael Cerularius, responded by excommunicating the Bishop of Rome. The basic issues plainly were those carnal strivings of ambitious men for recognition and supremacy. The technical reasons advanced for the breach, however, were the Roman use of unleavened bread in the Lord's Supper, omitting the "Hallelujah" from the liturgy during Lent, the dispute whether the confession is to be that the Holy Ghost "proceeded from the Father" only or "from the Father and the Son," and permission of the Greek clergy to marry as over against the Roman insistence on celibacy! And so came to completion a schism that has remained unhealed to this very day.

The Orthodox Church

We have already traced the roots of Eastern Orthodoxy in the earth, growing side by side with the Western Latin Church, though often in conflict with it. Five men are listed whose theology "still defines Orthodox spirituality"—Dionysius the Areopagite (c. 400), Maximus the Confessor (c. 580–662), John of

Damascus (c. 655–749), Gregory Palamas (c. 1296–1359) and just prior to him, Simeon "the New Theologian" (949–1022).

Simeon, considered "a forerunner of Orthodox Renewal," writes: "Whom am I, O my Lord, Master and God, that you should come down and become incarnate and should die for me so that you might set me free from death and corruption and make me a partaker of divinity?" Then Simeon admonishes: "When you address yourself to the Lord with this kind of attitude, immediately you will find the Lord embracing you mystically and kissing you and putting a right spirit within you, a spirit of freedom and of the forgiveness of your sins; indeed, He will crown you with His *charismata* and render you glorious in wisdom and knowledge."[22] Consequently, Simeon writes, "We are able to manifest the working of miracles and the grace of prophecy and diverse kinds of tongues and interpretation of tongues, helps and the administration of cities and people, and the full knowledge of future blessings, and the gaining of the kingdom of Heaven, adoption and the putting on of Christ and the knowing of the mysteries of Christ…we who are believers are able to know and to believe and to say all these things, being taught by the Holy Spirit alone."[23]

Modern-day Orthodoxy, however, seems much less assured of their salvation than Simeon. In a December 1996 article in the *Orthodox Observer*, entitled "Believers Must Work toward Spirituality," Fr. Constantelos, Professor of History at Richard Stockton State College in Pomona, New Jersey, writes: "…man is capable of becoming partaker of divine nature by imitating Jesus Christ, who set the example, prepared the way, and became the prototype. Thus the Fathers of the Church taught that 'God became human that the human might become God,' and that 'God became what we are in order to make us what God is'…An Orthodox Christian will never say 'I am saved' but always 'through the grace and the help of God I hope to be saved, for I am in the realm and process of salvation.' "

22. Simeon, *Moral Chapters*, 8, 166.
23. Simeon, *Theological Chapters*, 1, 195.

Modern-day Orthodoxy—the church of icons and incense, candles, and priests in resplendent robes and sacraments and tradition and chanting and bowing—seems to have traveled a long way from simple first-century Christianity. So much so that nineteenth-century Church historian Adolf von Harnack surprisingly wrote, "The Orthodox Church is in her entire structure alien to the gospel and represents a perversion of the Christian religion...."

The present Orthodox Church is actually not a single church but rather a family of 13 self-governing churches, united on the sacraments, doctrine, liturgy, and church government, but each administering its own affairs. The head of each of the 13 churches is called a "patriarch" or "metropolitan." The Patriarch of Constantinople (Istanbul, Turkey), however, is honored as the "ecumenical," or universal, patriarch. The five largest Orthodox churches in the world are the Russian, Romanian, Greek, Serbian, and Bulgarian Orthodox Churches. Sadly, the Orthodox Church in the former communist bloc has become one of the greatest opponents to the twentieth-century evangelism of Europe for Christ.[24]

Daniel B. Clendenin, author of *Eastern Orthodox Christianity: A Western Perspective,* raises a foundational concern: "The doctrine of justification by faith is virtually absent from the history and theology of Orthodoxy. Rather, Orthodoxy emphasizes *theosis* (literally, 'divinization'), the gradual process by which Christians become more and more like Christ."[25]

---

24. For example: "The upper chamber of the Russian parliament unanimously approved legislation today restricting the rights and activities of minority religions...." This legislation was "sought by the Russian Orthodox Church, which has felt threatened by the growth of minority faiths...on Russian soil since the fall of communism...." (*Washington Post*, September 24, 1997).

25. Daniel B. Clendenin, *Eastern Orthodox Christianity: A Western Perspective* (Grand Rapids, MI: Baker Books, 1994). Notwithstanding this, in 1987, former Campus Crusade for Christ staff member Peter Gillquist led 2,000 evangelicals in joining the Antiochian Orthodox Church. Another well-known modern-day convert to Orthodoxy is Franky Schaeffer, son of the late Francis Schaeffer.

Absolute Papal Power and Its Demise

The next 200-year period (1073–1294), known as the era of absolute papal power, extended from Gregory VII to Boniface VIII. Here we find the papacy at its height of power. Gregory VII (1073–1085) in his most renowned action, forced Emperor Henry IV of Germany to stand barefooted in the snow at Canossa, dressed as a humble penitent, begging the pope's forgiveness for having resisted him. (In revenge, however, Emperor Henry ultimately banished Pope Gregory to die in exile in 1085, and appointed an antipope, Clement III, in his place.) And in 1177, Emperor Frederick Barbarossa knelt in Venice to kiss the feet of Pope Alexander. Both of these events paved the way for the papacy to reach the height of its power in the time of Pope Innocent III (1198–1216), who crowned himself "vicar of Christ" on earth and stood all-powerful with every ruler under his authority. King John of England and the powerful Philip of France were brought, humiliated, to their knees before him.

The height of the absolute power of the papacy continued for yet another century until the time of Boniface VIII (1294–1303). Boniface made an ambitious declaration in his bull, *Unam Sanctam,* that reveals how far the notion of absolute power had gone. He declared "...that for every human creature to be subject to the Roman pope is altogether necessary for salvation." In the decree dated November 18, 1302, the pope also declared: "That which was spoken of Christ: 'Thou hast subdued all things under his feet' may well be verified in me. I have authority of the King of Kings, I am all in all and above all so that God Himself, and I, the vicar of God, have but one consistory and I am able to do almost all that God can do...What therefore can you make of me BUT GOD?"[26] It is little wonder many believers would regard these claims as blasphemous, a prophetic fulfillment of Second Thessalonians

---

26. *The Catholic Encyclopedia* (New York: Encyclopedia Press, Inc., 1917).

2:4 (NIV)—where the antichrist "sets himself up...proclaiming himself to be God." And indeed within Boniface's reign itself not only was this claim to absolute supremacy challenged, but the whole structure of papal absolutism began to crumble as sand castles before the rising tide of resistance. In 1303, Boniface VIII was dethroned by Philip the Fair, King of France, to die shortly thereafter in prison.

For the next 70 years, from 1309–1376 (a period known as the "Babylonian Captivity"), the papacy existed in exile in France under French political control. Scarcely had this scandal ended when a greater scandal, known as "The Great Schism," began. For the next 40 years (1378–1417), Catholicism had two popes and two colleges of cardinals, each anathematizing the other. In 1409, an ecumenical council was convened at Pisa at which a new pope, Alexander V, was elected, then leaving Catholicism with three popes, each anathematizing the others. The Council of Constance finally ended the schism in 1417 by deposing all three previous popes and electing a fourth pope, Martin V! The result of all these public maneuverings was a visible shaking of papal credibility, and the conclusion drawn by many was that its absolute authority was a myth. A new wind was beginning to blow, as the first signs of spring were beginning to appear after the long, bleak, dark winter. God was sovereignly beginning to stir in the earth!

Chapter 8

Clouds Heavy With Rain

The Dawn of the Reformation

(A.D. 1100–1500)

From a historical perspective, it is interesting to note that the extreme claims of the medieval absolute papacy gained a foothold in that age of intellectual and spiritual darkness known as the *Dark Ages*. And a powerful fact of history is that freedom from the authoritarian claims of the medieval papacy came during the period of history known as the Renaissance, a time of intellectual and spiritual and moral enlightenment. This was the scholastic rebirth of Europe, and this period runs parallel to a growing demand for reformation within the Church. Both the Reformation and the Renaissance run parallel to the decline of the papacy; each contributed to the others, as darkness was swallowed up in light. Plainly stated, the more illumination men have, the less they can be induced to believe what is not true.

The Crusades (1096–1270)

It may well be that the most fatal move of Pope Gregory VII (Hildebrand) was the initiation of the concepts that ultimately gave birth to the eight Crusades to free the Holy Land from the hands of the Turkish infidels. To that end, probably only the first crusade was of any success, and that at a great price. Six hundred thousand men left Europe in 1096. Of these, only 60,000 completed the journey and reached Jerusalem three years later. Ultimately, we can assess the value of these Crusades as one of the more pronounced causes in the eventual erosion of the absolute papacy. The Crusades sparked geographical exploration, ushering in the era of the exploits of Marco Polo (1295), Christopher Columbus (1492), Vasco de Gama (1487) and Ferdinand Magellan (1520). Concerning his passion to discover the New World, Christopher Columbus wrote in his diary: "It was the Lord who put it into my mind. I could feel His hand upon me. The fact that it would be possible to sail from here to the Indies. All who heard of my project rejected it with laughter, ridiculed me, but there was no question that the inspiration was from the Holy Spirit, because He comforted me with rays of marvelous inspiration from the Holy Scriptures."

This many-faceted exploration, in turn, sparked trade and commerce, which, in turn, sparked industry and the rise of a new class of merchants, bankers, and craftsmen. These, then, sparked new forms of strong national government—too strong to be controlled by the Church. The Crusades also stimulated the intellectual curiosities of Europe, which gave birth to a growth of freedom of thought and the rise of the universities and scholasticism and the printing press, all of which helped to smash those chains of darkness and superstition that held Europe shackled to untruth. Overall, the sleeping giant of Europe was beginning to arouse itself from its deep slumber and commencing to shake off its dull sloth. This was truly an era of rebirth, and clouds heavy with rain were appearing on the horizon.

Scholasticism and the Universities

The 1100's saw a distinct turning point in the cultural and intellectual development of Europe. Through the Crusades, and the attendant contact with the Graeco-Arabian culture, scholasticism arose in Europe. This new intellectual inquiry, as we have already noted, would ultimately culminate in the Renaissance and the Reformation. All across Europe universities sprang up and formed new centers of culture and learning. Bologna and Paris were the foremost models, with others springing up under their shadow, such as Montpellier in France, Glasgow, Prague, Vienna, Heidelberg, Cologne, Copenhagen, Oxford, and Cambridge. Foremost among the scholastics themselves were Anselm of Canterbury (1033–1109); the mystic, Bernard of Clairvaux (1091–1153); Hugo of Saint Victor (1097–1141); Peter Lombard (1100–1164); Bonaventura (1221–1274); Roger Bacon (1214–1294); William of Occam (1280–1347); Marsilius of Padua (d. 1342); and Thomas Aquinas (1227–1274).

John W. Kennedy comments on Thomas Aquinas: "The authority of the Roman Church found its complete, logical expression in the theology of Thomas Aquinas, whose influence has continued right up to the present day....It was he, probably more than any other, who lent sanction to the use of indulgences, a practice which led to such corruption and moral evil as to be one of the immediate factors which brought about the upheaval of the Reformation. According to Aquinas, the merit of Christ and the saints formed a pool of good works whose benefits could be transferred by...the Church to penitent sinners in order to mitigate, in this life or in purgatory, the penalties due to their evil deeds."[1] On a more positive moral note, the account is given of a conversation between Pope Innocent IV and Thomas Aquinas as bags of treasure were being carried through the gates of the Lateran. "You see," observed the Pope, with a smile, "the day is past when the church could say, 'Silver and gold have I none.' " "Yes, Holy Father," was

---

1. John W. Kennedy, *The Torch of the Testimony* (Gospel Literature Service, 1965; Goleta, CA: Christian Books, reprint), 122.

Aquinas' reply, "and the day is past when the church could say to the lame man, 'Rise and walk!' "

Raymond Lull, Missionary

At this juncture of history, we must pay particular attention to the missionary labors of Raymond (Raimon) Lull (1235–1315). Born of a noble Spanish family on the Island of Majorca, the brilliant Lull renounced his dissolute life, having been arrested by a vision of the crucified One. In deep repentance, he was converted to Christ and gave himself in full consecration to the Lord and to spreading His Word among the Muslims. His single prayer was, "To Thee, O Lord, I offer myself, my wife, my children, and all that I possess." Imprisoned in Tunis, he was then banished from the country. Returning a second time to North Africa, he was again imprisoned and deported. At 80 years old, he returned a third time, only to be stoned to death at Bugia, east of Algiers. His life's motto was: "He who loves not, lives not; he who lives by the Life cannot die."

(Both *Operation World*[2] and George Otis, Jr., with the *Sentinel Group,* reported that thousands have turned to Christ among the Kabyle—many through supernatural revelations of the Lord Jesus in the very area where Raymond Lull, the great missionary pioneer, was martyred. Raymond Lull's poured out life and intercessions were ultimately honored by the Father— 600 years later. Praying breath is never spent in vain!)

The Widespread Revival Move of God

"Heretical churches" (as the institutional Christians viewed them) spread from the Black Sea to the Atlantic Ocean. Simple fellowships of believers, similar to the "Friends of God" in the Balkans, were particularly numerous in northern Italy and southern France. Wherever believers would go, they would find others of kindred heart and would be united with them in fellowship around Christ—all to the consternation of the institutional clergy. Preachers arose who fearlessly denounced the

---

2. Patrick Johnstone, *Operation World* (Grand Rapids, MI: Zondervan, 1993), 88.

ecclesiastical sins of their day, declaring from the Scriptures a new life in Christ. Among these were Peter of Brueys and his companion in labor, Henry of Cluny. Peter was arrested and burned to death at St. Giles in 1226. Prior to that, in 1167, these believers convened a leadership conference in St. Felix de Caramen near Toulouse. Leaders came from as far east as Constantinople, simply drawn together around Jesus Christ in the fellowship of the Holy Spirit. We will now focus on the histories of the twelfth century Waldenses and the Albigenses of the Southern Alps, part of this widespread revival movement so opposed by the institutional Church.

The Albigenses and the Waldenses

The Albigenses in southern France and the followers of Peter Waldo of Lyons, the Waldenses, in northern Italy were two reform-minded groups that sprang up within the 1100's, crying out against the spurious, extra-biblical elements in Catholicism and pleading for a return to New Testament purity and simplicity. Eddie Hyatt, summarizing the thoughts of historian Philip Schaff, paints a fascinating portrait of the Waldenses: "The Waldenses recognized the responsibility of both men and women to preach, to baptize, and to administer the Lord's Supper. For them, the basis of ministry was the anointing or gifting of the Spirit rather than institutional appointment or ordination. Ministry was, therefore, open to all since it was the direct, free activity of the Holy Spirit which gave the right to bind and loose, to consecrate and bless."[3] As Peter Waldo sent out his preachers two by two across France, Flanders, Germany, Poland, Bohemia, Austria, and Hungary, hundreds of thousands shifted their allegiance from the formal and dying church of the day to Christ Himself.

The "heretical" Albigenses were purged from France by Innocent III, and the Waldenses were excommunicated and

---

3. Eddie L. Hyatt, *2,000 Years of Charismatic Christianity* (Tulsa: Hyatt International Ministries, Inc., 1996), 73.

severely persecuted by Pope Alexander III. Omer Englebert in his biography of St. Francis noted the grave "heresies" of the Waldenses: "placing the authority of the Bible above that of the Pope, [making confession] to virtuous laymen rather than to priests of evil life, and rejecting Purgatory, indulgences, and the veneration of the saints...."[4] But by the early 1300's "it was reckoned that there were 80,000 true Christians in Bohemia alone. This remarkable spiritual revival was partly the result of the labors of three reformers—Conrad of Waldhousen, Milic of Moravia, and Matthias of Janow; they prepared the way for the movement that was led by John Hus."[5]

William of Occam (1280–1347), the English Franciscan whose concepts strongly influenced Luther two centuries later, had written and taught at the reform-minded University of Paris that the pope is *not* infallible, that Holy Scripture is the *only* infallible source of faith and conduct, and that the pope and the Church are subordinate to the state in all secular matters.

John Wycliffe (1320–1384), "the morningstar of the English Reformation," a Roman Catholic priest and an able scholar at Oxford University, taught that justification was by faith in the crucified Savior *alone* and that the Scripture was the *only* source of truth. On matters of the Church, he further declared that "the *only* head of the Church is Christ. The pope, unless he rule in the spirit of the gospel, is the vicar of Antichrist.... The power-grasping hierarchy...who claim special religious sanctity are without Scriptural warrant." He rejected transubstantiation.[6] He denied the infallibility of the Roman Church, and he spoke out against confession, purgatory, the worship of saints, and the veneration of relics as all being unscriptural.

---

4. Omer Englebert, *St. Francis of Assisi, A Biography* (Ann Abor, MI: Servant Books, 1979), 59.

5. William E. Allen, *The History of Revivals of Religion* (C. Antrim, N. Ireland: Revival Publishing Co., 1951), 9-10.

6. The concept that the bread and wine in the Lord's Supper are *literally* changed into the body and blood of Christ.

Wycliffe also gave to the British people the first complete English version of the Vulgate Bible, and he also sent out lay evangelists, nicknamed the Lollards (a slur meaning "the Babblers") to instruct the people in the holy truths of God's Word.

Wycliffe declared: "The sacred Scriptures are the property of the people; and one which no one should be allowed to wrest from them. Christ and His apostles converted the world by making known the Scriptures, and I pray with all my heart that through...the things contained in this book, we may all together come to the everlasting life."[7] John Wycliffe was condemned by one of the French-puppet Avignon popes, Gregory XI, in 1377, but was protected from execution by the English parliament. After his death, the enraged Catholics exhumed his body, cremated it, and scattered his ashes to the four winds— almost in a prophetic foreshadowing of the widespread Reformation soon to appear on the horizon.

John Hus (1369–1415), a powerful preacher of the gospel and professor at the University of Prague and a follower of John Wycliffe, headed up the ongoing move for reform and revival in Bohemia. Because of his fiery preaching, Hus was summoned before the Council of Constance and the notorious Pope John XXIII. Hus, protected by the King of Bohemia and supported by many of the Bohemian people, had been promised "safe conduct" by the Emperor of the Holy Roman Empire, Sigismund, if he would appear at Constance. But he was betrayed, and at Constance he was condemned as a heretic and burned to death at the stake. John himself, however, was forced to resign as Pope by the same council, rather than face an investigation for his own personal crimes. Needless to say, the martyrdom of John Hus stirred the deepest of resentments in Bohemia.

Dominican monk and Prior of St. Mark's Convent, Girolamo Savonarola (1452–1498) also sought reform in the city of Florence, where between 1494 and 1498 there was a significant

---

7. Wycliffe, as quoted by William E. Allen, *History of Revivals and Worldwide Revival Movements* (Antrim, N. Ireland: Revival Publishing Co., 1951), 10.

revival, bringing many to deep repentance. One reported concerning the effects of Savonarola's sermons, "such terror and alarm, such sobbing and tears, that people passed through the streets without speaking, more dead than alive."[8] Another reported, "the churches were filled with people at prayer and the Bible was diligently read...even the Sultan of Turkey commanded Savonarola's sermons to be translated into Turkish for his own study...." Michelangelo, famed sculptor, painter, and poet, was also a frequent listener to the fiery Savonarola, whose denunciation of the corruption of the Church brought him Alexander VI's papal ban. Alexander VI had decreed that this Dominican monk must die, "even if he be another John the Baptist." Savonarola was hanged on May 23, 1499. Pope Alexander was later exposed for his own personal immorality.

The Brethren of the Common Life, of whom Erasmus and Thomas à Kempis, author of *The Imitation of Christ,* are perhaps the most widely known, sought reformation of the Church from *within* by teaching. Erasmus was educated, in part, by the Brethren of the Common Life, although he was not a member of that order. His greatest contribution was the production of a Greek New Testament, with an accompanying new translation in Latin. Thus was the authority of the Scriptures further established in the earth.

By the mid-1400's Queen Isabella of Spain, the wife of Ferdinand (who together had commissioned Columbus) and Cardinal Ximenes had effected great reform within the Spanish Church. All across Europe voices of dissent from without and a longing for reform from within the Catholic Church indicated that a new dawning was on the horizon. Reformation was in the air. These were the first sounds of the abundance of rain!

The Reformation of the 1500's

The Old Testament prophet Joel describes the decay of the people of God in his day in these graphic terms: "What the

---

8. As quoted by Allen, *History of Revivals and Worldwide Revival Movements, op. cit.*

locust swarm has left the great locusts have eaten; what the great locusts have left the young locusts have eaten; what the young locusts have left other locusts have eaten....The vine is dried up and the fig tree is withered; the pomegranate, the palm and the apple tree—all the trees of the field—are dried up. Surely the joy of mankind is withered away."[9] This experience of Israel directly parallels the experience of the Christian Church in its first-century decline to the depths of the Dark Ages. Later, in the Book of Joel, the prophet describes the longing of Israel for restoration, much like the longing we find in the twelfth through fifteenth centuries of Christianity: "Let the priests, who minister before the Lord, weep between the temple porch and the altar. Let them say, 'Spare Your people, O Lord. Do not make Your inheritance an object of scorn....' "[10] And God answered Israel of old, even as He answered the Church in the Reformation of the sixteenth century: "I will repay you for the years that the locusts have eaten—the great locust and the young locust, the other locusts and the locust swarm—My great army that I sent among you."[11] And so the Reformation began in Germany, in the 1500's, in the era of the Augustinian priest, Dr. Martin Luther.

The Reformation in Germany: Martin Luther

The young, brilliant, but restless, Augustinian monk, Martin Luther, had been directed by John Staupitz, his concerned vicar at Erfurt, to the study of the Holy Scriptures for his soul's salvation. Staupitz further turned him to the Lord Jesus Christ who alone could take away his sin and grant him fellowship with God. On the heels of years of tormenting, soul-searching struggle, while reading Romans, the peace of God came to young Martin's soul. Through his further studies of Paul, Augustine, and William of Occam, he came to see even more clearly that men are saved by God through Jesus Christ alone,

---

9. Joel 1:4,12 NIV.

10. Joel 2:17 NIV.

11. Joel 2:25 NIV.

not by their own good works, and that salvation depends solely on God's grace. Luther saw in God's salvation an *extrinsic* righteousness, a righteousness totally outside of, and apart from, the believer, and a righteousness found only in Christ Jesus Himself that is continually *imputed* to the account of a believing man. In this illumination, the Holy Scriptures became to Luther the sole authority for all faith and practice. Luther's spiritual experience and perception did not cause him to break with Rome. Luther was a pious Catholic priest, and as such, his burden was for reformation within the Church.

The Indulgence Issue

Pope Leo X had been in need of large sums of money to complete the magnificent St. Peter's Cathedral in Rome, begun in 1506 under Pope Julius II. To secure the money, he proclaimed a general sale of indulgences, the remission of purgatorial punishment. Leo's chief salesman was Dominican monk John Tetzel, who traveled across Germany hawking: "Soon as the money in the casket rings, the troubled soul out of purgatory springs."

To Luther, now sensitive to the unmerited grace of Jesus Christ by which men are freely forgiven of their sins, this profane and blasphemous practice of selling remission had to be purged from the Church. In conformity with academic etiquette, Luther nailed his 95 objecting theses to the door of the Castle Church in Wittenberg on All Saints' Day, October 31, 1517, as a basis for debate that he would have the right to conduct. As if in a windstorm, tens of thousands of copies of the theses were circulated in the German vernacular all across Germany. And so it was on All Saints' Eve that a spark was ignited that would eventually see all Europe ablaze with reformation. I shall quote in part from several of these valid, but inflammatory, theses:

> "(27.) They preach vanity who say that the soul flies out of Purgatory as soon as the money thrown into the chest rattles.

"(32.) On the way to eternal damnation are they and their teachers, who believe that they are sure of their salvation through indulgences.

"(82.) Why does not the Pope deliver all souls at the same time out of Purgatory for the sake of most holy love and on account of the bitterest distress of those souls... [rather than] that most miserable thing, money, to be spent on St. Peter's..?

"(86.) Why does not the Pope build St. Peter's...with his own money—since his riches are now more ample than those of Crassus,[12]—rather than with the money of poor Christians?"

In the summer of 1519, at age 36, Luther went to Leipzig, accompanied by 200 students and the scholarly Philip Melancthon, his lifelong friend and successor. Luther had tenderly described his shy and retiring friend Melancthon in these words: "I am rough, boisterous, stormy, and altogether war-like. I must remove the stumps, cut away the thistles and thorns, and clear the wild forests; but master Philip comes along, softly and gently, sowing and watering with joy."

Later on, when Philip Melancthon lay dying, Luther prayed fervently for him, declaring over him in faith: "Be of good courage, Philip, you shall not die." Melancthon recovered and later testified, "I should have been a dead man had I not been recalled from death itself by the coming of Luther." Luther himself testified, "God gave me back my brother Melancthon in direct answer to prayer."

Luther appeared with his colleague, Andrew Karlstadt, at Leipzig to debate against John Eck, professor at Leipzig University. Eck forced Luther to admit that popes and councils could err and that not all Hussite doctrine was heretical. Luther himself was promptly accused of Hussite heresy. Within a year Luther was excommunicated by papal bull and his writings

---

12. A Roman general.

ordered burned. Luther replied by publicly flinging the bull of excommunication, along with the false *Decretals* and certain papal books of law, into a bonfire outside of Wittenberg. Luther now stood as a free man—free from ties to the papacy and councils and traditions, free in his conscience to receive the holy Word of God as his sole rule of faith. And it seemed as if much of Germany stood with him.

In 1520, Luther wrote his three most powerful treatises. In his "To the Christian Nobility of the German Nation," Luther appealed to all Germany to unite against the abuses of Rome. In his "On the Babylonian Captivity of the Church," he attacked the unbiblical doctrines of the Church, especially the extra sacraments. And in his "The Liberty of a Christian Man," he emphasized the priesthood of all believers.

On April 18, 1521, Luther was then summoned to Worms to appear before Charles V, the young new Emperor. Charles, himself a devout Catholic and King of Spain, had hoped to consolidate his fractured empire by dealing with the schismatic "Protestants," a name given to those who *protested* against the Roman Church. Charles needed their support against the Turks, hence the practical purpose for this imperial Diet at Worms.

At Leipzig in 1519, Luther had defied the Pope and the Holy Roman Catholic Church and now, before the Diet of Worms, Luther stood to defy the emperor and the Holy Roman Empire. When asked before the emperor if he would recant he could only reply, "Unless I am refuted and convicted by testimonies of the Scriptures...I cannot and will not recant anything....Here I stand. I can do no other. So help me God. Amen."

Luther's stand at Leipzig had won him excommunication from the Church. Now his stand at Worms won him the ban of the empire. In the whole realm, all were forbidden to shelter him or to read his writings. To save his life, Frederick the Wise, Elector of Saxony, kidnapped Luther away to the castle of Wartburg. Here he was confined for almost a year, during which time he translated the New Testament from Greek into the German vernacular, a work of prime importance to the German Reformation.

In the spring of 1522, Luther returned, under cover, to Wittenberg to quell the unsettling and frenzied attacks of his former colleague, Karlstadt, against the rites and ordinances of the Catholic Church and to still the untempered and fanatical zeal of the Zwickau "prophets," Klaus Storch among them, whom Luther declared had "swallowed the Holy Ghost, feathers and all." These were expelled from Wittenberg that very year.

Luther's conservatism on spiritual gifts has been interpreted by some as opposition to them, but in the fourth stanza of his great hymn, *"Ein' Feste Burg"* ("A Mighty Fortress"), Luther declares: "The Spirit and the gifts are ours/Through him who with us sideth."

Historian Hyatt quotes Souer's work in German, *A History of the Christian Church*, (page 406 of volume 3) which describes Luther as "a prophet, evangelist, speaker in tongues and interpreter, in one person, endowed with all the gifts of the Holy Spirit."

Luther was a man of moderation, but some feared he had not gone far enough in his reformation. Luther's concepts of the State Church, coupled with his urging of the civil authorities to crush the Peasant's War without mercy—a war in which over 100,000 people lost their lives as they revolted against the hard social and economic injustices of the land—cost Luther much popularity among the peasants, a good number of whom became Anabaptists, a movement we shall consider shortly.

One of the gravest errors of Luther in the latter part of his life was his outburst of anti-Semitism, as recorded in his tract *Concerning the Jews and Their Lies*. With sorrow we quote his unholy words:

> "What then shall we Christians do with this damned, rejected race of Jews? Since they live among us and we know about their lying and blasphemy and cursing, we cannot tolerate them if we do not wish to share in their lies,

curses, and blasphemy....We must prayerfully and reverentially practice a merciful severity....Let me give you my honest advice:

"First...to set fire to their synagogues or schools and to bury and cover with dirt whatever will not burn, so that no man will ever again see a stone or cinder of them. This is to be done in honor of our Lord and of Christendom.

"Second, I advise that their houses also be razed and destroyed.

"Third, I advise that all their prayer books and Talmudic writings, in which such idolatry, lies, cursing, and blasphemy are taught, be taken from them.

"Fourth, I advise that their rabbis be forbidden to teach henceforth on pain of loss of life and limb.

"Fifth, I advise that safe conduct on the highways be abolished completely for the Jews. For they have no business in the countryside, since they are not lords, officials, tradesmen, or the like. Let them stay at home. [We might ask at this juncture, 'What home?' since, according to Luther's second point, all their homes would have already been destroyed.]

"Sixth, I advise that usury be prohibited to them, and that all cash and treasure of silver and gold be taken from them, and put aside for safe keeping.

"Seventh, I recommend putting a flail, an ax, a hoe, a spade, a distaff, or a spindle into the hand of young, strong Jews and Jewesses and letting them earn their bread in the sweat of their brow."

(Thus it becomes more than believable, although extremely painful to admit, how Adolf Hitler some four centuries later would use Luther's advice as a guide for implementing the first phases of his "final solution" against the Jews.)

The Diets of Speier in 1526 and 1529 and the final Peace of Augsburg in 1555 finally granted toleration to Lutheranism in Germany. Each state in Germany would be allowed to hold the religion of its ruling prince, whether Lutheran or Catholic.

The Reformation in Switzerland

In Switzerland, under Ulrich Zwingli (1484–1531), brilliant priest at the great Cathedral Church of Zurich, the Reformation took a more radical form than under Luther, in its sweeping abolition of medieval Catholic traditions, images, relics, robes, candles, etc.

Standing on the cardinal Reformation truths of justification by faith alone and the sole authority of the Scriptures, a Reformation Church was established in Zurich in 1522. It was unfortunate for the solidarity of the Reformation that, at a conference in 1529, even though Luther and Zwingli agreed on 14 main points of theology, they could not agree on the final one—the nature of the Lord's Supper. Although both reformers rejected the Catholic doctrine of transubstantiation, Luther held to the *literalness* of our Lord's words, "This is My body...This is My blood." Zwingli, however, held the bread and wine to be merely *symbols* that reminded men of Christ's flesh and blood. Unfortunately, on this disagreement the two reformers bitterly parted. In 1531, when the Protestant city of Zurich was attacked by the armies of the Catholic Swiss Cantons, Zwingli himself died on the battlefield of Cappel. His enemies cut his body into four pieces and flung them into the fire.

Geneva, in French Switzerland, became the next center of the Swiss Reformation under the brilliant French-born devout Catholic, John Calvin (1509–1564), whose spiritual life was impacted by the evangelical teachings of the learned Jacques Le Fevre and his disciple, the renowned preacher of the gospel, William Farel. Geneva soon surpassed Zurich in influence. John Calvin's greatest contribution to the Reformation was his *Institutes of the Christian Religion,* the first really systematic exposition of reformed theology, written when Calvin was but 26 years old. In his *Institutes,* Calvin sought to defend the Protestants as those who were loyal to the Apostles' Creed.

Calvin taught that the Reformation represented no new creed, but rather represented a return to apostolic simplicity; the Reformation was, in effect, a restoration of New Testament Christianity.

In his theology, John Calvin was a well-defined Augustinian. Like Augustine, Calvin defined God in terms of His sovereign will and His irresistible grace. Calvinism has come down to us in the succinct "T-U-L-I-P" formula: Total depravity by birth; Unconditional election (God saves only those whom He will); Limited atonement (Christ died only for the elect); Irresistible grace; and the Perseverance of the saints ("eternal security").

For a total of 25 years, and during two separate stays, John Calvin labored in Geneva. Geneva was known not only for its Reformed Church with its Presbyterian form of government through a consistory of elders, but also for its severe form of civil discipline, both of which were attributed to John Calvin. In five years, Geneva, with only 16,000 inhabitants, witnessed 57 executions and 76 banishments, and to the further grave discredit of the Reformation, Servetus, a famed Spanish physician and reformer, was burned at the stake because of his modalistic understandings of the nature of the Godhead. (Unfortunately, as with various groups down to this day, Calvin's revelation of grace apparently failed to transform the heart or foster mercy and forgiveness.)

The Anabaptists

The Anabaptist movement had its origins in Zurich in early 1525 among such godly men as Conrad Grebel and Felix Manz, who simply called themselves "brethren." They are not to be confused with the more fanatical "Zwickau prophets," mentioned before, or the apocalyptic false prophets of Munster who appeared just after the Anabaptist movement began. The Anabaptists held the conviction that Luther and Zwingli had not gone far enough in the Reformation. They objected to infant baptism, the Mass, and the State Church concept. They also called for a deeper return to apostolic simplicity according to the Holy Scriptures. *Anabaptist* literally means *those who baptize anew or again.* Anabaptists, in their rejection of infant baptism, rebaptized those who joined them. It was not unusual for the Anabaptists to dance, fall down under the power of the Spirit, and speak in other tongues. (Contemporary Mennonite author John H. Yoder declared that the Pentecostal movement "is in our century the closest paralleled to what Anabaptism was in the sixteenth."[13])

Unfortunately, many Anabaptists met with persecution and death. Felix Manz was executed by drowning in the River Limmat in early 1527, and Zwingli himself was a party to the proceedings. In Germany, Luther also urged "the use of the sword against them by right of law." Both the Catholics and the Protestants alike shamefully pursued the Anabaptist brethren to cruel death for centuries to come.

Two prominent branches of the Anabaptist movement that have come down to us from the Reformation are the followers of the Dutch Catholic priest, Menno Simons (1496–1561), called the *Mennonites* (of whom the Amish are but a stricter expression), and the followers of the Tyrolese hat maker, Jacob Hutter, called *Hutterites*—originating in Austria, Moravia, and Poland. Jacob Hutter was himself burned alive at the stake on February 26, 1536, at Innsbruck in the Tyrol. These were severely persecuted movements. John Horsch, in his book *The Hutterian Brethren,* writes: "Some were tortured terribly on the rack, so that they were torn apart and died. Some were burned to ashes...some were roasted on beams...some were torn with red-hot irons...some were hung on trees...some chopped to pieces...Thus the devil works, who is a murderer from the beginning." In the Anabaptists, however, we can see the Lord of the Church reviving and restoring yet more of the simplicities of the Christian life: believer's baptism, Spirit-filled church life,

---

13. Yoder, as quoted by Davis, "Anabaptism as a Charismatic Movement," 221, in Hyatt, *History of Revivals and Worldwide Revival Movements, op. cit.,* 89.

separation of state and church, living a life of non-violence, and the community of goods. It is unfortunate that Luther and Zwingli were so blinded in their insights as to be unable to see these as but a further step in the restoration of the life of the true apostolic Church upon the earth.

Spread of the Reformation

Lutheranism spread north from Germany into Denmark, Norway, Finland, Sweden, and the Baltic countries, eventually to become the State Church of those Scandinavian countries. The Swiss Reformation of Zwingli and Calvin spread south, east, and west into France, the Netherlands, Belgium, Scotland, Hungary, Spain, and Italy.

In France, despite severe persecution, the Protestants had over 2,000 congregations by 1560. But on the fateful night of August 24, 1574, under the direction of the Catholic Queen Mother, Catherine de Medici, some 22,000 Protestants were slaughtered in the St. Bartholomew's massacre. Huguenot blood ran red in the streets of France for the sake of the restoration of the simplicity of the gospel—forgiveness of sins by faith in Christ *alone,* the *sole* authority of the Holy Scriptures, and the priesthood of *all* believers.

Huguenots, concentrated in the Cevennes Mountains of southern France, experienced a powerful move of the Holy Spirit in their midst during this period. They testified, "God has nowhere in the Scriptures concluded Himself from dispensing again the extraordinary gifts of His Spirit unto men." An unusual work of the Spirit was seen in the Spirit of prophecy that rested on young children. Children as young as three years old prophesied the word of the Lord with fluency and clarity.

The diabolical *Inquisition* under the Catholic monarch, Philip II of Spain, sought to crush the emerging Reformation in the Netherlands. Beheading and burning at the stake became commonplace, but the Dutch endured and the Dutch Reformation succeeded. In Spain and Italy, however, the Reformation fires were all but completely stamped out by torture, imprisonment, and death in the bloody Inquisition of 1559 and 1560 under Pope Paul IV. The Waldenses of northern Italy, however, having survived from the pre-Reformation era, became a branch of the Reformed Presbyterian Church of the Swiss Reformation.

Hungary, likewise, ultimately embraced the Reformation and, in spite of the hostilities of Emperor Charles V in the 1500's and the severe persecutions by the Hapsburgs in the 1600's, the Hungarian Presbyterian Church emerged as one of the largest Presbyterian churches, though much of the rest of Hungary was ultimately won back to Catholicism under the Jesuits, whose history we shall shortly note.

Other countries of mid and southern Europe—southern Germany, Poland, Austria, and Bohemia—though initially set aflame by the Reformation, were eventually won back to Catholicism by repression, bloody slaughter, and the fierce efforts of the Jesuits, Ignatius Loyola's *Society of Jesus.* Ignatius of Loyola himself, while an officer in the Spanish army, had a remarkable conversion. Longing to be rid of his sins, he had cried out to God to show him the way of salvation. After much inward struggle, he found the saving grace of God. He determined that as he had served the King of Spain, he would now serve the Kingdom of God. At the monastery of Montserrat, he hung his weapons on the Virgin's altar, dedicating himself to the service of Mary and of Christ.

Loyola's *Jesuits* became the very soul of the Counter-Reformation. But, in succeeding generations, so glaring were the intrigues and plots of the Jesuits that they were ultimately banished from almost every Roman Catholic country for interference in European politics. (In 1773, Pope Clement XIV finally abolished the Order because of the scandal. But interestingly enough, some 40 years later, in 1814, Pope Pius VII annulled the decrees of his predecessor and restored the Jesuits.)

The Council of Trent (1545–1563)

In 1545, Emperor Charles V prevailed upon Pope Paul III to convene the Council of Trent. His hope was to effect the needed doctrinal and moral reform within the Catholic Church and to gain reconciliation with the German Lutherans. The Diet of Regensburg had been convened four years earlier and had produced the startling Catholic declaration: "We are not just, or accepted by God, on account of our own works or righteousness, but we are reputed just on account of the merits of Jesus Christ only." Surprisingly, Luther's terse rejection of this Regensburg agreement was as follows: "Popish writers pretend that they have always taught what we now teach concerning faith and good works, and that they are unjustly accused of the contrary: thus the wolf puts on the sheep's skin till he gains admission into the fold!" Reconciliation, to Luther, was apparently impossible, and for reasons we shall shortly see.

The Council of Trent in its *Canons on Justification* clearly anathematized semi-Pelagianism by its plain condemnation of the proposal "that man can be justified before God by his own works, which are done either in the strength of human nature or through the teaching of the law, apart from the divine grace through Jesus Christ." However, in the *Tridentine Profession of Faith,* issued in 1564, in the papal bull of Pius IV, the Catholic episcopacy again defined itself thusly:

> "I acknowledge the sacred Scripture *according to that sense* which Holy Mother Church has held and holds, *to whom it belongs to decide* upon the true sense and interpretation....I profess likewise that true God is offered in the Mass, *a proper and propitiatory sacrifice for the living and the dead....*I hold unswervingly that there is a purgatory and that the *souls there detained are helped by the intercessions of the faithful,* likewise also that the saints who reign with Christ *are to be venerated and invoked,* that they offer prayers to God for us and *that their relics are to be venerated....*I affirm that *the power of indulgences has been left by Christ in the Church....*I recognize the Holy Catholic and Apostolic *Roman Church as the mother and mistress of all Churches;* and I vow and swear *true obedience to the Roman Pontiff,* the successor of blessed Peter, the chief of the Apostles and *the vicar of*

*Jesus Christ....*This true Catholic Faith, *without which no one can be in a state of salvation...*I...profess and truly hold...vow and swear, God helping me, most constantly to keep...to my life's last breath...."[14]

The Reformation of the sixteenth century could not but totally reject these confessions of the papacy.

The Catholic Revival

We have already noted the counter-reformation measures taken by Ignatius Loyola's *Society of Jesus* as well as those of the Council of Trent. The doctrinal decrees of this Council were clear and definite in their rejection of Protestant beliefs, though there were positive changes that the Council effected within the Roman Church.

To these reformation and counter-reformation measures can be added the Catholic Revival of the mid-1500's, which produced a new wave of mystical piety and spiritual devotion. Outstanding in this movement were Teresa de Jesus (1515–1582) of Avila and Juan de la Cruz (1542–1591) of Fontiveros, in Spain, and Jeanne Françoise Fremyot de Chantal (1572–1641) in France. These were characterized by extreme devotion to God and to the Church and to the Sacraments.

We take special note of Juan de la Cruz, John of the Cross, born Juan de Yepes, in the Castile region of Spain in 1542. A generation before, Torquemada's Inquisition had forced the family to convert from Judaism. Left fatherless as a little boy, John became a professional beggar. Alone on the streets and poverty stricken, he caught a vision of Jesus, lover of his soul. At age 21, John entered the Carmelite novitiate at Medina. In 1567, newly ordained as a priest, John met reform-minded Madre Teresa de Jesús—Teresa of Avila. David Hazard, in *You Set My Spirit Free,* describes this meeting: "It was like two forest fires converging."[15] Teresa was 52 at the time; John was 25.

---

14. Emphasis added.

15. David Hazard, *You Set My Spirit Free* (Minneapolis, MN: Bethany House, 1994), 13.

John left his order to join Teresa in her reform movement, taking the name, "John of the Cross." Only the Lord knew how much John would actually have to bear the cross of Christ in suffering and pain.

From 1576 until his death, John was severely persecuted by the hierarchy of the institutional Church simply because of his call to repentance and a return to the Lord. John was kidnapped several times, imprisoned, viciously beaten almost daily, locked in a cramped broom closet for months on end, all because he insisted on calling a fallen Church back to an unbroken fellowship with God! While in the Toledo Prison in 1578, John wrote *The Spiritual Canticle,* a personalized version of the Song of Solomon, which has been beautifully set to music by the twentieth century troubadour John Michael Talbot—

> *"Where have You hidden, Beloved?*
> *Why have You wounded my soul?*
> *I went out to the wilderness calling for You...*
>
> *"I have searched for my Love in the mountains*
> *I have searched among the meadows and the fields*
> *He has poured out a thousand graces in them*
> *So my heart might be healed...."*

John's three other major works also survive him: *The Ascent of Mount Carmel, The Dark Night,* and *The Living Flame of Love.*

Hated and hounded by the clergy, John fled across southern Spain. Wherever he went declaring the love that is ours in the Presence of God, miracles began to happen. John's explanation was simple: "God sends His Holy Spirit, issuing as from a hidden wellspring on high, to refresh and strengthen us in spiritual 'graces' to help us on our way—the path of humility, which is 'the way' of Jesus Himself." In his last letter, written just a month before his death, John shared one of his life's secrets with a suffering nun: "Have a great love for those who contradict and fail to love you, for in this way love is begotten in a heart that has no love. God so acts with us, for He loves us that we might love by means of the very love He bears toward us."

Teresa died in October of 1582, and John died in December of 1591 at the age of 49. As John lay dying, these words of hope were on his lips: "...It is by the merits of the blood of our Lord Jesus Christ that I hope to be saved."

Although hounded and persecuted by the clergy while he lived, in December of 1726, nearly a century and a half later, Saint John of the Cross would be canonized by Pope Benedict XIII.

Catholic reformation zeal also expressed itself in the work of foreign missions. Most famous of the Catholic missionaries was Francis Xavier (1506–1552), one of the original followers of Ignatius Loyola. He arrived in India in 1542 and died ten years later as he was entering China. In his ten years of missionary work, he claimed converts in the hundreds of thousands.

The Reformation in England

The Reformation was not solely a spiritual movement. Because of the centuries of what many saw as bondage to Rome, kings and their kingdoms viewed the Reformation as a means of gaining political freedom from the claims of the Roman papacy. Such was the case in England.

The Erratic Reign of Henry VIII (1509–1547)

Catherine of Aragon, daughter of Ferdinand and Isabella of Spain, had been married to Henry VIII's older brother, Arthur, who then died before receiving the British crown. Contrary to canon law, Pope Julius II was pressured by Ferdinand of Spain and Henry VII of England to endorse the second marriage of Catherine to Prince Henry (VIII). After 24 years of marriage to Catherine, Henry VIII had born to him five stillborn children and only one living daughter, Mary, but no male heir to the British throne. Henry and others surrounding him looked upon this as God's judgment for his marriage to his brother's widow.

The year 1526 saw Henry VIII attracted to Anne Boleyn, one of the ladies of his court. But Anne refused simply to be his mistress. In 1527, through Cardinal Wolsey, Henry VIII petitioned the pope for an annulment of his marriage to Catherine on the grounds that it had originally been sin. Although it may have been within the power of the pope to grant such a dispensation, it was not politically expedient for him to do so for fear of offending Catherine's nephew, Charles V, the powerful Emperor of Germany, King of Spain, and defender of the Roman Church against insurgent German Protestantism. King Charles simply would not have tolerated his aunt Catherine's being set aside, and the pope could not risk losing his allegiance.

But despite the pope and emperor, Henry VIII was determined to have Anne as his wife. This same Henry who earlier had opposed Martin Luther, thus earning for himself, in 1521, the papal title, "Defender of the Faith," now, in 1529, permitted Protestant books to circulate in the British court. In 1531, Henry charged the English Catholic clergy with treason for receiving orders from Rome—a foreign power. In 1532, the Parliament gave the king authority to abolish certain clerical payments to Rome. Parliament also passed the *Act of Submission of the Clergy,* placing the clergy of the Church of England under Henry's control. Also in 1532, Protestant Thomas Cranmer was appointed Archbishop of Canterbury, and Thomas Cromwell, an ardent Protestant, replaced Catholic Thomas More as Prime Minister. In 1533, the *Act in Restraint of Appeals* was passed, making it a crime for a British subject to appeal to any court in Rome.

In January 1533, Archbishop Cranmer secretly performed the wedding of Henry to Anne Boleyn, and in May, the archbishop held court to formally declare Henry's marriage to Catherine nullified. Anne Boleyn was declared Queen of England—the "Anne of a thousand days" (after which she was beheaded by Henry VIII). In 1534, the pope consequently excommunicated Henry, thus releasing his subjects from their allegiance. In November of that year, Henry responded by the *Act of Supremacy,* passed by Parliament, declaring himself "the only supreme head on earth of the Church of England," and that "the Roman Pontiff has no greater jurisdiction bestowed on him by God in the Holy Scriptures than any other foreign bishop." In 1535 the king abolished the smaller monasteries. By 1540, all monasteries were abolished and their properties were confiscated by the Crown. Henry, in turn, sold much of this property to those in his court, thus creating a new upper middle class. This newly created aristocracy would naturally oppose any return to Rome and thus became the very foundation for the new Parliamentarianism and Puritanism.

In 1536, the *Ten Articles of Religion* were published, setting forth the basics of the English Reformation. Archbishop Cranmer drew these *Ten Articles* mainly from the Lutheran Augsburg Confession. Copies of the Holy Scriptures were circulated everywhere, and men were enjoined to read it, to avoid whatever was not taught in it, including such things as making pilgrimages, offering money or candles to images, and saying prayers over beads.

Henry VIII himself exists in history as a man motivated principally by his own self-interests. The moral fiber of the Reformation in England certainly did not stem from him. His ambition was for a reformed Catholicism under his own control. When, in 1539, it appeared as if things were moving too fast, he forced Parliament to sanction the *Six Articles* forbidding anyone to teach Protestant doctrines in England. In 1536, Henry had William Tyndale, the Bible translator, burned to death in Brabant. In 1540, this "Nero of England" likewise had Thomas Cromwell executed and Bishop Latimer imprisoned. Many others who resisted him, Catholic and Protestant alike, were executed. Henry VIII died in 1547.

The Short, Youthful Reign of Edward VI

(1547–1553)

Edward VI, son of Jane Seymour (Henry's third wife), was but ten when he succeeded his father, Henry VIII, on January 28, 1547. He had been groomed in the Reformation faith by

Archbishop Cranmer and was surrounded by an able, Protestant-minded council. Consequently, the Reformation took a great stride forward under his brief six-year reign. In 1547, Henry's treason and heresy laws, including the *Act of the Six Articles,* were repealed. For the first time freedom of the press and freedom of speech were legally permitted. In March of 1549, the *First Prayer Book*, prepared by Archbishop Cranmer, was authorized for the Church of England and in 1552, a revised *Second Prayer Book* emerged and with it a *Confession of Faith, the Forty-two Articles,* the official creed of the Church of England.

The English people themselves were still divided in their sentiments. Strong Catholic reactions still existed, which were to surface under the reign of Queen Mary. On the opposite side there were those who felt the Reformation in England had not gone far enough. These purists, or Puritans, wanted to pattern the English church after continental Calvinistic Protestantism, and would make their mark in the ongoing process of the restoration of the Church as it continued to emerge from its long years of Babylonian Captivity.

The Unhappy Reign of "Bloody Mary" Tudor (1553-1558)

Mary Tudor, sole surviving daughter of Henry VIII and Catherine of Aragon, succeeded Edward VI in 1553. She, like her mother, was a fanatical Catholic with strong Spanish ties, and her great aim was to restore England to the Catholic Church. Her marriage in 1554 to Philip II of Spain, son of Emperor Charles V, greatly antagonized the people of England, who felt their sovereignty as a nation thereby slipping away. The first parliament under Mary repealed the reforming acts of both her father, Henry VIII, and her half-brother, Edward VI. The outstanding Protestant bishops—Cranmer, Ridley, Coverdale, Hooper, and Latimer—were shortly imprisoned. In February of 1555, the Puritan bishop, Hooper, was burned alive at Gloucester. In October of the same year, Bishops Ridley and Latimer were similarly burned alive at Oxford for denying transubstantiation and the mass. Latimer's famed last words were: "...we shall this day, by God's grace, light such a torch in England as will never be put out." In March of the following year, Archbishop Cranmer was burned at the stake at Oxford. He had momentarily recanted under unspeakable pressure, but on the morning of his death, he unflinchingly testified before his enemies of his repentance for his lapse. Before the burning stake he then held the hand that had signed his recantation into the flames until it was burnt to cinders.[16]

In her brief reign of five years, no fewer than 290 martyrs were burned at the stake for the faith of the gospel of Jesus Christ. In the end Mary Tudor sat alone in tragedy—opposed by her people, hated by her husband, and even at variance with her pope whose cause she had so zealously championed.

The Reign of Elizabeth (1558–1603)

Elizabeth, daughter of Henry VIII and Anne Boleyn, succeeded "Bloody Mary" in 1558. She reigned for 45 years in favor of the Protestant cause. Although she probably could have favored the Roman Church, she was forced to depend on Protestant support for her reign. The pope, having never accepted the divorce of Henry VIII from Catherine of Aragon, dismissed her as a bastard and favored her cousin, Mary, Queen of Scots, as legal heir to the English throne. In 1559, under the *Act of Supremacy,* the Church of England was again wrested from the pope and placed under the control of the British

---

16. Catholic historians view the fate of the Protestant bishops under Mary Tudor in a different light: "Most of the bishops whom she executed richly deserved their fate; they were accomplices in many judicial murders in the reign of Henry VIII, since they had allowed many people whom they knew to be innocent, including one of their own number, to be executed. In particular, it can be taken for granted that Cranmer, if Mary had not burned him, would certainly have met death from Elizabeth, whose mother, Anne Boleyn, he had killed."

Crown. Under the *Act of Uniformity,* the *Second Prayer Book* of Edward VI was accepted as the standard Anglican liturgy.

Elizabeth, in the process of serving her own interests, appears in history as a mixture of good and evil. Although she hated Rome, she equally hated John Knox, the Scottish Reformer. Though she upheld the principles of the Reformation (oftentimes out of expediency to protect her own throne), she opposed the Puritans, several of whose propagandists she hanged. Though Rome had tried every conceivable way to regain its stronghold in England, the back of its intrigue was finally broken in the defeat of Philip's Spanish Armada off the coast of England. Consequently, during Elizabeth's reign, the solidarity of England's Reformation was clearly established.

The Reformation in Scotland

The Reformation in Scotland came principally through the strenuous labors of the Catholic priest, John Knox (1505–1572). The soil of the Scottish Reformation, however, had been well prepared by others. Through Scottish travelers and students on the continent and in England, Scotland had already been well influenced by the teachings of Wycliffe's Lollards and those of the Bohemian martyr John Hus and William of Occam. Now Lutheran ideas and ideals streamed into Scotland and stood in stark contrast with the publicized depravities of various ones among the Catholic clergy. One of the heralds of Lutheran ideology, the sainted Patrick Hamilton, was ruthlessly burned at the stake at St. Andrews in 1528 by order of Roman Archbishop Beaton. An inquisition followed, which was aimed at rooting out all Protestant heresy. In 1546, the godly gospel preacher and converted priest George Wishart was also burned at the stake by the Roman Cardinal Beaton, nephew to the archbishop. Shortly thereafter the cardinal himself was brutally murdered by the resistance and his body hung out of the window of St. Andrews.

By 1547, John Knox had emerged as a powerful Protestant preacher; however, he was exiled by the Catholics and made a galley slave for 19 months. After his release, he fled to England for five years, but when Catholic "Bloody Mary" ascended the English throne he fled to Frankfurt and then to Geneva where he became an ardent disciple of John Calvin. Meanwhile the situation in Scotland continued to foster opposition to Rome.

It is not possible to understand the Scottish Reformation without understanding something of the political tension that gripped Scotland, which was caught between the Catholic French throne and the vacillating English throne (one time Protestant, one time Catholic). Both France and England sought to rule Scotland. John Knox was fervently anti-Catholic and anti-French.

In 1557, a number of Scottish nobles severed their relationship with the Catholic Church and pledged themselves "to establish the most blessed Word of God and His Congregation." In 1559, Knox returned to Scotland. His agonizing cry before God was, "O Lord, give me Scotland, or I die." When he first came to St. Andrews and preached his first sermon the people declared of him, "Other men sawed the branches off the Papacy. This man lays his ax to the trunk of the tree." And this Knox zealously did, declaring the Roman Church of his day to be "the Synagogue of Satan," and the pope to be "the Anti-Christ." Wherever he went his preaching ignited open and widespread revolt against the Catholic Church. The French sought to interfere by force to quell the rebellion, but were forced to withdraw in 1560, when the Queen of England sent her army to intervene, leaving the government of Scotland in the hands of the Council of Lords. Also in 1560, the Scottish Parliament officially proclaimed the Reformed faith the religion of Scotland under the Calvinistic Scottish Confession. The Reformation had triumphed in Scotland.

As we have seen, within 50 years the Reformation had flowered all across continental Europe and the British Isles. A generation of men and women had been deeply touched by the fire of Almighty God. The Lord had begun the recovery of His glorious life in His people.

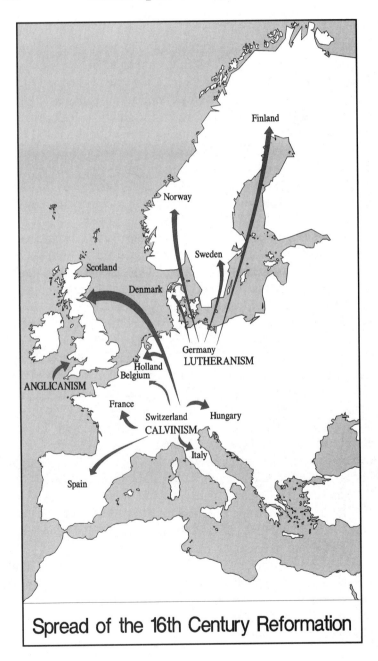

Spread of the 16th Century Reformation

Chapter 9

Fresh Rains
Are Falling

Progressive Revival and Restoration
in the 1600's and 1700's

Reaching Out Yet Further

Within 20 years of the inception of the German and Swiss Reformations, The *Anabaptist* movement began to rise on the Continent. Deep in the hearts of its godly followers lay the conviction that Luther and Zwingli had not gone far enough in their recovery. And so these men found themselves reaching out yet further for the simplicity and purity of apostolic life. Likewise, within 20 years of the inception of the English Reformation, believers called *Puritans* were found longing for a more complete, purer restoration of apostolic simplicity in England. These purists objected to the elaborate worship and rituals of the Church of England and continually appealed for simplicity in worship and for scriptural purity in all matters of faith and morals. Then, going even beyond the Puritans, we find a party of non-conformists—the Independents or Congregationalists—appearing around 1580.

Associated with these Independents were the names of Robert Browne, Henry Barrowe, and John Greenwood. Barrowe and Greenwood were imprisoned for their faith, and in 1593, they were hanged for the cause of Christ. The Independents severed all ties with the Anglican Church, rejecting both Presbyterianism and Episcopalianism and maintaining that the local church was the true basis for all Church life and government. This marks the beginnings of both Congregationalism and the different aspects of the Baptist movement.[1] Under severe persecution, many of these Independents fled to Holland, and many ultimately gained passage on the *Mayflower* as it sailed in 1620 to the New World. That first small company of Pilgrims, led by their elder, William Brewster, landed in Plymouth, New England, to establish a colony where they could freely worship God and give full expression to what they saw in His Holy Word.[2] Strong opposition had come from James I, "King of Great Britain, France and Ireland,"[3] who strongly advocated that oppressive Stuart doctrine, "the Divine

---

1. English Baptists differed from the Anabaptists of Europe in their rejection of certain Anabaptist apocalyptic and revolutionary extremes. The Baptists differed from the English Independents in that the Baptists rejected infant baptism in favor of believer's immersion. For the most part, regular Baptists were Calvinistic in doctrine, although in 1791 there was an Arminian division called "Free-will Baptists." In the 1600's there also arose certain "Seventh-day Baptists," known as such because they observed the Sabbath. Perhaps the most impressive of the early Baptists was the author of *Pilgrim's Progress,* John Bunyan (1628–1688), imprisoned for his faith for 12 years in Bedford jail during the Stuart reign.

2. "The difference between Puritans and Pilgrims could be expressed in the two words reformation and restoration. The Puritans sought to reform the church as it existed in their day. The Pilgrims believed that the ultimate purpose of God was to restore the Church to its original condition, as portrayed in the New Testament" (from a review of *Sharing History Through Prayer and Fasting* by Derek Prince in the "Intercessors For America" Newsletter, October 4, 1997).

3. The title given to him in the dedication preface of the 1611 Authorized King James Version of the Bible.

Right of Kings." In his absolutism, James declared of the Puritans that he would "make them conform, or harry them out of the land or worse." It was this King James who, in 1611, authorized that version of the Bible that still bears his name and remains impressive in both its beauty and style.

Ongoing Revival in Scotland and Ireland

Historian Richard M. Riss in the introduction to his book, *A Survey of 20th-Century Revival Movements in North America*, comments: "After the time of the Reformation, there were many significant local revivals, particularly in Scotland and in Ireland."[4] He then lists the following: a revival of "considerable depth" in Ayr, Scotland, between 1590 and 1606 under the ministry of John Welch, son-in-law of Scottish Reformer John Knox. John Welch was a man of intense prayer, who spent seven or eight hours every day in continual prayer. In 1596, revival came to the Scottish General Assembly. Between 1625 and 1630 revival fires burned in Stewarton, in the west of Scotland under the ministry of David Dickson of Irvine. In 1625 and 1626, revival awakenings ignited in Northern Ireland under John Welch's son, Josiah Welch, and several others.

Around that same time there were revivals in Edinburgh and Inverness, Scotland, under Robert Bruce of Kinnaird, and in 1625, there was a remarkable revival in Ulster, Ireland, birthed out of "many days and nights in prayer." In June of 1630, at Kirk of Shotts in Scotland, a large number of godly souls gathered for several days of prayer, including one whole night of prayer. When John Livingston preached, the Spirit of God so moved upon the congregation that many were smitten to the ground under great conviction and hundreds were converted to Christ. The history of the Presbyterian Church records that "many of the most eminent Christians in that county could date either their conversion, or some remarkable

---

4. Richard Riss, *A Survey of 20th-Century Revival Movements in North America* (Peabody, MA: Hendrickson Publishers, 1988), 10.

confirmation...from that day." There were also revivals across Scotland between 1650 and 1661 and in London in 1665.

In 1642, England was plunged into a civil war that brought about the collapse of the monarchy and the institution of the Protectorate of Oliver Cromwell. Cromwell vehemently opposed Rome, but he also opposed the imposition of any one form of worship on the land. Consequently, between the year 1642 and the year 1660 (when the monarchy was again restored), the gospel had free course, and the spiritual life of the nation was strengthened. These were indeed "seasons of refreshing" from the Presence of the Lord. God was clearly not only the God of reformation and restoration but also the God of renewal and revival.

Jacobus Arminius (1560–1609)

When, in 1609, the Netherlands declared its independence from Catholic Spain, Calvinism was proclaimed the state religion of the Dutch Republic. Some ministers, however, could not accept the Augustinian extremes of Calvinism,[5] and in the process of debate Jacob Arminius, professor at Leyden, advanced his almost-Pelagian[6] views. In opposition to Calvinism, Arminianism advocated the following views: (1) conditional election—God elects men on the basis of His foreknowledge of their choice; (2) unlimited atonement—Christ died for all men; (3) cooperation of the human will with divine grace; (4) resistible grace; and (5) the possibility of falling from grace—conditional security. Though condemned in 1618 by the Synod of Dort, Arminianism reappeared in full vitality as the fiber of Wesleyan Methodism a century later.

The Rise of Mysticism and Pietism

In order to understand the rise of evangelical *mysticism* under George Fox and the Quakers, and the rise of evangelical *pietism* under men such as Philip Spener, August Francke,

---

5. See Chapter 8 for the five basic tenets of Calvinism.
6. See Chapter 6 for the basic tenets of Pelagiansim.

Count von Zinzendorf, and the Wesleys, we must understand something of the sterile orthodoxy into which the Reformation had degenerated. The century after Luther and Calvin was a century of Protestant scholasticism. Lutheran historian Lars P. Qualben describes this century thus: "The Bible became an arsenal from which doctrines were to be proved. The gospel was treated as doctrine rather than as a power of God unto salvation, and Christianity was presented as a religion of right thinking without a corresponding emphasis on the right condition of the heart. This one-sided emphasis on right thinking made the age of orthodoxy an age of great theological controversies."[7] This sterility created the need that both *mysticism* and *pietism* met in the ongoing thrust of the Holy Spirit in the earth.

The Mystical George Fox and the Quakers (1624–1691)

George Fox, of Leicestershire, son of a Presbyterian weaver, was trained in the Puritan religion and influenced early in life by the Anabaptists. Having been disillusioned by the organized Church and its sterile, intellectual ministry, he left home to wander about until his transforming experience in 1646, at the age of 22. At that time Fox saw in a revelation the importance of the "inner light" abiding within every man, which, if followed, would lead him to the Light of life, Christ Jesus.[8] In Fox's own case, "when all his hopes...in all men were gone, then he heard a voice which said: There is One, even Christ Jesus, that can speak to thy condition....[This happened]...that he might give the Lord alone the glory, and that Jesus Christ might have the preeminence."[9] The following year, Fox's wanderings gave birth to a purposeful, itinerant

---

7. Lars P. Qualben, *A History of the Christian Church* (New York: Thomas Nelson & Sons, 1933), 357.

8. See John 1:9.

9. Major Douglas, *George Fox—The Red Hot Quaker* (Cincinnati: God's Bible School Book Store, n.d.), 13.

ministry that lasted for 40 years throughout England, Scotland, Holland, and America.

Two characteristics stand out in Fox's stormy ministry. The first was his severe denunciation of the existing religious order. Early in his career, while at Leicester, Fox rose to his feet in a certain congregation and publicly declared, "Dost thou call this place a church, or this mixed multitude a church?...The church is the pillar and the ground of the truth, made up of living stones and lively members; a spiritual household of which Christ is the head; but He is not the head of a mixed multitude, or of an old house composed of lime, stones and wood."[10] Thus Fox began his relentless defiance of organized Christianity and its sterile religious forms. He denounced the clergy, insisting that every member is a priest unto God, whether man or woman. He excluded any liturgy, even music and singing. His followers would come together to "wait upon the Spirit" and would only speak, pray, or exhort when moved upon by the Spirit. He likewise refused the sacraments, accepting them only as spiritual and not as literal realities.

The second earmark of Fox's prophetic ministry was its dynamic charismatic nature. "As he prayed, the power of God came down in such a marvelous manner that the very building seemed to rock, and some of those present declared: 'This is like that in the days of the apostles, when at Pentecost the house where they met was shaken!' "[11] Quaker Edward Burroughs told of the power of God present in Quaker meetings: "We received often the pouring down of the Spirit upon us...and we spoke with new tongues, as the Lord gave us utterance, and as His Spirit led us...."

In 1648, a dissolved Anabaptist congregation at Nottingham, England, gathered around Fox. And by 1652, the first Quaker community was formed in Preston Patrick, northern England. "Quakers," who quaked under the power of God,

---

10. *Ibid.,* 17.
11. *Ibid.*

were initially so named out of derision, but the name was soon adopted by Fox's followers. "Friends," the name of simplicity from the Book of Third John, was the name originally chosen by the group. By 1656, Fox had 56 associate itinerant preachers with him, and by 1660, the Quakers, then "the fastest growing movement in the Western world," had over 50,000 adherents. And by 1661, there were more than 4,000 dissenting Quakers in English prisons! *The Blasphemy Act* prohibited the type of public disturbances that the Quakers created. An additional offense was their refusal to take oath, bear arms, or perform civil service. Quaker missionaries traveled to continental Europe, Asia, Africa, and the West Indies; and in 1682, William Penn, the most eminent trophy of Quakerism, founded a Quaker colony in Pennsylvania, having obtained a grant from Stuart Charles II for release of a debt owed by the British Crown to Penn's father. William Penn wrote of George Fox, "He had an extraordinary gift in opening the Scriptures. But above all he excelled in prayer. The most living, reverent frame I ever beheld, was his in prayer."[12]

In the face of certain unsettling extremes, usually present in every charismatic revival, Quakerism began to be shaped by Fox in 1660. Guidelines were established for the formation and discipline of local congregations under the elders as leaders of the flock. Although it was not his original intention to organize the movement, by the time of his death in 1691 a mold was cast around the "Society of Friends" that would characterize it to this day. Quaker synods sprang into existence. Congregations were formally organized, and a system of Quaker doctrine was forged by Robert Barclay, the able theologian of the movement. But, in all, these evangelical mystics had staked out yet a further plane in the recovery of the dynamic life of the apostolic church on the earth.

---

12. Penn, as quoted by William E. Allen, *History of Revivals and Worldwide Revival Movements* (Antrim, N. Ireland: Revival Publishing Co., 1951), 22.

On yet another note: one of the best known Catholic mystics of the late seventeenth and early eighteenth centuries was Madame Guyon. Although imprisoned by the King of France in the Bastille, her godly influence spread far beyond the walls of that awful dungeon, right down to this present day.

Seventeenth-Century Pietism

Running parallel to the rise of George Fox and his mystical Quakers in England, we find the emerging of German Pietism on the Continent.

One did not have to go very far into history to sense a missing note in the ongoing of the Continental Reformation. Regardless of what personal spiritual experiences Martin Luther and John Calvin may have had themselves, the Reformation was basically not an "experience" oriented movement. Reformation thinking ultimately centered more in men's *standing* in grace rather than in a personal *experience* of that grace. In the sixteenth and seventeenth centuries men quickly forgot Luther's concern that "the heart of religion lies in its *personal pronouns.*" Justification became more positional than practical.

Because of the severity of the Reformation's reaction against Catholicism's "works-righteousness," the Reformation pendulum tended to swing to the opposite pole and get stuck! And so seventeenth-century Lutheran Pietism, as framed by Philip Spener and August Francke, was really just a plea for a renewal of *personal* religion on the basis of Luther's principles. The Pietists were a revival movement within intellectual Lutheranism, seeking a simple religion of the heart and a simple fellowship together. Pietism called for experiential justification, personal holiness, and apostolic evangelism. Here were "a band of men, whose hearts God had touched!"

God had indeed touched the heart of Philip Jacob Spener (1635–1705), Lutheran clergyman and initiator of German Pietism. Spener, as a young man, had been influenced by the writings of the English Puritans Richard Baxter and John Bunyan, as well as, by Jean de Labadie, apostle of the "household church" movement in Geneva. What was begun by Spener was then completed by August Hermann Francke (1663–1727) at the University of Halle, the great pietistic center destined to supply Europe with pietistic teachers, pastors, missionaries, and godly laymen. Pietism was basically an "in-church" movement, designed to renew the dead orthodoxy of Lutheranism. Pietists taught that the regeneration of man took place, not in baptism, but in a specific experience of conversion. Pietistic emphasis centered in building up the life of the believer in home Bible studies and prayer meetings, called *collegia pietatis* ("fellowship of piety"), hence the term "Pietism," and in the involvement of all believers, rather than just the clergy, in the work of winning the lost and building up the believers. One of the sons of the Pietist movement was the historian Gottfried Arnold (1666–1714), founder of the "Philadelphia Gatherings." And one of their converts was Gerhard Tersteegen, the anointed hymnist.

Strong emphasis was placed by the Pietists on foreign missions among the Jews, as well as to the Orient and to the New World. There was also a vision for fellowship between those of different denominations in a love that transcended doctrinal differences. The movement also soon spread northward into the Scandinavian countries of Denmark and Norway. In Norway, the renewal produced Hans Nielsen Hauge (1771–1824), famed Lutheran lay-preacher and revivalist. To its opponents, the danger of Pietism lay in its tendencies toward subjectivism in spiritual experience (perhaps almost losing the objective element of justification by faith), and in its moralism that tended almost to Pharisaism, especially in the judging of those unlike itself.

Thus we have observed both the Continental Pietists with their hope for renewal within the structure of institutionalism and the English Quakers with their vision for a restoration of the Body of Christ apart from institutionalism.

Eighteenth-Century Pietism

Saxon Count Nicolaus Ludwig von Zinzendorf (1700–1760) was raised a pietist and trained at Francke's University of

Halle. Even as a boy he was characterized by the trait that was to mark his whole spiritual life: passionate devotion to the Lord Jesus Christ. His whole life was summed up in his beautiful testimony: "I have one passion. It is Jesus, and Jesus alone!"

In the wake of the Counter-Reformation, homeless Moravian and Bohemian Protestants, many with roots going back to John Hus, were invited by Zinzendorf to settle on his estate at Herrnhut in Saxony. Though differences seriously divided the settlers and threatened to disrupt the community, Zinzendorf, in 1727, prevailed on the brethren to repent and to seek unity in those things that they had in common. He was a man who, by his own example, led the way. He declared of one of his most ardent opponents: "Although our dear Christian David was calling me the Beast and [Herrnhut Minister] Mr. Rothe the False Prophet, we could see his honest heart nevertheless, and knew we could lead him right...." Christian David, a modest carpenter at Herrnhut, joined with Zinzendorf in seeking revival at Herrnhut.

And revival did come to the repentant saints at Herrnhut in August of 1727. The following account is taken from the "History of the Moravians" by A. Bost:

> "On the Lord's day, the 10th of August, the minister Rothe was seized, in the midst of the assembly, with an unusual impulse. He threw himself upon his knees before God, and the whole assembly prostrated themselves with him...singing and prayer, weeping and supplication, continued till midnight. All hearts were united in love...On the 18th of August, all the children at the boarding school were seized with an extraordinary impulse in the Spirit, and passed the whole night in prayer...no words can express the powerful operation of the Holy Spirit upon these children."[13]

One participant commented: "A sense of the nearness of Christ was given to us all at the same moment...What the Lord did...was inexpressible. The whole place appeared like a visible tabernacle of God with men."

---

13. Bost, as quoted by Allen, *op. cit.,* 15-16.

On August 25, 1727, a continual prayer meeting was begun that would last for over a century! Bost comments: "They considered that, as in the ancient Temple the fire on the altar never ceased to burn, so in the Church, which is now the Temple of God, the prayers of the saints ought always to ascend to the Lord."[14] Count von Zinzendorf himself observed that "at this juncture supernatural gifts were manifested in the church and miraculous cures were wrought," and Moravian historian John Greenfield wrote that "Christian women and young people were filled with the Spirit and prophesied."[15]

Zinzendorf, in accord with his pietistic conviction of *ecclesiola in ecclesia*,[16] originally intended the refugees to melt into the Saxon Lutheran State Church, while they maintained additional meetings in accord with Spener's plan of *collegia pietatis*. But the Moravians were ultimately destined by circumstances beyond their control to stand as a distinct Church body within Christendom, the *Unitas Fratrum*, the United Brethren, with distinctive doctrines, practices, and Church government.

The Moravian Brethren were characterized by three outstanding qualities: their passionate zeal and devotion for the Lord Jesus Christ Himself; their burden for a fraternity of all true believers that transcended all denominational barriers and reached even into the Roman and Greek Catholic communities; and their fervent revival zeal for foreign missions that took them into various parts of continental Europe, England, America, the West Indies, Greenland, South America, Africa, and Labrador.

John Wesley and the Methodists

No movement in the restoration of the apostolic church on the earth is more impressive than early Methodism with its

---

14. *Ibid.*

15. John Greenfield, *When the Spirit Came* (Minneapolis, MN: Bethany, 1967), 60.

16. "The Church within the Church."

quest for the inner fire of the Holy Spirit, its deeper life "cell-group" concept, and its evangelistic social revolution. And no leader stands more impressive than its stilted, abrupt apostle, John Wesley of Epworth, England, whose life spanned most of the eighteenth century. Known for his methodicalism in all life's functions (from which Methodism derived its name), the story is told of Wesley's host finding him asleep on the top of the stairs one evening. Having been but a bit late for his bedtime exactly on the hour, he did not quite make it into bed!

Against the backdrop of English rationalism and the general spiritual and moral decline of English society, Methodism—with its far-reaching spiritual effects—altered the course of England's history and spared the nation from moral bankruptcy.

The roots of Methodism are found in four colorful personalities: John Wesley (1703–1791), its master-builder; George Whitefield (1714–1770), its dynamic orator; Charles Wesley (1708–1788), its great hymn-writer and author of over six thousand hymns; and John Fletcher (1729–1785), its able theologian. Fletcher's most important work was his *Checks to Antinomianism*, a defense of the Arminian theology of Wesleyian Methodism. In a letter to Charles Wesley, dated January 5, 1763, Fletcher also revealed his strong Pentecostal passion: "What I want is the light and mighty power of the Spirit of God. As to my parish…we look for our Pentecost…."

John Wesley was the son of an Anglican rector, Samuel Wesley, and Susannah, his wife. The fifteenth of 19 children, he was barely saved with Charles, his brother, from a burning rectory in 1709. Ever after, John was to view himself as a "brand snatched from the burning." In 1728, John was ordained an Anglican priest. In 1729, the Wesleys, with several others, formed the "Holy Club" at Oxford, a "cell-group" for the deepening of spiritual life. And in 1735, George Whitefield joined their pietistic ranks. Within the year the Wesley brothers left England to serve as missionaries in the newly established colony of Georgia. Soon after reaching Savannah, John met August Spangenberg, the Moravian, who—along with

Peter Bohler (who encountered Wesley after his return from Georgia)—pointedly spoke to him about his own personal relationship with God. "Do you know Jesus Christ?" Spangenberg asked. John could but answer, "I know He is the Savior of *the world*," to which Spangenberg responded: "True, but do you know He has saved *you*?"

Having returned from America to England, John's inner transformation took place on May 24, 1738, three days after the conversion of his brother Charles. On that Wednesday evening at an Anglican "society" at Aldersgate Street in London,[17] John heard Luther's preface to the *Commentary on Romans* read. He testifies, "About a quarter before nine, while he was describing the change which God works in the heart through faith in Christ, I felt my heart strangely warmed. I felt I did trust in Christ, Christ alone for salvation; and an assurance was given me, that He had taken away my sins, even mine, and saved me from the law of sin and death."

Desiring to know more about the Moravians, John Wesley departed for Germany less than three weeks after his conversion, where he spent time with Zinzendorf. He dialogued particularly on the issues of personal holiness. Upon returning to England, John took up the burden of itinerant preaching at the urging of George Whitefield who, in his outdoor meetings near Bristol, had gathered audiences that at times numbered 20,000. Whitefield had been preaching on the necessity of biblical conversion and spiritual regeneration as opposed to baptismal regeneration. This won for him great hostility among the Anglicans who closed their pulpits to him, forcing him to take up open-air preaching.

In both private prayer meetings and in public preaching services, John Wesley saw unusual happenings. On January 1, 1739, at a New Year's prayer meeting, he records: "About three in the morning, as we were continuing instant in prayer,

---

17. On the order of a modern-day "in-church" cell-group created for the cultivation of spiritual life.

the power of God came mightily upon us, insomuch that many cried out for exceeding joy, and many fell to the ground. As soon as we were recovered a little from the awe and amazement at the presence of His Majesty, we broke out with one voice, 'We praise Thee, O God; we acknowledge Thee to be the Lord'."[18] Twenty-four year old George Whitefield, who was present at this meeting wrote, "It was a Pentecostal season indeed... we were filled as with new wine... overwhelmed with the Divine Presence...." And they went forth empowered for a new mission. Bishop Ryle comments, "They did not wait for sinners to come to them, they pursued them everywhere...like men storming a breach... no sinner was safe anywhere!"

In Wesley's public meetings, scenes such as these were not uncommon: "Immediately one, and another, and another sunk to the earth: they dropped on every side as thunderstruck. One of them cried aloud. We besought God in her behalf, and He turned her heaviness into joy. A second being in the same agony, we called upon God for her also: and He spoke peace unto her soul....One was so wounded by the sword of the Spirit, that you would have imagined she could not live a moment. But immediately His abundant kindness was shown, and she loudly sang of His righteousness."[19]

George Whitefield initially questioned these unusual manifestations. But Wesley records: "The next day [Whitefield] had opportunity of informing himself better: for no sooner had he begun, in the application of his sermon, to invite all sinners to believe in Christ, than four persons sunk down close to him, almost in the same moment. One of them lay without sense or motion; a second trembled exceedingly; the third had strong convulsions all over his body, but made no noise, unless by groans; the fourth, equally convulsed, called upon God, with strong cries and tears. From this I trust we shall all suffer God to carry on His own work in the way that pleaseth Him."[20]

---

18. Wesley, Vol. I, 170.
19. Wesley, Vol. I, 188-189.
20. Wesley, Vol. I, 210.

In a letter to James Hutton dated April 30, 1739, Wesley also records: "Immediately the power of God fell on us: one, and another, and another sunk to the earth; you might see them dropping on all sides as thunderstruck. One cried out aloud. I went and prayed over her, and she received joy in the Holy Ghost. A second falling into the same agony, we turned to her, and received for her also the promise of the Father." It is of interest to note that John Wesley himself seemingly never fell down or shook, etc. He just observed this in others, mainly women, as he ministered—and for the most part concluded these were valid responses to the power of God.

John Wesley was not always well received. In October of 1743, in Walsall, an enraged mob cried out, "Drown him! Hang him! Crucify him!" Some shouted, "Strip him, tear off his clothes!" to which Wesley mildly responded, "That you need not do: I will give you my clothes if you want them." He was miraculously spared.

For the next nearly 50 years John Wesley would travel, mostly on horseback, over 250,000 miles, preaching some 40,000 sermons, often to 20,000 persons at a time, leaving behind about 140,000 Methodists and 1,500 traveling preachers. Wesley's dual message was justification by faith in the blood of Christ Jesus and sanctification by faith in the fire of the Spirit of God. Wesley did not judge the validity of his work by the unusual phenomena that occurred but by the lives changed by the power of God. "These are my living arguments for what I assert," he declared. Wesley's vision for "Christian perfection" was born out of the influence of the writings of William Law on his life—in particular, Law's *Treatise on Christian Perfection* and *Serious Call to a Devout Life*—as well the writings of other Christian mystics.[21]

---

21. One of the clearest explanations of Wesley's understandings of "Christian Perfection" appears in Vinson Synan's *The Holiness-Pentecostal Tradition: Charismatic Movements in the Twentieth Century* (Grand Rapids, MI: W.B. Eerdmans, 1997). In chapter one, "The Double Cure," Synan convincingly outlines that Wesley's view was not one of "sinless perfection," but rather one of a "life of daily victory over conscious willful sin."

John Wesley's original attempt, as with Zinzendorf, was not to create a new Church. He formed strict "societies" for the furtherance of the spiritual life of his converts. These he divided into "bands" and then into "classes" of about 12 members. These were to supplement Anglicanism, but Anglicanism soon forced Methodism's hand; and Methodism, like the Moravians, was destined to stand as a distinct church body in the earth. Methodism initially forked into two main streams— Calvinistic Methodism under the leadership of the young Welshmen, Howell Harris, Daniel Rowland, Griffith Jones, and George Whitefield with his sponsor Lady Huntington; and Arminian Methodism under the Wesleys. Wesleyan Methodism was the larger and more vital of the two branches. To John Wesley, Calvinism, which had dominated English social, religious, and political life over much of the previous century, seemed paralyzing to moral effort and, for a season, not a little hostility existed between Wesley and Whitefield on the subject. In all, Methodism stood as a strong spiritual force on both sides of the Atlantic in the ongoing recovery of the manifest presence of God upon the earth in the eighteenth century.

The Great Awakening of the 1700's

Running concurrently with the Pietistic revivals on the Continent was the Evangelical Awakening throughout the British Isles. A high point of this Awakening was the Cambuslang revival that broke out on February 18, 1742, under the ministries of William McCulloch and George Whitefield, setting off fires of revival across all Scotland. At one communion service upwards to 50,000 people assembled. "They seemed charged with divine electricity, a Pentecostal power which astonished even Whitefield."[22] Whitefield recorded of these days: "Such a commotion surely never was heard of…it far out did all that I ever saw in America. For about an hour and a half

---

22. Pollock, as quoted by Colin C. Whittaker, *Great Revivals*, (Springfield, MO: Radiant Books, 1984), 59.

there was such weeping, so many falling into deep distress."[23] Similar powerful revivals took place throughout Wales. Howell Harris described the March 1743 meetings of Daniel Rowland in Wales: "O! how did my soul burn with sacred love when I was among them! They fell almost as dead by the power of the Word, and continue weeping for joy, having found the Messiah...." Not only did God move mightily by His Spirit through the emerging instrument of Methodism, but others of the more established Church bodies experienced a real visitation from God in this awakening. The emphasis was on "conversion"— a transforming experience of regeneration—and on Christian growth.

Anglicanism was affected by the Awakening, as were the Congregationalists and the Baptists. Apart from the Wesleys and George Whitefield, this awakening produced such godly men as Charles Simeon (1759–1836) of Cambridge, and such outstanding hymn writers as Isaac Watts (1674–1748), author of *Jesus Shall Reign Where'er the Sun;* Augustus Toplady (1740–1778), author of *Rock of Ages;* William Cowper (1731–1800), author of *There Is a Fountain Filled With Blood;* and John Newton (1725–1807), author of *Amazing Grace.* This was also the era of Johann Sebastian Bach (1685–1750), Ludwig von Beethoven (1770–1827) and George Frederick Handel (1685–1759), and their inspired masterpieces of praise and adoration to God.

Running parallel to both the continental Pietistic revivals and the Evangelical Awakening of the British Isles, we further note the Great Awakening on the American side of the Atlantic among the 13 colonies. In yet another quarter of a century, in 1775, the colonies would begin their revolution against England. In 1776, the Declaration of Independence would be signed, and in 1789 the Constitution of the United States would emerge as a new and great nation "under God" was birthed on the earth!

---

23. Whitefield, as quoted by Whittaker, *op. cit.*

Because of new immigrations, basically all the European denominations eventually took root on American soil—the Congregationalists at New Plymouth in 1620; the Dutch Reformed at New York on the heels of Henry Hudson of the Dutch East India Company in 1623: the Lutherans at New York in 1623; the Roman Catholics at Maryland in 1634 by George Calvert (first Lord of Baltimore and founder of Maryland); the Baptists at Rhode Island in 1639 by Roger Williams; the Presbyterians on Long Island, New York, in 1640; the Quakers at Massachusetts in 1656 (in 1681, Quaker William Penn founded the colony of Pennsylvania as a "holy experiment" in freedom of religion); the Mennonites by 1638; the Moravians at Georgia in 1735; and the first Methodist works began in New York and Maryland around 1744. The Church of England ceased to exist in America when England recognized the independence of the American Colonies. Its successor, the Protestant Episcopal Church, was organized in 1789.

Outstanding men, such as Dutch Reformed T.J. Frelinghuysen (1691–1748) in New Jersey, and Presbyterian William Tennent, Sr. (1673–1745) in Pennsylvania (who laid the foundations for what would later become Princeton University), and Congregationalist Jonathan Edwards (1703–1758) in New England, a personal friend of George Whitefield, became the instruments in the hands of God in this great revival of the Great Awakening that swept thousands into the Kingdom of God.

The revival that began in Northampton, Massachusetts, in 1734 under Jonathan Edwards continued in full strength for about eight years, and then in a lesser degree for yet another 15 years. Assisted by Gilbert Tennet and George Whitefield, the revival spread throughout New England. On the evening of the day preceding the outbreak of the revival, some Christians met and spent the whole night in prayer. When the Spirit fell in Northampton, Edwards notes, "There was scarcely a person in the town, old or young, left unconcerned about the great things of the eternal world. The work of conversion was carried on in a most astonishing manner, and increased more and more; souls did, as it were, come by flocks to Jesus Christ. This work of God soon made a glorious alteration in the town…the town seemed to be full of the presence of God…."[24]

William Conant records the impact of the revival on New England and beyond: "It cannot be doubted that at least 50,000 souls were added to the churches of New England, out of a population of about 250,000…a fact sufficient…to determine the destinies of the country….[as] floods of blessing poured over the land."[25] During these days, Jonathan Edwards's wife, Sarah, often experienced unusual manifestations of the Lord's presence. On one occasion, she noted: "My soul was so filled with love to Christ, and love to His people, that I fainted under the intenseness of the feeling."[26] Similar phenomena accompanied waves of revival all across New England. Of the Great Awakening, Edwards himself reports, "It was a very frequent thing to see a house full of outcries, faintings, convulsions and such like, both with distress, and also with admiration and joy."

George Whitefield, arriving from England, assisted in the great revival. (This was but one of seven times Whitefield sailed across the Atlantic to preach the gospel, forging a sovereignly ordained "revival link" between England and the United States, which would continue through the end of the twentieth century.) Whitefield preached to many thousands not only in New England, but in Philadelphia, New York, and on the famous Boston Common. At Nottingham, Delaware, on May 14, 1740, 12,000 people gathered. Thousands cried out under conviction, almost drowning Whitefield's voice. Men and women dropped to the ground as though dead, then

---

24. Edwards, as quoted by Allen, *op. cit.,* 17.

25. Conant, as quoted by Allen, *op. cit.,* 18.

26. These experiences, writes Guy Chevreau, in defining the 1994 "Toronto Blessing," "seem to be eighteenth-century equivalents to the falling, resting and 'slain' experiences witnessed at the Airport Vineyard" (*Catch the Fire,* [Marshall Pickering], 1994, 77).

revived, then dropped again, as Whitefield continued preaching. President Calvin Coolidge commented: "America was born in a Revival of Religion—and back of it were John Wesley and George Whitefield." It was estimated that 30,000 souls were converted through Whitefield's revivals in America.

Jonathan Edwards made his mark on America for generations to come; he was an able evangelist in the harvest fields of the Lord. Edwards was also the first truly great American philosopher in his own right, strongly influenced by the English empiricist John Locke. Edwards died in 1758, just shortly after assuming the presidency of Princeton.

The Close of a Glorious Century

The year 1790 ushered in a fresh decade of revival, birthing the Second Great Awakening in America, known in Britain as the Second Evangelical Awakening.

The ground was deluged with the presence of God! In the United States there were extensive revivals in Pennsylvania, as well as in the New England states, New York, New Jersey, Ohio, Kentucky, Tennessee, the Carolinas, and Georgia. There was a tremendous visitation in Virginia at Hampton-Sydney College and in Brunswick County, Virginia, under Methodism's Francis Asbury. Harlan Page wrote of the revival in New York City: "The Lord appears now to be coming down on all parts of this great city...Thousands of Christians here are praying as they never prayed before. Conversions are occurring in all parts of the city. Churches are daily crowded to overflowing, and a most fixed and solemn attention is given to the...truth."

In England, the Great Yorkshire Revival of the mid-1790's among the Methodists tripled their constituency to almost a quarter of a million people. And at the turn of the century there were remarkable revivals in Scotland under the ministry of Alexander Stewart. These were indeed "floods upon the dry ground," as the Lord answered the cries of His thirsty people!

The Birth of Modern Apostolic Missions: The Fruit of Revival

Foreign missions, for the most part, were very limited ventures in the 1500's and 1600's among the Reformation churches. The sentiment by the turn of the 1700's was even less enthusiastic. The Divinity Faculty of Wittenberg had denounced missionary advocates as false prophets. In 1722, the hymnologist Neumeister of Hamburg closed his Ascensiontide sermon by giving out the hymn:

> *"'Go out into the world,'*
> *The Lord of old did say;*
> *But now: 'where God has placed thee,*
> *There he would have thee stay!'"*

Dr. George Smith has summarized the prevailing mood aptly: "Here and there one man was reached and roused, his eyes opening to the fact that millions were dying without the gospel; his ears opening to the cry of want and woe which, like the moan and sob of waves on the seashore, tells of storm and wreck. Now and then a man went forth, while as yet the Church as a whole seemed locked in icy indifference and insensibility!"[27]

In the face of this apathy and even hostility, the Halle-Danish mission, fruit of German Pietism, began its missionary activities in the early 1700's, furnishing some 60 foreign missionaries during that century. We have already noted the missionary zeal of the Quakers and the Moravians, with their century-long prayer meeting. These, within 150 years, sent out no less than 2,170 missionaries. Dr. Warneck, German historian of Protestant Missions wrote of the Moravians that they "called into being more missions than the whole evangelical church had done in two centuries." But it was to be the Evangelical Awakening that would birth modern apostolic missions. Schools of learning such as Princeton and Columbia were established to equip a

---

27. "The New Acts of the Apostles," 74.

new generation of harvesters and missionary societies, and their missionaries were set ablaze by the fires of revival.

"A Corn of Wheat"

David Brainerd (1718–1747) labored among the Indians in the Delaware River region of the 13 English colonies. His missionary career spanned but a brief three to four years; then he succumbed to consumption, broken in health by the hardships and privations he had endured for the sake of his "beloved Indians." Stories were told of his prayers of intercession on behalf of the Indian nations, as he knelt for hours in the snow, deep within the forests. When he would finish, the place where he prayed was often circled in blood, crimson against the snow, consumptively coughed up by him as he wrestled in prayer. As a result of his labors and intercession, the revival power of God fell among the Indians in the summer of 1745. David Brainerd recorded in his journal:

> "The power of God seemed to descend…'like a rushing mighty wind,' and with an astonishing energy bore down all before it…I never saw a day like it in all respects: it was a day wherein I am persuaded the Lord did much to destroy the kingdom of darkness among this people....I long to be a flame of fire, continually glowing in the divine service, preaching and building up Christ's kingdom to my latest, my dying hour."[28]

David Brainerd died at age 29 as dawn broke on Friday, October 9, 1747, in the home of his dear friend, Jonathan Edwards. Edward's saintly daughter Jerusha was buried next to her beloved David at peaceful Northhampton in Massachusetts, following him in death but four months later. One of his parting words to her had been, "Jerusha, if I thought I should not see you, and be happy with you in another world, I could not bear to part with you...[but] we shall spend a happy eternity together."

---

28. Brainerd, as quoted by Allen, *op. cit.*, 20-21.

A.C. Dixon wrote: "The prayer and consecration of that one man, David Brainerd, did more for the great missionary revival of the nineteenth century than did any other single force." Indeed that holy, sacrificial, poured-out life of David Brainerd was destined to fall into the ground and die, but in his place many would spring up to fill the face of the earth with fruit. And such a one was William Carey.

William Carey (1761–1834) was born in Northhamptonshire in England, worked as a cobbler, and then became a Baptist minister. Concerned for the heathen, it was he who was told by one of his Calvinistic ministerial brethren, "Sit down, young man, and respect the opinions of your seniors. If the Lord wants to convert the heathen, He can do it without your help." His persistence, however, led to the founding of the Baptist Missionary Society in 1792; and the next year Carey, "the father of modern missions,"[29] set out for India. His watchword was, "Expect great things from God, attempt great things for God."

Henry Martyn, "Cambridge's greatest missionary,"[30] was another life inspired by David Brainerd. Sent forth by the Church Missionary Society to Calcutta in 1806, he finally died in Persia at the early age of 31, having won only one soul to the Lord, but inspiring many by his sacrifice.

The London Missionary Society, formed in 1795, sent Robert Morrison (1782–1834), the first Protestant pioneer missionary, to China. They also sent martyr John Williams (1796–1839) to the South Sea Islands, Robert and Mary Moffat to South Africa, and martyr James Chalmers to New Guinea.

William Ellis won much of Madagascar to Christ. David Livingston, son-in-law of Robert and Mary Moffat, died on his knees after 30 years in Central Africa.

---

29. Robert Hall Glover, *The Progress of Worldwide Missions* (New York: Harper, 1960), 94.

30. A.M. Renwick, *The Story of the Church* (London: InterVarsity Fellowship, 1958), 180.

In 1829, the Church of Scotland sent Alexander Duff to India. And, in 1866, the China Inland Mission, a firstfruits among faith missions, was founded by J. Hudson Taylor, "the man who believed God."[31] An army of apostolic men and women had been raised up in revival power, in the words of the Moravians, "to win for the Lamb that was slain, the reward of His suffering."

---

31. For J. Hudson Taylor's stirring biography, see Marshall Broomhall's *The Man Who Believed God* (Chicago: Moody Press, n.d.).

St. Francis of Assisi
1182–1226

Martin Luther
1483–1546

John Calvin
1509–1564

John Wesley
1703–1791

Jonathan Edwards
1703–1758

George Whitefield
1714–1770

Charles Finney
1792–1875

Charles H. Spurgeon
1834–1892

Dwight L. Moody
1837–1899

Charles H. Mason
1866–1961

John G. Lake
1870–1935

Frank Bartleman
1871–1923

Chapter 10

The Floodgates of Heaven Are Opened

Revival and Restoration During the 1800's

The First Half of the 1800's

The first half of the 1800's saw the continuation of the marvelous movings of the Holy Spirit begun in the 1700's. Historians call this powerful fresh wave, the "Second Great Evangelical Awakening," as we have already noted.

Volume II of the *New History of Methodism* recorded:

"The early years of American Methodism witnessed an almost continuous revival. Scarcely a society was formed which did not grow out of a revival....In no period of the early history were revivals more general than during the years from 1784 to 1808. [The American Methodist Church was formally organized in Baltimore in 1784 under the oversight of Francis Asbury and Richard Wright. Their commission came from John Wesley himself: 'We believe that God's design in raising up the preachers called Methodists in America is to reform the continent and spread scriptural holiness over these lands'.] At one time all of Maryland was ablaze with revival. Similar signs and wonders were seen in Virginia. In New England revival followed revival, some of them of great power. In 1800 one of the most remarkable spiritual movements of American history began in Kentucky, and spread through Tennessee and Ohio with the amazing swiftness of a prairie fire."[1]

Historian Winthrop Hudson similarly observed that this move of God swept "back and forth across the country for almost two generations after 1800."[2]

In June of 1800, a four-day "sacramental meeting" was held at Red River, Kentucky, by James McGready, a Presbyterian pastor. These meetings had been preceded by four years of prayer and fasting. On the final day of these special meetings a revival broke out that was destined to change the course of the nation. The floor was "covered by the slain," and the most notorious infidels cried out, "What shall we do to be saved?" A month later, another "sacramental service" was held by McGready at Gasper River, and "the power of God seemed to shake the whole assembly." The cries of the penitent drowned the preacher's voice and people all over the congregation fell prostrate on the ground. These were the beginnings of many camp meetings to follow, the most famous of which was the one convened by Barton W. Stone, a Presbyterian pastor, on August 6, 1801, at Cane Ridge in Bourbon County, Kentucky, where between 10,000 and 25,000 gathered. Interestingly, Stone had originally been urged to serve the Cane Ridge Church by Daniel Boone, the noted frontiersman.

James B. Finley, who at that time was not a professing Christian, reported the following about Cane Ridge: "The noise was like the roar of Niagara...Some of the people were singing, others praying, some crying for mercy...while others shouted...At one time I saw at least five hundred, swept down in a moment as if a battery of a thousand guns had been

1. *New History of Methodism*, Vol. II, 106.
2. Winthrop S. Hudson, *Religion in America,* 2nd ed. (New York: Charles Scribner's Sons, 1973), 135.

opened upon them...I fled for the woods...."[3] Several of the more unusual happenings at Cane Ridge were the "holy laughter, and the barking like dogs," as those so moved were "treeing the devil."[4]

Commenting on these camp meetings and the ensuing tidal waves of revival, Peter Cartwright, a Methodist preacher, stated, "The work went on and spread almost in every direction...til our country seemed all coming to God." Historian James Boles stated that this movement actually birthed the southeastern United States "Bible Belt."[5]

Revival Among Native Americans

James B. Finley (1781–1856), who had been converted at Cane Ridge and became a Methodist circuit rider, had a successful ministry among the Wyandot Indians of Ohio. He described an 1828 camp meeting held among them:

"The Indians being more expert in pitching tents than the whites, they, of course, were ready at an earlier hour to engage in religious exercises. It is characteristic of the Indian to devote exclusive attention, for the time being, to whatever pursuit he may take in hand. So in regard to religion, the time devoted to God was the most sacred. After singing one of their Christian songs, only as Indians can sing, they fell simultaneously upon their knees and lifted up their faces toward heaven. While they were praying the Spirit came down upon them, and the power of God was manifested in the awakening and conversion of souls. The tears and groans and shouts [were] a sign that the Great Spirit was at work upon the hearts of these sons and

---

3. Charles A. Johnson, *The Frontier Campmeeting* (Dallas, TX: S.M.U., 1955), 64-65.

4. The later twentieth century "Toronto Blessing" experienced similar laughter and animal noises as various ones "roared like lions," prophetically celebrating the victory of the Lion of the Tribe of Judah over satan.

5. James Boles, *The Great Revival, 1787–1805* (Lexington: University of Kentucky Press, 1972), as quoted by Lewis Drummond, *Eight Keys to Biblical Revival* (Minneapolis, MN: Bethany House Publishers, 1994), 52.

daughters of the forest. The whole encampment was in a flame of religious excitement, the Lord having taken his own work into his own hands...."[6]

Sadly, Finley's ministry there ended when the U.S. government coerced the tribe to sell its land and move west. (It was this ongoing abusive, treacherous, and murderous treatment of Native Americans that eventually brought down the great Indian cultures and so demoralized these indigenous nations that by the end of the twentieth century only less than one percent of the remaining nearly two million American Indians living in the United States would be born-again Christians.)

Yale College, Dartmouth, Williams, and other colleges experienced mighty moves of the Holy Spirit, and likewise the University of Georgia at the turn of the century was touched where "they lay for hours in the straw prepared for those 'smitten of the Lord' or they shouted and talked in unknown tongues."[7] It was these college and university outpourings of the Spirit that rolled back the evil influences of the "French Enlightenment." A "Concert of Prayer for Colleges" then began in June of 1815, seeking God "for a revival of religion in all the colleges of the United States."

American church growth was impressive in these years. Historian Richard Riss observes that Methodism grew "from only 15,000 members in 1784 to slightly less than one million in 1830. The Baptists doubled in number from 1802 until 1812, and the Presbyterians grew from 18,000 in 1807 to almost 250,000 in 1835."[8]

The fire fell in the early 1800's in the British Isles as well as in America. The island of Skye in the Hebrides was the scene of a powerful revival, as well as the Scottish island of Arran under the anointed ministry of Neil McBride. Shortly thereafter

6. James B. Finley, "Sketches of Western Methodism" (1854).

7. E. Merton Coulter, *College Life in the Old South* (New York: Macmillan, 1928), 194-195.

8. Richard Riss, *A Survey of 20th-Century Revival Movements in North America* (Peabody, MA: Hendrickson Publishers, 1988), 14.

Breadalbane in Scotland experienced an awakening under John McDonald, followed by revival on the island of Lewis, followed by the revival at Kilsyth, Scotland, under William Chalmers Burns. As Burns retold the story of the revival at Kirk of Shotts, the Spirit of God came mightily upon the people. "They broke forth simultaneously in weeping and wailing, tears and groans. Some were screaming out in agony; others—among these, strong men—fell to the ground as if they had been dead."[9]

In 1814, the Cornwall Revival was thus described: "Revival had spread like a prairie fire. A service began in the Methodist chapel on Sunday, 27 February and the Holy Spirit was present in such power that the meeting could not be closed until the following Friday morning. People came and went but the meeting continued. During the course of that week it was claimed that thousands had professed Christ."

The Revivals Under Charles G. Finney

Outstanding among the revivalists of this era was the youthful lawyer from upstate New York, Charles Grandison Finney (1792–1875). Finney was converted to Christ "on a Sabbath evening in the autumn of 1821"[10] at age 29. He describes his conversion thus: "As I went in and shut the door after me, it seemed as if I met the Lord Jesus Christ face to face....He said nothing, but looked at me in such a manner as to break me right down at His feet. As soon as my mind became calm enough to break off from the interview, I returned to the front office....But as I turned and was about to take a seat by the fire, I received a mighty baptism of the Holy Ghost. The Holy Spirit descended upon me in a manner that seemed to go through me, body and soul....No words can express the wonderful love that was shed abroad in my heart.

---

9. William E. Allen, *History of Revivals and Worldwide Revival Movements* (Antrim, N. Ireland:Revival Publishing Co., 1951), 34

10. Charles G. Finney, *Short Life of Charles G. Finney* (Belfast, N. Ireland: Revival Publishing Co., 1948), 8.

I wept aloud with joy and love....I literally bellowed out the unutterable gushings of my heart."[11]

The following spring, Finney put himself under the care of the presbytery as a candidate for the Presbyterian ministry. Soon revivals broke out under his fervent and intense preaching all across New York State, Pennsylvania, Massachusetts, Ohio, and in other states. In an hour when Calvinism had crippled the vitality of the churches, Finney's message was predominantly Arminian as he appealed to men to *respond* to the grace of God in repentance and faith. His doctrines are clearly outlined in his *Systematic Theology.* Finney described one particular meeting near Antwerp, New York, in these words: "An awful solemnity seemed to settle upon the people; the congregation began to fall from their seats in every direction and cry for mercy. If I had a sword in each hand, I could not have cut them down as fast as they fell. I was obliged to stop preaching." Hundreds of thousands were swept into the Kingdom of God across the United States. Actually revivals were breaking out on both sides of the Atlantic—not only in the United States, but also in Europe, in the Netherlands in 1840, and in Germany in 1844.

Joseph Smith and the Mormons

Joseph Smith, Jr. (1805–1844), as a boy of 15 in Manchester, New York, "on the morning of a beautiful spring day in 1820" had his first "heavenly visitation." In a generation that was destined to see the conversion of many hundreds of thousands to Christ, God supposedly told young Smith, "They are all wrong....they draw near to me with their lips, but their hearts are far from me." In this attitude of separationism and isolationism, which would characterize his *Church of Jesus Christ of the Latter-Day Saints,* Smith embarked on a path of prophetic revelation that would take him and those with him deeper and deeper into deception and error. In 1827, Smith, the starry-eyed dreamer, allegedly dug up near Manchester certain gold plates—the *Book of Mormon*—supposedly translated by

---

11. *Ibid.*

means of two peep stones into a supplement to the Bible. The first Mormon Church was organized in 1830 in Fayette, New York. At Kirtland, Ohio, Brigham Young joined the church.

In their book, *Mormon Enigma: Emma Hale Smith*, two Mormon women, Linda King Newell and Valeen Tippetts Avery, describe the dedication of the Kirtland temple on March 27, 1836:

> "Between nine hundred and a thousand [people] crowded in...For these Saints it was a glorious day and their hearts echoed the silent prayer, 'Lord, accept our offering'...At nine o'clock the service began with psalm reading and a hymn....When Joseph [Smith] gave the dedicatory prayer, he asked God to accept the building as fulfillment of the command to construct it...When the prayer ended the assembled saints broke into joyous song:
>
> *"The Spirit of God like a fire is burning;*
> *The latter day glory begins to come forth;*
> *The visions and blessings of old are returning;*
> *The angels are coming to visit the earth.*
>
> *"We'll sing and we'll shout with the armies of heaven;*
> *Hosanna, Hosanna to God and the Lamb!*
> *Let glory to them in the highest be given,*
> *Henceforth and forever: Amen and amen!*
>
> "Don Carlos Smith [Joseph Smith's brother] blessed the bread and wine for the Lord's Supper...The congregation shouted, 'Hosanna, Hosanna, Hosanna to God and the Lamb'...Brigham Young spoke in tongues; David W. Patten interpreted....Heavenly beings appeared to many.... Solemn assemblies were called. Endowments were given. The Elders went from house to house, blessing the Saints...."[12]

---

12. Linda King Newel and Valeen Tippetts Avery, *Mormon Enigma: Emma Hale Smith* (Chicago: University of Illinois Press, 1994), 58-60. (It is interesting, when we consider the purpose of this book, to note that it won two Mormon awards: The Mormon History Association's Best Book Award and John Whitmer Association [RLDS] Best Book Award.)

By the time of these Kirtland phenomena, the Mormon church was already steeped in deception, having accepted Joseph Smith's *Book of Mormon* as part of the Holy Scriptures. Joseph Smith himself was also well on his way to establishing his infamous doctrine of "celestial marriage including a plurality of wives." (The main point in Newell and Avery's 394-page book, *Mormon Enigma*, was simply to show proof that Emma Smith *opposed* these sinful, polygamous practices and that Joseph Smith used the "celestial marriage" doctrine as a *religious cover-up* for his numerous adulterous affairs.)

In 1974, Dr. Reed Durham, a Mormon professor, delivered a lecture to the Mormon History Association, in which he documented the following: "All available evidence suggests that Joseph Smith the Prophet possessed a magical Masonic medallion, or talisman, which he worked during his lifetime and which was evidently on his person when he was martyred...a Jupiter talisman...Jupiter [the father of the Greek gods] being very powerful and ruling in the heavens...guaranteed to the possessor of this talisman the gain of riches, and favor, and power...."[13] These doctrinal, moral, and occult aberrations have caused evangelical Christians to consequently brand Mormonism as nothing short of an occult deception and a charismatic counterfeit.[14]

In 1838, the Mormon leaders embarked for Missouri, and in 1840, established Nauvoo, Illinois. Near here Smith, apparently wearing his Jupiter talisman, was killed in a shoot-out in 1844, leaving the movement divided between Brigham Young, who eventually settled in Salt Lake in Utah, and the immediate descendants of Joseph Smith, who eventually headquartered in Independence, Missouri, forming the *Reorganized Church of Jesus Christ of the Latter-Day Saints.*

The Utah Mormons have grown from just over 26,000 adherants in 1844 to 9.7 million in 1996, half in the U.S. and

---

13. Durham, as quoted by Barney Fuller, *The Burning of a Strange Fire* (Lafayette, LA: Huntington House, 1994), 53-55.

14. See Appendix VII for further Mormon doctrinal error.

half abroad, with a business empire worth $30 billion, created by investing the tithes of the faithful.[15]

John Nelson Darby and the Brethren

In this time of spiritual awakening across the earth, the Lord put a vision within the hearts of His own for a yet purer, ongoing restoration of the Body of Christ in its simplicity. Among these were John Nelson Darby (1800–1882), formerly a clergyman of the Anglican Church of Ireland, and those who stood with him, known simply as the "Brethren." Their vision for the church is summed up in the words of Anthony Norris Groves, a returned missionary, and an early leader among them: "Our aim is that men should come together in all simplicity as disciples, not waiting on any pulpit or ministry, but rather trusting that the Lord will edify us together by ministering to us, as He sees good, from ourselves." The 1860 revival in Tinevelly, South India, was spearheaded by an Indian evangelist, Aroolappen, a disciple of Anthony Norris Groves. Aroolappen wrote: "...the Holy Spirit was poured out openly and wonderfully. Some prophesied...some...trembled and fell down through the shaking of their bodies and souls...some of our people praised the Lord by unknown tongues, with their interpretations...some missionaries admit the truth of the gifts of the Holy Spirit. The Lord meets everywhere one after another, though some tried to quench the Spirit." One (Brethren) missionary wrote, "What God is now doing in the midst of us was altogether beyond the expectations of missionaries and other Christians: who can say what manifestations the Spirit of God will or will not make of His power?"[16]

On the Body of Christ itself, its unity and all inclusiveness, J.N. Darby wrote in 1840, "I could not recognize an assembly that does not receive all the children of God, because I know

---

15. *Time* Magazine, August 4, 1997.
16. Quoted by Arthur Wallis in *In the Day of Thy Power* (London: Christian Literature Crusade, 1956), 76-77.

that Christ received them....I see the Church in ruins...but I desire to bear with the weakness or lack of light that I may find in other Christians and do all that I can to unite those who love the Lord...."[17] In 1880, just two years before his death, however, he forebodingly wrote: "It would be still a question whether God was going to set aside the Brethren: if He does, certainly I would not go with any party in it. I have long felt that this party that assumes to be the godly ones is the one to be feared...Suffice it to say, with no party action will I have anything to do save to reject it."[18]

The first Brethren assembly was formed around 1827 in Dublin. The assembly at Plymouth, England, originating around 1830, became the source for the nickname, "Plymouth Brethren." Contrary to Darby's vision and burden, the Brethren soon did splinter into various factions, some "exclusive" and some "open," with Darby himself being a cause of various of the divisions.

Revered among the early Brethren was the godly George Muller (1805–1898), pioneer in faith and founder of five large orphanages, accommodating over 2,000 children in Bristol. Muller had been greatly impacted by pietism at August Francke's University of Halle on the Continent. Also, outstanding among the Brethren was Samuel Tregelles (1813–1875), eminent student in the Greek New Testament. The Brethren developed within Christendom as champions of the simplicity of church life, but, due to their "dispensationalism," they often find themselves sapped of first century vitality—depleted of the apostolic dynamic needed to match their apostolic simplicity.[19]

---

17. *Letters of J.N. Darby (1840–1880)*, Vol. 1 (New York: Loizeaux Bros., Inc.), 42.

18. *Ibid.,* Vol. 3, 116.

19. The concept that various of the gifts and ministries of the Holy Spirit were only for the early Church is part of "dispensationalism." Another of its features is the extreme distinction between the "Church" and the "Israel of God," which distinction renders all of the Old Testament and part of the New pertinent only for natural Israel and not the Church. "Dispensationalism"

Edward Irving and the Apostolic Church

This same era saw the emerging of Edward Irving (1792–1834), former Scottish Presbyterian minister, and the Catholic Apostolic Church. Unlike the Brethren, the Irvingites in their quest for restoration resembled more the second-century Montanists, complete with supernatural endowments and gifts of the Holy Spirit.[20] Unfortunately, like the Montanists, the Irvingites also had their share of charismatic idiosyncrasies. By 1835, they had established 12 apostles, and by 1836, they had organized all Christendom into "12 tribes," with an apostle for each apostolate, in anticipation of the imminent return of the Lord. The last of their apostles died in 1901.[21] In the heat of eschatological expectation and vision, the Irvingites also spawned what then became known as the theory of the "pre-tribulation" rapture, currently widely accepted among evangelicals. The Brethren joined with the Irvingites in its popularization, although outstanding Brethren such as George Muller were in open opposition to the new theory.[22]

The Campbells and the Disciples of Christ

The year 1832 saw the official birthing of the *Disciples of Christ* from a merger of the followers of former Presbyterian Barton Stone (1772–1844), who had convened the famous Cane Ridge Camp meeting in 1801, and those of former Presbyterian minister Thomas Campbell and his son Alexander

---

developed among the early Brethren and has become popularized in present-day evangelical and fundamentalist circles.

20. See Chapter 4 for a description of Montanism.

21. Larry Christenson, in his *A Message to the Charismatic Movement* (Minneapolis, MN: Bethany Fellowship, Inc., 1972), gives an excellent history and evaluation of the Irvingite movement. One of the more well-known followers of Edward Irving was Henry Drummond, a member of Parliament and a tongues-speaker.

22. The "pre-tribulation rapture" position has presently come under scrutiny in some evangelical circles as well as in various neo-Pentecostal circles, and a shift began in the 1970's to the position of Matthew, chapter 24.

(1786–1866). The Campbells were originally from Ireland, but had moved to Pennsylvania. Alexander had been influenced by Robert and James Haldane, Scottish revivalists and forerunners of the Brethren, at Glasgow as he was preparing for Presbyterian ordination.

The teachings of Robert and James Haldane had contributed to Alexander's vision for a return to New Testament simplicity. The Campbells stood firm against sectarianism and for the unity of all believers. In pursuit of this simplicity they adopted the rule, "Where the Scriptures speak, we speak; and where the Scriptures are silent, we are silent."[23] They never intended to create a new denomination but rather a union of all believers on the basis of this simple rule without any additional tests of creed or ritual. In their quest for simplicity, the *Disciples* upheld the necessity of water baptism "for the remission of sins,"[24] a position differing from the Baptists and the Brethren, who view baptism as symbolic. The *Disciples* also came together on the Lord's Day to break bread. In their views of church government they recognized but one church, the Church of Christ, governed by local elders.[25] For all its stand for unity and against division, the "Restoration Movement" unfortunately soon fractured into the *Christian Church*, the *Churches of Christ,* and the *Disciples of Christ,* developing in the process a high degree of sectarianism and exclusivity. The "Restoration Movement" went further in their dispensationalism than the Brethren, limiting even the "baptism in the Holy

---

23. An example of this was seen in their withdrawal from the Baptists in 1832. Campbell had refused to use any other than scriptural expressions regarding the Father, Son, and Holy Spirit.

24. Acts 2:38 KJV.

25. In practice, however, their itinerant ministers differ little from the one-man "pastors" of other denominations. Historian Lars P. Qualben states of Campbell that "his cherished system of a 'plurality of elders' had to yield gradually to the 'one-man-system' of professionally trained ministers," in the evolution of the development of the Church of Christ structure (Lars P. Qualben, *A History of the Christian Church* [New York: Thomas Nelson & Sons, 1933], 569).

Spirit," as well as the supernatural gifts and ministries of the Holy Spirit, to the first-century apostles. However, in their amillennial[26] understandings of the Church as the true Israel of God, they differed radically from Brethren dispensationalism. The *Disciples of Christ* movement stands presently as one of the larger bodies within present-day American Protestantism.

The Second Half of the 1800's

The second half of the 1800's began as powerfully as the first half of the century. Charles Finney recorded: "This winter of 1857–58 will be remembered as the time when a great revival prevailed throughout all the Northern States." Revival also broke out in Ontario, Canada, in late 1857, under the ministry of evangelists Phoebe and Dr. Walter Palmer. The Fulton Street prayer meeting (1857–1860), convened by a simple New York merchant Jeremiah Lanphier, actually helped spark revival around the globe. By February 1858, many churches and public buildings in downtown New York City were filled with tens of thousands of people praying. Newspapers began covering "The Progress of the Revival" on a daily basis, and at the peak of the revival, conversions numbered 50,000 a week. Out of a total population of 30,000,000 people, 1,000,000 people were converted to Christ across the nation. One account further declared that between 1857 and 1859 2,000,000 converts were added to the Church. The following account of the revival was given:

> "Such a time as the present was never known since the days of the Apostles...Revivals now cover our land, sweeping all before them, exciting the earnest cry from thousands, 'what shall we do to be saved?' Ministers...baptized with the Holy Ghost...preach with new power...The large cities and towns...from Maine to California are sharing in this great and glorious work. It really seems as if the Millennium was upon us in its glory."[27]

---

26. Accepting no literal millennium of a thousand years, believing rather that the millennium is the present Church age.
27. Quoted by Allen, *op. cit.*, 35.

By March of 1858, 6,000 were also gathering daily for prayer in Philadelphia, and thousands were attending five different prayer meetings in Washington, D.C. Edwin J. Orr in *Awakening* quotes from a contemporary newspaper article: "There are several New England towns in which not a single adult person can be found unconverted."[28]

In Charleston, North Carolina, in 1858, the revival under John Girardeau "went on night and day for eight weeks."

In places such as Binghamton, New York, the revival fervor took on a distinctly Pentecostal flavor where "some shouted, some laughed, some wept, and a large number lay prostrate from three to five hours, beyond the power of shouting or weeping."[29]

Not only all across America, but all across the British Isles the Holy Spirit was poured out in fresh power. In 1859, in Ireland, the Spirit descended in power and "even strong men staggered and fell down under the wounds of their conscience," bringing 100,000 to Christ—the greatest move of God since the days of St. Patrick. Paisley comments on the 1859 Ulster Revival: "So suddenly, so powerful and extraordinary were the manifestations of the Spirit's Presence...about one thousand people were suddenly, sensibly and powerfully impressed and awakened." In the same year as well, God moved in Wales, where it was estimated that there were 100,000 converts, with a total of at least 1,000,000 people converted to Christ all across the United Kingdom. The revival presence of God had likewise broken out in England and in Scotland. Port Glasgow was the scene of a powerful revival. One witness reported, "In the evening the place of meeting was crammed. There must

---

28. Orr, as quoted by Colin C. Whittaker, *Great Revivals* (Springfield, MO: Radiant Books, 1984), 83.

29. Quoted by Vinson Synan, *The Holiness-Pentecostal Tradition: Charismatic Movements in the Twentieth Century* (Grand Rapids, MI: W.B. Eerdmans, 1997), 20.

have been more than two thousand present. One cried out, and then another, and another...."[30]

Similar moves of the Holy Spirit came to Sweden and Norway, where a quarter of a million people came to Christ in 12 months; and as well in Australia, the West Indies, India, and South Africa! What has been called, "the greatest revival in the history of South Africa" began in 1860 in a church pastored by Andrew Murray, accompanied by the same phenomena recorded in the Book of Acts. Andrew Murray, in his little booklet *The Secret of Power From on High,* expressed this concern: "How often only half the Gospel is preached—conversion and forgiveness of sins, and souls are led no further into the truth; the knowledge and appropriation of the life of the Spirit within us is not mentioned." Dr. Murray then admonished: "Begin at once to pray the Father to grant you the gift of the Holy Spirit anew each day...." During the mid-1800's the floodgates of Heaven were indeed opened upon men!

The Holiness Revivals

Historically, the ministry of Charles G. Finney and his associates, Asa Maham and Thomas Upham, became the foundation for the Holiness revivals of the later 1800's and the consequent Pentecostal revivals of the 1900's. It was these men, among others, who inaugurated the great American Holiness movement of the 1800's with its strong emphasis on a definite conversion experience, a specific baptism in the Holy Spirit, and heart purity, or Christian perfection in this present life. Revivalist Phoebe Palmer and her husband Dr. Walter Palmer, already mentioned, were leading proponents of these emphases, as well as Dr. Charles Cullis, a Boston physician, one of the fathers of the American "faith homes" for the healing of the sick and the tending of the homeless. In 1875 Cullis also published Hannah Whitall Smith's powerful book, *The Christian's Secret of a Happy Life.*

---

30. Paterson, as quoted by Allen, *op. cit.*, 38.

Unfortunately, John Wesley's Methodism of a century before had become, by the mid-1800's, the most organized denomination in America next to the Roman Catholic Church. In 1787 when the American Methodist superintendent, Francis Asbury, changed his title from *superintendent* to *bishop*, John Wesley had reprimanded him, "How can you, how dare you, suffer yourself to be called Bishop? I shudder, I start, at the very thought! Men may call me a knave or a fool, a rascal, a scoundrel, and I am content, but they shall never by my consent call me a bishop! For my sake, for God's sake, for Christ's sake put a full end to this!" But unfortunately this was to be only the beginning. Methodism's increased organizationalism eventually caused its spiritual decline. As early as 1807, when Lorenzo Dow returned to England from America with reports of the American camp meetings, British Methodism resisted this fresh move of the Holy Spirit, precipitating the formation in 1811 of English *Primitive Methodism*. H.B. Kendall observed: "At some of these English [Primitive Methodist] Camp Meetings from ten to twenty thousand persons are said to have been present. Again and again there were scenes of Divine demonstration and the power of the Holy Ghost." Remarkable spiritual gifts were also manifested by many of these early Primitive Methodists.

By the mid-1800's, indictments had been widely sounded that Methodism had indeed become too formal, too liberal; that "heart religion" was fading out; and that Wesley's doctrines of entire sanctification and heart purity were being neglected. In response to this, the holiness agitation reached its climax in the latter part of the 1800's, having birthed the "National Camp Meeting Association" in 1867, and spawned many, many new holiness bodies, thereby fracturing Methodism, but also reviving the original flames of Wesleyan pietism. These "sparks" ignited revival fires in countless places across the United States of America. The *Wesleyan Methodist Church of America* was formed in 1843 as a protest against both slavery and the Methodist episcopacy. Vinson Synan comments that "Orange Scott and other leaders of the new sect charged that by compromising with the evil of slavery the Methodist Episcopal Church had renounced its duty to become, like its founder, John Wesley, 'evangelically anti-slavery.' "[31] Wesley had called slavery "the sum of all villainies," and rule 42 of the "Methodist Discipline of 1784" had formulated an elaborate plan to root out "the abomination of slavery."

In 1807, the British government passed a law declaring the trading of slaves "hereby utterly abolished"—mainly due to the tireless efforts of William Wilberforce, a man who "despised the cruelty of slavery."[32]

In objection to "new school" Methodism, which they considered destructive to Wesleyan standards, the *Free Methodists* had also been formed in 1860 at Pekin, New York, under the inspiration of B.T. Roberts. (In June of 1968, the *Wesleyan Methodist Church* merged with the *Pilgrim Holiness Church,* which was formed in 1922 to become the 135,000-member *Wesleyan Church.*)

The Civil War (1861–1865)

Discerning Church historians are not slow to sense in the devastating ravages of the Civil War the judgments of a holy God against the abominations of slavery. In 1863, Abraham Lincoln wrote these words: "May we not justly fear that the awful calamity of civil war which now desolates the land may be a punishment inflicted upon us for our presumptuous sins, to the needful end of our national reformation as a whole people?" Though the South fought for "states' rights" in the face of the interference of "big Federal Government," the evil of slavery was at the root of the war. Out of a nation of over 30 million people, ten percent of whom were black slaves, armies were raised of over 2,500,000 men. Between the firing of the first confederate cannon at Fort Sumter on April 12, 1861, and the

---

31. Synan, *op. cit.*, 19.

32. Joel Freeman and Don B. Griffin, *Return to Glory* (Woodbury, NJ: Renaissance Productions, Inc., 1997), 77.

surrender of General Robert E. Lee at Appomattox Court House on April 9, 1865, a nation was torn apart and over 630,000 men were killed in battle (a number greater than the combined American casualties of World War I, World War II, and the Vietnam War.)

The great revival of 1858 had been the last great outpouring before the Civil War, but unfortunately the South had been virtually untouched by it. Only after its crushing defeat did the South experience several years of "revival...from one border to the other" in 1865–1867. The Methodist Episcopal Church and the Baptists had both split in the early 1840's over the issue of slavery. The Southern Baptist Convention and the Northern Baptists separated over the slavery issue and have continued to remain separated. The several branches of the Presbyterian Church had also split over slavery (the New School and the Old School in 1857 and 1861, respectively). The year 1861 seemed to be the "time for judgment to begin with the family of God."[33] It began April 12, 1861, to be exact.

The Birth of the Black American Church

Author Albert J. Raboteau observes: "During the seventeenth and much of the eighteenth century there was a great deal of indifference, reluctance, and hostility to the conversion of the slaves. Not until the successive waves of religious revival known as the Great Awakening began in the 1740's did incidents of slave conversion occur in any sizable numbers."[34] The Great Awakening indeed heralded "the dawning of the new day" in the history of the conversion of slaves to Christ. Edwards, Whitefield, Tennent, and other revivalists noted with joy the presence of black people flocking to their preaching. Whitefield, in 1740, recounted an occasion in Philadelphia when "nearly fifty negroes came to give me thanks for what God had done to their souls." Presbyterian Samuel Davies, a

---

33. 1 Peter 4:17 NIV.
34. Albert J. Raboteau, *Slave Religion* (New York: Oxford University Press, Inc., 1978), 66.

future president of Princeton, wrote in 1757: "...at the last sacramental solemnity, I had the pleasure of seeing the table graced with about 60 black faces." In 1786, there were 1,890 black Methodists out of a total membership of 18,791. Within four years the number of black Methodists grew to over 12,000—almost one-fourth of the total Methodist membership. The majority of black Methodists lived in Maryland.

The camp meetings of the early 1800's likewise embraced blacks, who eagerly participated in the revival. John Thompson, born as a slave in Maryland in 1812, describes the appeal of the gospel to the slave community: "It brought glad tidings to the poor bondman; it bound up the broken-hearted; it opened the prison doors to them that were bound, and let the captive go free. As soon as it got among the slaves, it spread from plantation to plantation, until it reached ours, where there were but few who did not experience religion." Fear of slave rebellions unfortunately haunted southern whites, who then hindered attempts to convert the slaves in the South.

The first separate black church in America appears to be a Baptist Church, founded around 1775, in Silver Bluff, South Carolina. In 1780, a Methodist ministerial conference in Baltimore boldly declared that "slavery is contrary to the laws of God, man, and nature—hurtful to society; contrary to the dictates of conscience and pure religion, and doing that which we would not others should do to us and ours." In 1784, Methodism further mandated "to extirpate this abomination from among us," but unfortunately because of fierce pressure from the slaveholders, the Methodists were not able to see that commitment fulfilled.

Consequently, in 1787, a group of Negro Methodists withdrew from the Methodist Episcopal Church in Philadelphia. Their reasons were because of the painful practices of discrimination. They built a chapel and ordained a black preacher. In 1793, Methodist Bishop Francis Asbury dedicated their chapel, Bethel Chapel, in Philadelphia. The African Methodist Episcopal (A.M.E.) Church was formally organized in 1816.

In the same year Richard Allen was consecrated as its first bishop by Bishop Asbury. Prior to the Civil War, the A.M.E. Church was confined to the North. Following the war, however, its membership increased rapidly in the South, and today it is represented in virtually every state in the Union. It is the second largest Methodist group in the United States. Vinson Synan, describing the great holiness revivals of the later 1800's, comments on the "remarkable revival in the Bethel Church in Philadelphia, the mother church of the movement...The meetings were bi-racial, interdenominational, and supportive of female spiritual leadership."[35] Other black churches birthed around the same time as the A.M.E. were the African Methodist Episcopal Zion Church in 1821, the African Union First Colored Methodist Protestant Church, Inc. and the Colored Methodist Episcopal (renamed in 1954 the Christian Methodist Episcopal Church.) Interestingly, it is believed that 1821 was also the year that Harriet Tubman was born, the "black Moses" who devoted herself to the dangerous task of leading 3,000 slaves to freedom through the Underground Railroad.

Birthed in the fires of revival, and shaped by the struggles of the Civil War era, the black Church has become a powerful spiritual force in the United States of America.

Other Happenings of the Late 1800's

William Booth, an ordained minister in the Methodist New Connexion body in England, regretfully left that pulpit in 1861 to become a freelance evangelistic preacher. In 1878, the Salvation Army was officially formed with General Booth at the lead: a veritable army of God all across England, Europe, and America in this time of renewed Wesleyan zeal and fire. Booth wrote, "What I wanted to see was an organization with the salvation of the world as its supreme ambition and object...." Specifically concerning "the gift of tongues," "the gifts of healings," and "miracles," Booth wrote: "There is not a word in the Bible which proves that we may not have

---

35. Synan, *op. cit.*, 28.

them at the present time...I long for them myself. I believe in their necessity, and I believe they are already among us. The poor infidel world should be made to see all of God that is possible, in order that it may believe."[36]

At least 200 independent (and, at times, mutually exclusive) religious bodies in the United States bear the name, Church of God, in one form or another. Many of these have their origins in this time of the holiness revivals of the latter 1800's. Among these, we specifically note the following: A.J. Tomlinson's Church of God of Prophecy, with its roots dating back to 1886, and the Church of God with headquarters at Anderson, Indiana, which was consolidated in about 1880 as a movement toward unity within existing churches.

The mid-1890's saw the birth of the "Five-Baptized Holiness Church," which is considered by Vinson Synan to be "an important link in the chain that later produced the modern Pentecostal movement." The year 1894 saw the emerging of the Church of the Nazarene, one of the larger divisions from Methodism. (The Nazarenes then merged with the Association of Pentecostal Churches in America, an East Coast Holiness group, in 1907 and with the southern Holiness Church of Christ in 1908. All three thus formed the Pentecostal Church of the Nazarene. In 1919, the word "Pentecostal" was then dropped from their name to disassociate themselves in the public mind from any connection with twentieth-century Pentecostalism and its practice of "speaking in tongues," which teaching and practice are quite vigorously opposed by the Church of the Nazarene.)

In 1885, under the oversight of preacher Charles H. Mason (1866–1961) and author and songwriter Charles P. Jones (1865–1947), yet another Holiness group was birthed, which would eventually became the largest African-American Pentecostal denomination in the United States and in the world, the Church of God in Christ. Mason, a son of slaves, traveled to

---

36. William Booth, *The War Cry*, November 21, 1914.

Azusa Street in 1907 where he received his "baptism in the Holy Spirit." He was called by his followers a "Greater than the Apostle Paul." C.P. Jones, regrettably, rejected the Pentecostal experience and message of C.H. Mason, and in the division which followed became the leader of the Church of Christ (Holiness) U.S.A.[37]

The Christian and Missionary Alliance, with belief in "Christ as Savior, Sanctifier, Healer, and coming Lord," originated in 1881 in New York under the able leadership of A.B. Simpson. Simpson had been influenced by the healing ministry of Dr. Charles Cullis and veteran healing evangelist Ethan O. Allen. (By the early 1970's the missionary-oriented Alliance had more than three times as many churches abroad as in North America. The late A.W. Tozer, the famed modern-day pietistic author, was editor of the *Alliance Weekly*, a publication of the C.M.A.)

Among yet other Holiness bodies, the Pentecostal Holiness Church, organized in 1909 at Anderson, South Carolina, was committed to the theological standards of Methodism. (The Congregational Holiness Church was founded in 1921 by a group of ministers withdrawing from the Pentecostal Holiness Church, seeking to retain Wesleyan doctrines and yet establish more democratic church policy.) And so the sparks continued to be scattered abroad so that the Pentecostal fires of revival were to be found everywhere by the dawning of the 1900's.

Also prominent in the latter 1800's, and running parallel to these Holiness revivals, were the evangelistic labors of Congregationalist pastor Henry Ward Beecher, Billy Bray, Billy Sunday, "Gipsy" Smith, Sam Jones, and Dwight L. Moody. Their soul-winning labors greatly strengthened the spiritual life and growth of the Christian Church both in America and in Britain. It was believed that at this time "in the United States more than a million people were converted to God in one year."

---

37. In 1996, the Church of God in Christ numbered over 4,000,000 members in the United States; the Church of Christ (Holiness), numbered some 15,000.

In 1871, though running a Sunday school with an attendance of nearly 15,000 children, a greater hunger and thirst filled the heart of D.L. Moody. He said, "I was crying all the time that God would fill me with His Spirit." And God did! "One day, in the city of New York...I had such an experience of His love that I had to ask Him to stay His hand...." In 1875, R. Boyd, a Baptist minister, went to a meeting in London where Moody had just spoken. He recalls, "When I got to the rooms of the Young Men's Christian Association, Victoria Hall, London, I found the meeting on fire. The young men were speaking with tongues, prophesying...Moody had addressed them that afternoon."

During Moody's revival meetings in Boston in 1877, the Lord worked miracles of deliverance and healing, launching A.J. Gordon, the pastor of the Clarendon Street Baptist Church, into the healing ministry. A.J. Gordon (1836–1895) was the founder of Gordon College. He wrote, "It is still our privilege to pray for the baptism of the Spirit...until we be endured with power from on high." In 1882, D.L. Moody was invited to conduct a mission at Cambridge in England. The famed "Cambridge Seven" emerged when this British University was stirred to the depths by the ministry of Moody. Most prominent among the "Seven" was cricketer Charlie Thomas (C. T.) Studd (1860–1931), founder of the Worldwide Evangelization Crusade (W.E.C.).

R.A. (Rueben Archer) Torrey (1856–1928) was D.L. Moody's associate and the first superintendent of Moody Bible Institute. Both Moody and Torrey experienced and taught a distinct "baptism in the Holy Spirit," empowering them for service. Dr. Torrey described one notable event: "At three o'clock we gathered in front of Mr. Moody's mother's home, four hundred and fifty-six of us in all, all men from the eastern colleges. We commenced to climb the mountainside. After we had gone some distance Mr. Moody said...'I can see no reason why we should not kneel down here now and ask God that the Holy Spirit may fall on us as definitely as He fell on the Apostles at Pentecost...'

We knelt down on the ground; some of us lay on our faces on the pine needles. The Holy Ghost fell upon us. It was a wonderful hour. There are many who will never forget it."[38]

To this era also belongs Fanny Crosby, the most prolific hymn writer "in recorded Christian history." Fanny was mightily baptized in the Holy Spirit in November of 1850. Her hymns were often sung in the Moody-Sankey revivals. Presbyterian minister A.T. Pierson wrote during these times: "If in these degenerate days a new Pentecost would restore primitive faith, worship, unity, and activity, new displays of divine power might surpass those of any previous period."

The prince of British preachers, C.H. (Charles Haddon) Spurgeon was born in Kelvedon, Essex, England, on June 19, 1834. At the age of 16 he was born again. His simple testimony was: "I looked to Him; He looked on me; and we were one forever." At the age of 17, the "Boy Preacher" became the pastor of the Waterbeach Church, and in 1854, at the age of 20, he was called to be Baptist pastor of New Park Street Chapel in London. Over the next 40 years Spurgeon preached to immense audiences, and won tens of thousands of souls to Christ. The 1859 revival was a high-water mark. Spurgeon wrote, "The times of refreshing from the presence of the Lord have at last dawned upon our land. A spirit of prayer is visiting our churches. The first breath of the rushing mighty wind is already discerned, while on rising evangelists the tongues of fire have evidently descended."[39]

Spurgeon's godly wisdom concerning revival was reflected in his words: "Observe how sovereign the operations of God are....He may, in one district, work a revival and persons may be stricken down and made to cry aloud, but in another place there may be crowds and yet all may be still and quiet, as though no deep excitement existed at all....He can bless as He wills and He will bless as He wills. Let us not dictate to God. Many a blessing has been lost by Christians not believing it to

---

38. Torrey, as quoted by Phil Saint, *Amazing Saints* (Logos, 1972).
39. Spurgeon, as quoted by Whittaker, *op. cit.*, 100.

be a blessing because it did not come in the particular shape that they had conceived to be proper and right."

Spurgeon had earnestly prayed: "O God, send us the Holy Ghost! Give us both the breath of spiritual life and the fire of unconquerable zeal. O Thou art our God, answer us by fire, we pray Thee! Answer us both by wind and fire...The kingdom comes not, and the work is flagging. Oh, that Thou wouldst send the wind and the fire!...God, send us a season of *glorious disorder*...Oh, for the fire to fall again...Give us now both hearts of flame and tongues of fire to preach Thy reconciling word, for Jesus' sake! Amen!"[40] And God answered! In those years a million people were converted to Christ in the United Kingdom!

Fruit of the vast spiritual awakening of this period was further seen in the birthing of the deeper life Keswick movement in 1874 with its conventions for special teaching on the Spirit-filled life. Beginning at Keswick in the British Isles, "Keswick" deeper-life conventions have spread around the world, greatly strengthening the inner life of the Church of Jesus Christ. And in early 1881, the first Christian Endeavor Society was formed in Portland, Maine, which birthed literally millions of young people's meetings out of which came multitudes of ministers, missionaries, and church workers.

Earlier, in 1844, George Williams, a young London draper's assistant, founded the Young Men's Christian Association (Y.M.C.A.), which was, in its day, a worldwide instrument in the hands of the Lord to further His cause, especially among youth. Selections from *My Utmost for His Highest,* the famed golden book of Oswald Chambers, were taken from talks delivered by the mystic Chambers in the early 1900's in the Y.M.C.A. huts at Zeitoun, Egypt, just before his death.

The period between 1885 and 1889 also saw the amazing "Woodworth revivals," the phenomenal labors of Mary Woodworth-Etter. She describes one of her meetings at Oakland, California, in 1889 in these words: "The power of God was

---

40. Spurgeon, as quoted by Wallis, *op. cit.,* 249.

over all the congregation...the Holy Ghost would fall on the people while we were preaching...Men and women fell, all over the tent, like trees in a storm; some would have visions of God. Most all of them came out shouting the praises of God."

John Alexander Dowie also arrived in America from Australia in 1888; he was originally from Edinburgh. In 1893, he began his work in Chicago. The outstanding healing of Ethel Post, a 13-year-old girl with cancer of the mouth and throat, took place in his Chicago meetings. Dr. Lilian Yeomans, a witness to the miracle, reported, "The malignant growth withered away and fell out of the girl's mouth and throat, and she was completely and permanently healed." This was indeed an era of *great* spiritual advance in the renewal, revival, and restoration of the Lord's Church!

Winds of Adversity

The 1800's were unfortunately not only years of revival and reform (on issues of slavery, prohibition, and women's rights), but these years were also marked by materialism, rationalism, and modernism. From the pen and the lips of Karl Marx (1818–1883) came a flood of agnostic and atheistic socialist thought that would seek to enslave half the world, murdering tens of millions of true Christian believers in the process. Interestingly, Marx's sister-in-law was a committed Christian. But to Marx, religion was "the opium of the people," and his ideology was totally incompatible with the claims of the Christian Church. In Marx' godless communistic ideology was the demonic counterfeit of the true community of the Body of Jesus Christ that the Lord was restoring to His Church.

In 1859, Charles Darwin published his *Origin of Species,* followed by his *Descent of Man.* Thus was spawned Darwin's famed "theory of evolution," which was destined to chip away at the solidarity of the foundations of Holy Scripture and its inspired account of the creation of man.[41] Added to these

---

41. The heart-rending story of Darwin's recantation at the end of his days is told in Appendix V.

materialistic gusts of communism and evolution were also the stormy results of Voltaire's eighteenth-century rationalism and Nietzsche's nineteenth-century anti-Christ philosophy. To Voltaire (1694–1778), reason was God. To Nietzsche (1844–1900), God was dead. "God is dead, He spoke to us and now is silent....We have killed him—you and I. All of us are his murderers...." And then came Sigmund Freud (1856–1939) with his new view of "animal man"—all gathering together to form the strong winds of adversity that would blow upon hearts in opposition to the true simplistic faith of our Lord Jesus Christ. Out of this storm of rationalism and its resultant materialism came the tide of theological modernism and liberalism (along with its "social gospel") in which the solidarity of the Scriptures was attacked and the cardinal doctrines of the Christian faith were ridiculed.

One of the early citadels of modernism was Union Theological Seminary of New York City and one of its early champions was Baptist minister Harry Emerson Fosdick. Against this veritable spiritual Goliath of modernism and liberalism a simple "David" was divinely raised up—Fundamentalism, which was armed with its five smooth stones: (1) the verbal inerrancy of Scripture, (2) the deity of Christ, (3) the virgin birth, (4) the substitutionary atonement, and (5) the physical resurrection and bodily return of Christ.[42] Champion among the early fundamentalists was the godly Presbyterian professor J. Gresham Machen (1881–1937).

We have observed so far that the latter 1800's produced two very divergent streams of historical influence in the earth. First of all, we noted the Holiness-revival school, which for the purposes of our study we wish to single out as the vessel of God

---

42. It is unfortunate that evangelical fundamentalism must presently be equated in many places with "dispensationalism," which, in effect, many believe, accomplishes the same end as outright modernism. (Modernists simply deny the inerrant inspiration of the Holy Scriptures. Dispensationalism avows these same Scriptures to be divinely and inerrantly inspired, but renders many of them presently of none effect in the Church by "dispensationalizing" them away for Israel in the future or the early Church in the past.)

in the ongoing process of the revival and restoration of His Church upon the earth. In every sense of the word the Wesleyan Holiness and the deeper-life revivals were the forerunners of the Pentecostal visitation of God in the early 1900's, out of which the mid-twentieth-century outpourings came, and on its heels the renewals and revivals of the latter 1900's. The second, and very much opposite stream that flowed in the latter 1800's was, as we have seen, the stream of rationalism, materialism, liberalism, and modernism. Historian Lars P. Qualben tersely sums up the differential between these two streams in these words: "In marked contrast to the American Holiness Movement and its 'twice-born' adherents is the modernistic movement and its 'once-born' adherents. The former asserts the depravity of human nature and the need of a new spiritual birth; the latter asserts that human nature is essentially good and that salvation is insured by developing the good in man."[43] Qualben then also cites Ralph Waldo Emerson (1803–1882), Henry Wadsworth Longfellow (1807–1882), and President William H. Taft (1857–1930) as prominent in this stream of liberal humanism and modernism.

Revivals of Errors and Extremes

To these two peculiar earmarks of the latter 1800's, we may also add a third—the revival of ancient errors and extremes. A marked peculiarity of the latter 1800's was its reduplication of the heresies and excesses of the declining Church of the second, third, and fourth centuries.

We have already noted the reduplication of some of the Montanist extremes of A.D. 150 in the charismatic Irvingite movement of the earlier 1800's.[44] Some of these extremes continued to surface well into the twentieth century in every segment of Pentecostalism.

Origen's universalism[45] of the fourth century was duplicated throughout the latter 1700's and the 1800's in the form of

---

43. Qualben, *op. cit.,* 472.
44. See Chapter 4 concerning the issue of Montanism.
45. See Chapter 5 concerning Origen's universalism.

the Universalists. (In May 1961, the anti-Trinitarian Unitarian Churches and Universalist Churches in North America were consolidated as the Unitarian Universalist Association of just over 200,000 members.[46])

First-century Judaism[47] was birthed anew in what was destined to become the largest branch of the apocalyptic Adventist Movement initiated by William Miller (1782–1849), a New York Baptist who declared 1844 to be the year of the second advent of our Lord. Gathered around this expectation of the imminent return of our Lord and also a strong adherence to the laws of Moses (particularly the seventh-day sabbath) were James White and his prophetic wife, Ellen G. White, whose writings Seventh-Day Adventists hold "in highest esteem" and accept "as inspired counsels from the Lord." In 1855, the Adventists set up headquarters at Battle Creek, Michigan, with a publishing house called the Review and Herald Publishing Association. In 1860, they officially adopted the name Seventh-Day Adventists, and in 1903, they moved their headquarters to its present location in the Washington, D.C. area. (There were, in 1997, 9,000,000 Adventists worldwide, with about ten percent of these in North America.) In all the main points of doctrine and practice Adventists are essentially evangelical and fundamentalist.

---

46. In 1997, a Unitarian Universalist took his doctrinal stand against Coach Bill McCartney's *Promise Keepers*, in these words: "I do not believe in the Trinity...I do not believe that the Bible is God's written revelation to people...I do not believe in the virgin birth or the bodily resurrection of Jesus...I do not believe that the Holy Spirit is dwelling in people like yourself...I do not believe in original sin...I believe we can live good, moral lives by studying Buddhist, Islamic, Jewish, or Hindu scriptures...if heaven exists, all of us will be blest with universal salvation..." (*An Open Letter to Coach Bill McCartney, Founder and CEO of the Promise Keepers,* by Roger Fritts, September 28, 1997, Cedar Lane Unitarian Universalist Church, Bethesda, Maryland).

47. See Chapter 2 concerning the issue of Judaism.

Ancient Gnosticism[48] revived in 1879 in the founding of the First Church of Christ, Scientist in Boston by Mary Baker Eddy, author of *Science and Health with Key to the Scriptures*, the "inspired" textbook of Christian Science. Christian Scientists "acknowledge and adore one supreme and infinite God." They "acknowledge His Son, one Christ; the Holy Ghost or divine Comforter; and man in God's image and likeness." They view the atonement "as the evidence of divine, efficacious Love, unfolding man's unity with God through Christ Jesus the Way-shower," who was "endowed with the Christ, the divine spirit without measure." Christian Scientists, in classic gnostic terms, likewise uphold "the allness of Soul, Spirit and the nothingness of matter."

Fourth-century Arianism[49] with its blatant denial of the deity of our Lord Jesus Christ revived in the apocalyptic Russellite movement of the 1880's, so named after its initial organizer and first president, Pastor Charles Taze Russell. (After Russell's death in 1916 the mantle of leadership fell to Judge Rutherford, who governed the sect as president until his death in 1942, to be succeeded by Nathan H. Knorr, who, in turn, was succeeded by Fredrick W. Franz in 1977. The fifth Watchtower president, Milton G. Henschel, was installed on December 30, 1992. The title Jehovah's Witnesses was assumed in 1931, and the additional designation, Watchtower Bible and Tract Society, was taken in 1956.)

The Watchtower movement reaches worldwide with about 4.5 million baptized witnesses[50] actively engaged in the door-to-door preaching of their anti-Trinitarian, Arian gospel—declaring Jesus to be merely "the highest of God's Creation," "a perfect man, nothing more, nothing less." Jehovah's Witnesses

---

48. See Chapter 3 concerning Gnosticism.
49. See Chapter 6 concerning the error of Arianism.
50. The "1992 Service Year Report of Jehovah's Witnesses Worldwide" (Watchtower).

likewise deny the bodily resurrection of our Lord Jesus Christ, declaring "the man Jesus must remain dead forever."

A Violent Thunderstorm

The 1800's also marked two significant additions to Roman Catholic dogma. In 1854, without consultation with his Council, Pope Pius IX, at the instigation of the restored Jesuits, declared the doctrine of the Immaculate Conception of the Virgin Mary—that she was born without original sin. Pius IX in his bull, *Ineffabilis Deus,* declared "the most Blessed Virgin Mary was, from the first moment of her conception, by a singular grace and privilege of almighty God and by virtue of the merits of Jesus Christ, Savior of the human race, pre-served immune from all stain of original sin....Wherefore if any shall presume...to think...anything contrary...let them...know well that they are condemned...have suffered shipwreck concerning the faith, and have revolted from the unity of the Church...."

The second and by far most controversial addition to Roman dogma was the formalizing of the previously assumed doctrine of the infallibility of the pope. As a violent thunder-storm raged above St. Peter's in Rome on July 18, 1870, Pius IX and the bishops of the First Vatican Council decreed a far more violently stormy doctrine: "That the Roman Pontiff, when he speaks *ex cathedra* (that is, when fulfilling the office of Pastor and Teacher of all Christians on his supreme Apos-tolical authority, he defines a doctrine concerning faith or morals to be held by the Universal Church)...is endowed with that infallibility...And therefore, that such definitions of the Roman Pontiff of themselves—and not by virtue of the con-sent of the Church—are irreformable. If anyone shall presume (which God forbid!) to contradict this our definitions; let him be anathema." This power was invoked in the 1950 declaration that Mary was assumed bodily into heaven and it remains as a cardinal cause of disunity in ecumenical Christendom. It became an especially thorny issue in the twentieth-century renewal and revival movements that involve both Protestant and Catholic Spirit-baptized believers. This decree originally created much opposition in the Roman Church. John Doellinger of Munich voted against it at the council, and for this he was excommunicated. He and others of like mind formed themselves into the Old Catholic Church.

A number of Catholic hierarchical contemporaries of Pius IX, including the French bishop, the Dean of Sorbonne, wrote that Pius IX, who politically steered this doctrine through Vatican I, was "mad." And indeed, according to history, his brash actions at the council left much to be desired for a father of the Church, and the instigator of one of its most controversial doctrines.

And so we have considered the nineteenth century, out of the diversity of which rises the momentous twentieth century, the century of the most pronounced pentecostal visitations since the first century—a century sovereignly destined to see the fuller stages of the sovereign renewal, revival, and restoration of the true, holy, and apostolic Body of Jesus Christ on the earth.

Chapter 11

The Early and Latter Rains of the Twentieth Century

Part I
The First Half of the Twentieth Century

It seems as if two mighty seasons of revival helped shape the whole of the twentieth century for God. The first was the powerful Welsh Revival of 1904 in which God used a simple young man named Evan Roberts. This move was then accompanied by worldwide outpourings of the Holy Spirit. On American soil, God then came to Los Angeles, California, in 1906, in the Azusa Street outpouring. He used a simple black man, William Seymour, a rag-tag group of hungry people, and a "day of small beginnings." Thus it was that some hundreds of Spirit-filled believers at the beginning of the 1900's would grow to become hundreds of *millions* of Spirit-filled believers by the end of the 1900's and become one of the most powerful forces for revival and for world evangelism on the face of the earth.

The second mighty season of visitation took place mid-century. It appears as if many of the powerful events that helped shape the second half of the twentieth century had their roots unusually intertwined in the 1948–1950 outpourings of the Holy Spirit that took place in Argentina, the Hebrides, northern Canada, and across the United States, thus bringing the twentieth century to the level of the mightiest outpouring of the Holy Spirit and the greatest ingathering of souls since the beginning of time.

The Worldwide Awakening of 1904–1906
The Welsh Revival

The main instrument the Lord chose in the Welsh Revival of 1904 was Evan Roberts, a young, unassuming student preparing for the ministry. It was in the spring of 1904 that Roberts encountered the Lord in an unusual way: "I found myself with unspeakable joy and awe in the very presence of the Almighty God. And for the space of four hours I was privileged to speak face to face with Him as a man speaks with a friend...and it was not only that morning, but every morning for three or four months...and I knew that God was going to work in the land, and not this land only, but in all the world."[1]

And God did work—beginning in the late fall of 1904. The Lord had already begun to move in August, as the Spirit of God fell in power under the ministry of F.B. Meyer during the Welsh Keswick week, and in the same month the Spirit was poured out at Cardiff during R.A. Torrey's ministry. Torrey wrote: "When we left, the meetings went right on without us...for a whole year—meetings every night and multitudes converted."

In the course of the revival in Wales, Roberts, then in his mid-twenties, and his "Revival Party" of young people conducted thousands of meetings. It was estimated that 100,000 souls were converted to Christ. Taverns went bankrupt, police became unemployed in many districts, and coal mines were

---

1. W.T. Stead, *The Story of the Welsh Revival* (New York: Fleming H. Revell, 1905), 55-56.

disrupted as the pit ponies couldn't understand commands anymore. They didn't recognize their owners' redeemed language.

The motto of the Welsh Revival was "Bend the church, and save the world"; and prayer was the underpinning of this great move of God. During the revival, a Wiltshire evangelist stood up and said: "I have journeyed into Wales with the hope that I may glean the secret of the Welsh Revival." In an instant Evan Roberts jumped to his feet and replied: "My brother—there is no secret! *Ask and ye shall receive!*"

An eyewitness described the meetings: "Such marvelous singing...could only be created by a supernatural power, and that power the divine Holy Spirit. No choir, no conductor, no organ—just spontaneous, unsynchronized soul-singing... Singing, sobbing, praying...."

One historical researcher concluded that the Welsh Revival "was the farthest-reaching of all the movements...for it affected the whole evangelical cause in India, Korea, and China, renewed revivals in Japan and South Africa, and sent a wave of awakening over Africa, Latin America and the South Seas"—and of course, all across the United States of America.

Under a hailstorm of criticism in 1905, the Welsh Revival eventually began to diminish. The revival was spoken against as "a sham...a mockery, a blasphemous travesty of the real thing." Arthur Wallis, in his book, *In the Day of Thy Power*, wisely addressed the opposition that inevitably seems to dog the steps of every move of the Holy Spirit: "If we find a revival that is not spoken against, we had better look again to ensure that it *is* a revival."[2]

Winkie Pratney calls the end of Evan Roberts' public ministry "one of the strangest endings of a ministry in history."[3]

In the spring of 1906, Mr. and Mrs. Jessie Penn-Lewis sequestered the beleaguered Evan Roberts at their home in

---

2. Arthur Wallis, *In the Day of Thy Power* (London: Christian Literature Crusade, 1956), 26.

3. Winkie Pratney, *Revival—Its Principles and Personalities* (Lafayette, LA: Huntington House, 1994), 153.

Leicestershire where Mrs. Penn-Lewis and Roberts then co-authored the controversial book, *War on the Saints,* a commentary on some of the perceived fanaticisms of the Welsh Revival. In 1930, Evan Roberts moved to Cardiff. He concluded: "My work is devoted to prayer. By preaching I would reach the limited few but by and through prayer I can reach the whole of mankind for God...." He died in Cardiff in 1951—truly a "vessel unto honor."

Brian Edwards in his well-documented book, *Revival! A People Saturated With God,* comments on the sobering aftermath of the Welsh Revival: "Evan Roberts was so concerned not to meddle with the work of the Spirit that he allowed meetings largely to run themselves. The weakness of this is seen in the fact that a greater number of converts appear to have fallen away in the few years following the 1904 revival than in any other revival for which we have such records." Edwards then wisely observes: "The centrality of preaching is a sound curb to excess and error and is, after all, one thing God has clearly committed to his church...One reason why the revivals experienced by Whitefield, Wesley and, a century later, by Charles Haddon Spurgeon continued so long was that preaching was at the center."[4]

An International Outpouring

The twentieth century actually began with an unusual *international outpouring*, much of which drew encouragement from the Welsh Revival. By the turn of the century, in Uganda, there were "a hundred thousand souls brought into close contact with the Gospel...the power of God shone...in the center of the thickest spiritual darkness in the world." In 1901, Pandita Ramabai (1858–1920) in Mukti, India, saw 1200 converts baptized in two months, but news of the revival in Wales in 1904 stirred her hunger even more, and by 1905 fresh revival waves

---

4. Brian H. Edwards, *Revival! A People Saturated With God* (Durham, England: Evangelical Press, 1990), 214.

came, which flowed across all India. There were deep confessions of sin, joyful singing, dancing before the Lord, speaking in other tongues, and many conversions to Christ.

Pandita Ramabai became known as "the Mother of the Pentecostal Movement in India." In 1989, the Hindu government of India issued a postage stamp honoring her for her social impact on India.

In 1902, two missionaries in Calcutta heard Dr. Torrey speak on prayer. They were deeply moved. When they returned to the Khassia Hills of India, they gave themselves to prayer until revival broke out among them in 1905. Among the Welsh Presbyterians in the hills of Assam revival also broke out, inspired by the move in Wales in 1904. Also, at this time in India, at Dohnavur, Amy Carmichael wrote concerning the move of God: "It was so startling and dreadful—I can use no other word...Soon the whole upper half of the church was on its face on the floor, crying to God...The sound like the sound of...strong wind in the trees...the hurricane of prayer continued for over four hours....almost the whole compound got saved...."[5] All across India God was moving; the Christian population jumped by 70 percent, 16 times faster than the growth of the Hindu population.

In 1905, the Spirit of the Lord likewise came to Charlotte Chapel in Edinburgh, Scotland. "There was nothing, humanly speaking, to account for what happened. Quite suddenly, upon one and another came an overwhelming sense of the reality and awfulness of His Presence and of eternal things. Life, death and eternity seemed suddenly laid bare!"

News of the Welsh Revival in 1904 and the great revival in the Khassia Hills of India inspired Jonathan Goforth to believe God for revival in China, Manchuria, and Korea. When the Spirit fell in Pyongyang in 1906, one missionary wrote: "The room was full of God's Presence...a feeling of God's nearness

---

5. Carmichael, as quoted by Edwin J. Orr, *Evangelical Awakenings in Southern Asia* (Minneapolis, MN: Bethany, 1975), 133.

impossible to describe…man after man would arise, confess his sin, break down and weep…practically every church throughout the peninsula received its share of blessings….” Revival came to Korea in three waves—in 1903, 1905, and 1907, quadrupling the number of Christians in a decade. Of this Korean revival Goforth said: “The Korean movement was of incalculable significance in my life…Korea made me feel, as it did many others, that this was God’s plan for *setting the world aflame.*” Likewise in Japan, at the turn of the century, “the churches set themselves to pray for a work of God.” The call went out for prayer that “the Spirit of the Lord would prepare the way for a meeting of Pentecostal power.” A year later the missionaries were reporting a “Pentecost in Japan.” Japanese churches nearly doubled in a decade.

The Spirit was also poured out in South Africa, in Ceylon, in Brazil in 1910, in Norway in 1907, and then in England, in Australia, in New Zealand, and in Indonesia, where the Church tripled to 300,000 souls in a decade. The revival in Chile among the Methodists under Willis and Mary Hoover was inspired by reports of what God did through Pandita Ramabai in India. The Hoovers describe the beginnings on July 4, 1909: “Saturday night was an all night of prayer…the atmosphere seemed charged with the Holy Spirit and people fell on the floor, or broke out in other tongues, singing in the Spirit.” After two months attendance increased to almost 1,000, and the revival was spreading to other cities. The Pentecostal Methodist Church, founded by Hoover, now numbers over 600,000 members, and there are a total of nearly two million Pentecostals in Chile today, about 20 percent of the nation’s population.[6]

In Burma, the Baptists baptized 2,000 tribal people among the Karens, an ongoing expression of the great revival dating back to 1858. Between the mid-1800’s and the mid-1900’s, the Karens also saw 250,000 of their neighbors, the Kachin,

6. Vinson Synan, *The Holiness-Pentecostal Tradition: Charismatic Movements of the Twentieth Century* (Grand Rapids, MI: W.B. Eerdmans, 1977), 137.

converted to Christ. (All this was the fruit of the first missionary to this area, Adoniram Judson, the American Baptist missionary of 1817 who had only one Buddhist convert after seven years of hard labor.)

God was moving among other tribes. Among the Lahu people, some 60,000 were converted, and among the Wa headhunters 10,000 were baptized into Christ. In China, among the Lisus, tens of thousands were swept into the Kingdom of God as well.

The following report was also given concerning Armenia: "The years 1900-1901 are remembered amongst the Armenians living in S.E. Turkey as the years of the great religious revival. The revival appears to have started in the Aintab area and spread to all the Armenian areas along the south-east coast....Services continued until midnight and the churches were unable to hold all who wanted to attend. In the market place and wherever people gathered, conversation centered 'on the revival.' "[7] This revival prepared the Armenians for the fierce opposition and executions just ahead of them under the Communists. In 1915, the Turks massacred 1.5 million Armenians because they were Christian and considered a threat.[8]

In an unusual prophetic prediction at the turn of the twentieth century, praying John Hyde, missionary to India, compared the 1800's to the ministry of John the Baptist; but the 1900's, he foresaw, would be like the ministry of Jesus—much greater in power and effect. From 1904–1910 praying Hyde himself experienced revival at the Indian Sialkot conventions, and he lived to see his prophetic prediction begin to come true all across the world.

Throughout the twentieth century, in Latin America Christians were destined to increase from between 200,000 - 300,000

7. Rhoda Carswell, as quoted by Colin C. Whittaker, *Great Revivals* (Springfield, MO: Radiant Books, 1984), 125.

8. Patrick Johnstone, *Operation World* (Grand Rapids, MI: Zondervan, 1993), 65.

to an expected 80,000,000 - 90,000,000 by the year 2000.[9] Certain sections of Africa would increase from 2 percent Christian to nearly 50 percent. Though Korea had relatively few believers at the start of the twentieth century, now every morning around 5 a.m. about a million Korean Christians are in their churches praying. Even in a repressive society such as China, believers increased from 1,000,000 at the time of the Communist takeover to what the Communist government itself estimates could be 100,000,000 by the year 2000! God indeed stepped down from Heaven in the twentieth century!

On American Soil

Richard Riss, in *A Survey of 20th-Century Revival Movements in North America*, traces the impact of the Welsh Revival on America. In December of 1904, the Spirit was poured out on Welsh settlers in Pennsylvania, and in early 1905, Riss writes, "there was an explosion of revival in many parts of the United States and Canada"[10]—at Taylor University in Indiana, at Yale University in Connecticut, at Baptist Temple in Brooklyn, New York, and among the Methodists in Michigan. Revival also broke out in Denver under J. Wilbur Chapman and in Schenectady in upper New York State, where "all the evangelical churches in town had been moved, with packed congregations in each, and the movement continued for months on end."

The ministers of Atlantic City, New Jersey, reported that out of a population of 60,000, only 50 adults were left unconverted. These were years of great ingathering in the United States, as well as worldwide.

Revivals were also reported in Nebraska, Iowa, Minnesota, the Dakotas, the Carolinas, Georgia, New England, Virginia, Illinois, and Texas. At Asbury College in Kentucky, classes were canceled as days of repentance, confession, conversion, and

---

9. *Ibid.*

10. Richard Riss, *A Survey of 20th-Century Revival Movements in North America* (Peabody, MA: Hendrickson Publishers, 1988), 44.

consecration fell upon the student body. The revival soon spread throughout the whole town. One of the Asbury students, E. Stanley Jones, was deeply touched. He later became one of the well-known missionaries of the twentieth century. In early 1906, at Dr. Reuben A. Torrey's meetings in Canada, Oswald J. Smith and his brother Ernest gave their hearts to Christ. Oswald J. Smith would later become pastor of The Peoples Church in Toronto and a great twentieth-century advocate for the cause of missions. At the same time the Spirit of God fell at A.B. Simpson's Nyack Missionary Training Institute on the Hudson in New York. "For three weeks preachers, teachers and students were lying upon their faces...God had struck with mighty conviction...the mighty presence of God filled the place...the atmosphere was so holy...it was just about three months before the Spirit was poured out in Los Angeles."

The Birth of the Pentecostal Revival

Historian Richard Riss notes at this juncture: "In the wake of the Welsh revival, and a vital element of the world-wide awakening of 1904–1906, the early Pentecostal revival came as one of the greatest revivals of the modern period, perhaps almost as important in its effects as the Protestant Reformation of the sixteenth century. Originating within the milieu of the Holiness movement of the late nineteenth century, it brought into existence hundreds of ecclesiastical bodies and denominations worldwide, many of which quickly became some of the fastest growing religious organizations in the world."[11]

New Year's Day 1901 had been a "day of small beginnings" for the Pentecostal Revival in the United States. Charles Parham, a Holiness preacher and the founder of the short-lived Bethel Bible College in Topeka, Kansas, had been asked by Agnes Ozman (1870–1937), one of his students, to lay hands on her that she might receive the Holy Spirit after the pattern in

---

11. Riss, *op. cit.*, 47.

Acts.[12] When Parham prayed for her, she began to speak in other tongues and continued on in the phenomenon for days. Parham testified: "Humbly in the name of Jesus, I laid my hand upon her head and prayed. I had scarcely repeated three dozen sentences when a glory fell upon her, a halo seemed to surround her head and face, and she began speaking in the Chinese language, and was unable to speak in English for three days."[13] In the following month most of Parham's student body of some 40 people, including 12 who held credentials with Methodist, Holiness, or Friends churches, likewise "received."

In his *Tongues Like as of Fire*, Robert Chandler Dalton reported concerning those days in Topeka: "On one occasion a Hebrew rabbi was present as one of the students read the lesson from the Bible. After the service this rabbi asked for the Bible from which the lesson was read. The Bible was handed him and he said, 'No, not that one. I want to see the Hebrew Bible. That man read in the Hebrew tongue.'"[14]

Tim Peterson, in a private treatise entitled *The History of the Pentecostal Movement*, records: "When all this 'was noised abroad,' the crowds began to gather. Newspaper reporters from cities as far away as St. Louis, Missouri, came to see and hear. They were convinced and wrote front page reports with large headlines for the big dailies. Soon other reporters brought along government interpreters, professors of languages, and even foreigners, to hear and identify the languages being spoken through human beings by the Spirit of God."[15]

---

12. To the Holiness people "the baptism of the Holy Spirit" was a familiar phenomenon, but usually in relation to sanctification, or heart purity (Acts 15:8-9). In the Pentecostal revival of the 1900's, "the baptism" took on a new dimension—accompanied by "the evidence" of speaking with other tongues.

13. Quoted by Sarah Parham, *The Life of Charles F. Parham* (Baxter Springs, KS: Apostolic Faith Bible College, 1930), 52

14. Robert Chandler Dalton, *Tongues Like as of Fire*, 37.

15. Tim Peterson, *The History of the Pentecostal Movement* (Owatonna, MN: Christian Family Church and World Outreach Center).

October 1903 at Galena, Kansas, saw a further great leap forward in Parham's new ministry when the Lord apparently bore witness to His Word by numerous healings. Parham believed that healing was in the atonement and "as much part of the Gospel" as the forgiveness of sins. By 1905, "Pentecostal" or "Full Gospel" meetings had sprung up all across Kansas, Oklahoma, Missouri, and Texas. By the winter of 1905, Texas alone had 25,000 Pentecostal believers as a direct result of Parham's labors.

Charles Parham: Pentecostalism's Speckled Bird

Charles Fox Parham (1873–1929) appears in history as a speckled bird. On the one hand, he is seen as a great man of faith and spiritual power. On the other hand he has been charged with financial and moral sins and serious doctrinal error.

While historian Eddie Hyatt upholds Parham as one who "had always practiced both gender and racial equality,"[16] Tim Peterson in *The History of the Pentecostal Movement* states, "Parham spent the later years of his life as an avid supporter of the Ku Klux Klan, praising its members for their 'fine work in upholding the American way of life.' "[17]

Notwithstanding these issues, Vinson Synan makes this sweeping (and accurate) observation of him: "Parham's teaching laid the doctrinal and experimental foundations of the modern Pentecostal movement. It was Parham's ideas preached by his followers that produced the Azusa Street revival of 1906 and with it the worldwide Pentecostal movement."[18]

Perhaps because of the questions surrounding Parham's life, Pentecostal leaders distanced themselves from him, and various outstanding evangelical leaders opposed the fruit of his labors. G. Campbell-Morgan said of the emerging Pentecostal movement: "It was the last vomit of Satan." R.A. Torrey

---

16. Eddie L. Hyatt, *2000 Years of Charismatic Christianity* (Tulsa: Hyatt International Ministries, Inc., 1996), 157.

17. Peterson, *op. cit.*

18. Synan, *op. cit.*, 89.

declared, "It was emphatically not of God and founded by a sodomite," and Dr. A.T. Pierson bluntly announced, "It was anti-Christian." H.A. Ironsides lumped both the Pentecostal and Holiness movements together as "disgusting...delusions and insanities," and H.J. Stolee described Pentecostal worship as "mob psychology...hypnotism...and demon power...." Parham and his fledgling movement were destined to be a sign spoken against, but a sign nonetheless.

Charles Parham at Zion City, Illinois

Apart from the shaping influence Charles Parham had on William Seymour and on the spring of 1906 Azusa Street revival (which we will shortly consider), his greatest contribution to the Pentecostal Outpouring came from the revival meetings he held in the fall of 1906 at Zion City, Illinois. Parham came to Zion City seeking to stabilize the crumbling empire of a demented John Alexander Dowie who, in 1901, had already proclaimed himself to be "Elijah the Restorer" and in 1904 also announced that, as "the first apostle of a renewed end times church," he would "restore apostolic Christianity." By 1906, Dowie, having also suffered the effects of a debilitating stroke, was unable to hold his bankrupt and battered city together.[19] Parham was not well received by the officials of Zion City, but he launched out nonetheless.

According to the September 28, 1906, edition of *The Daily Sun* of Waukegan, Illinois, thousands attended Parham's meetings. "Hundreds experienced release from bitterness, despair, and anger, and were baptized in the Holy Spirit. They saw visions, and hundreds responded to the call to full-time ministry. The fire of revival lifted them out of the fire of despair."[20]

---

19. It was reported that the schismatic Dowie was smitten by the stroke during a communion service as he held the communion cup in his hand (1 Cor. 11:29-32), but the power of God for healing remained with him right up to his death.

20. Hyatt, *op. cit.*, 161.

Church historian Paul G. Chappell comments on the far-reaching fruits of Parham's meetings: "Some of Parham's Zion followers were responsible for spreading the message by traveling throughout the world, planting the pentecostal message...."[21]

Among those were Cyrus Fockler, who founded the Milwaukee Gospel Tabernacle, and D. Opperman, who joined the Apostolic Faith in Texas, both of whom were among the founders of the Assemblies of God and served on its first executive presbytery. Fred Volger, another recipient of Parham's labors at Zion, served as assistant general superintendent of the Assemblies of God for over 14 years. Fred Hornshuh, Sr., became one of the founders of the Open Bible Standard Churches, and Martha Wing Robinson founded the Zion Faith Homes. Related to the Zion City revival was also the first Pentecostal assembly in London and the first Pentecostal wedding conducted in England on October 11, 1911, when Alice Rowlands and Stanley H. Frodsham were joined in marriage by Smith Wigglesworth, a great man of faith for healing.

Marie Bugess Brown (1880–1971) received both a missionary call and her "baptism in the Holy Spirit" on October 18, 1906, at one of Charles Parham's Zion City meetings in the home of F.F. (Fred) Bosworth. That same night both Bosworth himself and John G. Lake were also filled with the Holy Spirit. Marie Burgess Brown moved to New York City where she founded and pastored Glad Tidings Tabernacle, which was destined to become one of the most prominent Pentecostal churches in America. In 1961, while she was still its pastor, Glad Tidings Tabernacle was noted as the "church with the largest missionary budget in the missionary-minded Assemblies of God."

F.F. Bosworth (1877–1958) launched an international ministry of faith and healing. It is estimated that over a million souls came to Christ through his ministry. His book, *Christ the*

---

21. Paul G. Chappell, *The Divine Healing Movement in America* (Ph.D. Diss., Drew University, 1983), 351.

Healer, remains a classic, and his influence, through his work with William Branham and T.L. and Daisy Osborne, impacted the healing revivals of the 1950's.

John G. Lake (1870–1935) emerged from Parham's Zion City Revival as "a giant firebrand in the Pentecostal Movement." He founded the Apostolic Faith Churches of South Africa—some 2,500 assemblies birthed in revival and the miracle-working power of God. Cecil Rhodes, the South African "empire builder," said of John G. Lake's preaching: "His message has swept Africa. He has done more toward South Africa's future peace than any other man"; and Mahatma Ghandi said of Lake's ministry, "Dr. Lake's teachings will eventually be accepted by the entire world." (Perhaps that word was destined to be fulfilled through David du Plessis, the "Mr. Pentecost" of the Charismatic Movement, who was saved in an Apostolic Faith Church in South Africa.)

John G. Lake also labored on the other side of the Atlantic, in Portland, Oregon. In 1923, he invited Charles Parham to Portland for an evangelistic crusade, during which Gordon Lindsay (1906–1973) was converted. Historian Hyatt notes that "Lindsay's ministry, together with that of his wife Freda (1914—) spanned the Pentecostal, healing, and Charismatic revivals, and through *Christ For the Nations* in Dallas, Texas, is still highly influential."[22]

It appears historically true that Charles Parham's decision to go to Zion City "precipitated one of the most important religious events of this twentieth century"—the 1906 revival at Zion City, Illinois.

Pentecost Comes to Los Angeles in 1906

During his time in Houston, Texas, Charles Parham was impressed to open a short-term Bible school on January 1, 1906. The most important person to be touched by Parham at this school was a son of slaves, a black Holiness preacher

---

22. Hyatt, *op. cit.*, 165-166.

named William Joseph Seymour (1870–1922). Vinson Synan describes him as "a short stocky man, with one eye damaged by smallpox."[23] Parham, in the face of southern segregation laws, "skirted the legal restrictions by arranging for Seymour to sit in an adjoining room where, through an open door, he was able to listen to the lectures."[24]

Convinced of Parham's teaching on the "Baptism of the Holy Spirit accompanied by the physical evidence of speaking in other tongues,"[25] Seymour left Houston to accept a call to pastor a newly formed Holiness congregation on Santa Fe Street in Los Angeles. His first sermon was from Acts 2:4, which earned for him a padlocked door on the meeting place by that very evening.

From there Seymour accepted hospitality at the home of Richard and Ruth Asberry[26] at 214 Bonnie Brae Street, where Seymour gave himself to prayer. Soon the Holy Spirit was poured out. Richard Asberry, William Seymour himself and others experienced the "Baptism of the Spirit with the physical evidence of speaking in other tongues." Carl Brumback described the event:

> "As though hit by a bolt of lightning, the entire company was knocked from their chairs to the floor. Seven began to speak in divers kinds of tongues and to magnify God…Soon it was noised over the city that God was pouring out His Spirit. White people joined the colored saints and also joined the ranks of those filled with the Holy Ghost."[27]

---

23. Synan, *op. cit.*, 93.

24. Hyatt, *op. cit.*, 153.

25. The Holiness position generally held that *the inner witness* of a clean heart was the evidence of the "Baptism of the Holy Spirit."

26. Three different spellings of their name have come down to us: Asberry (Richard Riss and Eddie Hyatt), Asbery (Vinson Synan), and Asbury (Tim Peterson).

27. Carl Brumback, *Suddenly…From Heaven: A History of the Assemblies of God* (Springfield, MO: Gospel Publishing House, 1961), 36.

Soon large crowds gathered at the Asberry home. Only after part of the floor collapsed were the meetings moved to an abandoned A.M.E. Church building at 312 Azusa Street in mid-April of 1906. Vinson Synan calls the meetings at Azusa Street among "the most far-reaching religious meetings of the twentieth century." Synan continues: "No sooner had Seymour begun preaching in the Azusa location than a monumental revival began. Scores of people began to 'fall under the power' and arise speaking in other tongues."[28] Services continued daily for 1,000 days.

News of the happenings were publicized in the *Los Angeles Times* (and in not-too-favorable language: "New Sect of Fanatics Is Breaking Loose"). The great San Francisco earthquake, in which nearly 10,000 lost their lives, hit at the very same time—in mid-April, 1906—and contributed to the mystique of the hour. Hundreds and then thousands began to flock to Azusa Street by the trainloads, from all across the United States and Canada and even from around the world. As they drew near to the building, people would fall down under the power of God, blocks away. Angels were seen, and fire was seen consuming the building just like the burning bush in Exodus. In the meetings there was complete integration of the races: "the color line was washed away in the blood."

Frank Bartleman, a Holiness journalist and one of the early participants in the revival, described the Azusa Street meetings in these words: "Suddenly the Spirit would fall upon the congregation. God Himself would give the altar call. Men would fall all over the house, like the slain in battle, or rush to the altar *en masse* to seek God...The services ran almost continuously. Seeking souls could be found under the power almost any hour, night and day...God's presence became more and more wonderful. In that old building...God took strong men and women to pieces, and put them together again for His

---

28. Synan, *op. cit.*, 85, 97.

glory. It was a tremendous overhauling process. Pride and self-assertion, self-importance and self-esteem could not survive there...No subjects or sermons were announced ahead of time, and no special speakers for such an hour. No one knew what might be coming, what God would do. All was spontaneous, ordered of the Spirit. We wanted to hear from God...." Bartleman continued: "Brother Seymour generally sat behind two empty shoeboxes, one on top of the other. He usually kept his head inside the top one during the meeting in prayer."[29]

News of the revival spread further by means of William Seymour's *Apostolic Faith Newsletter,* the circulation of which began in the fall of 1906 and grew to 80,000 per publication.

John G. Lake described William Seymour in these grand words: "God had put such a hunger into that man's heart that when the fire of God came it glorified him. I do not believe any other man in modern times had a more wonderful deluge of God in his life...and the glory and power of a real Pentecost swept the world...."[30]

Despite internal divisions and charges of occult spiritism and a resulting separation between Seymour and Parham, the Azusa Street revival continued in strength for three years, from 1906 to 1909. Unfortunately, the ongoing strife eventually caused it to diminish in effectiveness. Many whites left to begin their own churches. By 1914, the Azusa Street Mission was but a small local black congregation. On September 28, 1922, William Seymour died, a brokenhearted man. In 1972, Sidney Ahlstrom, the noted Church historian from Yale University, called Seymour "the most influential black leader in American religious history." Charles Parham died in 1929. The Azusa Street Mission itself was torn down in 1931, eventually making room for a parking lot.

---

29. Bartleman, as quoted by Riss, *op. cit.*, 56-57, and Peterson, *op. cit.*, respectively.

30. John. G. Lake, *Spiritual Hunger/The God-Men* (Dallas: Christ for the Nations, 1980), 14.

Vinson Synan gives an excellent historical perspective on the Azusa Street revival:

"The Azusa Street revival is commonly regarded as the beginning of the modern Pentecostal Movement. Although many persons had spoken in tongues in the United States in the years preceding 1906, this meeting brought the practice to the attention of the world and served as catalyst for the formation of scores of Pentecostal denominations. Directly or indirectly, practically all of the Pentecostal groups in existence can trace their lineage to the Azusa Street Mission...The Pentecostal Movement arose as a split in the holiness movement and can be viewed as the logical outcome of the holiness crusade that had vexed American Protestantism, the Methodist Church in particular, for more than forty years. The repeated calls of the holiness leadership...for a 'new Pentecost' inevitably produced the frame of mind and the intellectual foundations for just such a 'Pentecost' to occur. In historical perspective the Pentecostal movement was the child of the holiness movement, which in turn was a child of Methodism. Practically all the early Pentecostal leaders were firm advocates of sanctification as a 'second work of grace' and simply added the 'Pentecostal baptism' with the evidence of speaking in tongues as a 'third blessing' superimposed on the other two...the movement that Parham and Seymour unleashed in Topeka and Los Angeles was destined to begin a new and important chapter in the history of Christianity."[31]

Pentecostal Growth in the South

By the end of 1906, word of the Azusa Street Revival had spread across the nation and around the world. One of those deeply impacted by the report was G.B. (Gaston Barnabas) Cashwell, a Southern Holiness preacher. In the fall of 1906, he left this word with puzzled delegates of his denomination

---

31. Synan, *op. cit.*, 105-106.

assembled for their annual conference: "I realize that my life has fallen short of the standard of holiness we preach; but I have repented in my home in Dunn, North Carolina, and I have been restored. I am now leaving for Los Angeles, California, where I shall seek for the Baptism of the Holy Ghost."[32] Upon receiving his own personal "Pentecost," Cashwell returned to Dunn, where, according to Vinson Synan, he convened meetings that "would be for the Southeast what Azusa Street had been to the West," meetings that would draw much of the Southeastern Holiness movement into the Pentecostal experience, thus establishing the South as a Pentecostal stronghold, and Cashwell himself as the South's Apostle of Pentecost.

Firsthand witness G.F. Taylor described Cashwell's historic meetings in these words: "They went to Dunn by the thousands, went down for the Baptism with all the earnestness they could command, and were soon happy in the experience, speaking in tongues, singing in tongues, shouting, weeping, dancing, praising, and magnifying God. They returned to their respective homes to scatter the fire. A great Pentecostal revival broke out in practically all the churches. A revival had come, and nobody was able to stop it." In early 1907, Cashwell was instrumental in bringing Holiness preacher A.J. Tomlinson into the Pentecostal experience, and with him the Church of God of Cleveland, Tennessee.

In 1911, as a result of the Dunn Pentecostal revival, the Fire-Baptized Holiness Church merged with the Pentecostal Holiness Church. The Pentecostal Holiness Church maintained both the sanctification emphasis of the Holiness movement and the "speaking in tongues" emphasis of the Pentecostal movement. In 1909, a disillusioned Cashwell left the Holiness Pentecostal Church to become a Methodist. Seven years later, in 1916, Cashwell died. He was a man whose brief several years of Pentecostal ministry had "profoundly effect[ed] the religious future, not just of the south, but of the entire country."[33] The South thus

---

32. *The Pentecostal Holiness Advocate,* May 29, 1930, 1.
33. Synan, *op. cit.*, 128.

significantly became the mother of major Pentecostal denomi-
nations—the Church of God in Christ, the Pentecostal Holiness
Church, the Church of God of Cleveland, Tennessee, and the
Assemblies of God.

Pentecostal Growth Worldwide

The British Keswick Conventions of the late 1800's and
the Welsh Revival of 1904 (which was characterized by speaking in other tongues) gave Great Britain its openness to the
Pentecostal revival. The deeper-life labors of R.A. Torrey in
Germany likewise gave Germany its opening to Pentecostal-
ism. In January 1907, a young Swedish Baptist pastor, Lewi
Prethus, received "the baptism in the Holy Spirit" in Oslo,
Norway, through the ministry of a Methodist minister, Thomas
Barratt, who had received in America in late 1906. Prethus, in
turn, was one of the instruments of God to bring the Pente-
costal revival to Sweden. Also through Thomas Barratt,
Alexander Boddy, the Anglican vicar of All Saints' parish in
Sunderland, England, received. Jonathan Paul, a leader in the
German Holiness movement, also received under Thomas
Barratt. Smith Wigglesworth received his personal baptism in
the Holy Spirit after a visit to Boddy's parish and being prayed
for by Boddy's wife. Both Alexander Boddy and Jonathan
Paul profoundly affected both England and Germany, respectively, for the Pentecostal cause. Thus throughout the first
quarter of the twentieth century the Pentecostal revival spread
throughout Britain, Scandinavia, and central Europe:

> "By 1908, the movement had taken root in over 50
> nations. By 1914, it was represented in every American
> city of 3,000 or more, in every area of the world, from Ice-
> land to Tanzania, and Pentecostals were publishing litera-
> ture in 30 languages."[34]

By 1909, Pentecostalism had also spread as far as China
through missionaries connected with Azusa Street. By 1909,
the Pentecostal revival had also prospered in South Africa, as

---

34. Douglas G. Nelson, as quoted by Hyatt, *op. cit.*, 176.

previously mentioned, under John G. Lake, and in central Africa, the revival had taken root through English missionaries by 1915. Pentecostal manifestations appeared in Chile in 1909, as previously noted, and also in Argentina, and then in Brazil, in 1910, though two young Swedes from the United States, Daniel Berg and Gunnar Vingren. Since then, Brazil has continued to be an outstanding recipient of this new "rain from heaven" in this blest century. Beginning in 1911, with only 18 members, the Brazilian *Assembléias de Deus*[35] has become the largest national Pentecostal movement in the world, with 20,000,000 members.[36]

Further Developments in the Pentecostal Movement

By 1910, a shift in the Pentecostal movement had taken place in the United States—from Azusa Street in Los Angeles to Chicago, Illinois. William H. Durham, who had been baptized in the Holy Spirit in 1907 at Azusa Street, was at the forefront. Historian Thomas William Miller wrote: "When Durham returned to Chicago, a Pentecostal revival broke out which replicated, if it did not exceed, the supernatural events of the Azusa Street Mission. The North Avenue Mission was so full of the power of God, according to eyewitnesses, that a 'thick haze...like blue smoke' filled its upper region. When this haze was present, wrote pioneer Howard Goss, the people entering the building would fall down in the aisles. Some never got to sit in the pews. Many came through to the baptism or received divine healing."[37] E.N. Bell, later to become the first general superintendent of the Assemblies of God, received his personal Pentecost at the North Avenue Mission.

Through Durham's influence the Pentecostal Movement spread to Canada after A.H. Argue of Winnipeg visited Durham in Chicago and there received his Pentecostal experience.

---

35. With no official connection to the Assemblies of God of Springfield, Missouri.
36. Figure is from a 1997 count.
37. Miller, as quoted by Riss, *op. cit.*, 81.

Argue's ministry across Canada led to the forming, in 1919, of Canada's largest Pentecostal denomination, the Pentecostal Assemblies of Canada. An Italian immigrant to Chicago, Luigi Francescon, also received "the baptism in the Holy Spirit" at Durham's Chicago North Avenue Mission. Francescon helped establish the first Italian-American Pentecostal congregation in America in 1907, and in Brazil in 1909, and then, co-laboring with Giocomo Lombardy, in Italy. Persian immigrants also received "the baptism" under Durham and returned to Persia "to evangelize." Durham died in 1912 at the age of only 39, but he was nevertheless a man of great influence in the early Pentecostal movement, as we shall continue to note.

Australia, late in its Pentecostal initiation, was greatly affected by the campaigns of British evangelist Smith Wigglesworth in 1921, Aimee Semple McPherson in 1922, and A.C. Valdez in 1925. In 1920, Ivan Voronaev, who had received his Pentecostal experience in New York City, traveled to Russia and other Slavic lands founding the first Pentecostal churches. Voronaev was martyred by the Communists in 1943 in the Gulag; his body lies in an unknown grave in Siberia. The Pentecostal movement came to Korea in 1928, through Mary Rumsey, an Elim Fellowship American Missionary. In 1952, her work was turned over to the Assemblies of God. In the first class of their new Bible School was a young convert from Buddhism, David Yonggi Cho, who then started a new church under a tent in 1958. Yoido Full Gospel Church in Seoul is now the largest church in the world—with approximately 900,000 people.[38]

---

38. As David Yonggi Cho (formerly Paul Yonggi Cho) began his fledgling ministry in 1958, another Korean, Sun Myung Moon, was establishing his fledgling ministry in South Korea as well—the *Holy Spirit Association for the Unification of World Christianity,* known as the *Unification Church.* In 1992, according to the *One World Family Crusade,* "Rev. Moon declared he and his wife were the 'True Parents of all mankind, the Savior, the Lord of the Second Advent, the Messiah' " (taken from a fax dated August 1995, from the *One World Family Crusade*).

Apart from those immediately mentioned, there were several other pioneers of early Pentecostalism in America: Mrs. M.B. Woodworth-Etter, of whom we have already spoken, used much in establishing the Anderson *Church of God,* and the Englishman, Dr. Charles S. Price, whom we shall yet consider, who received the "baptism in the Holy Spirit" under Aimee Semple McPherson's preaching. Through the labor of these and others, there was to be found a ring of Pentecostal fire encompassing the whole world by the end of the first quarter of the twentieth century. Hundreds of thousands were swept into the Kingdom of God, gloriously filled with the Holy Spirit! In the truest sense of the word, the promised *rain* was falling upon the earth. The spiritual threshing floors were full of grain, and the vats were being filled with new wine and oil.

Pentecostal Fragmentation

From its humble beginnings, the Pentecostal movement was destined to experience both phenomenal growth and grave fragmentation—both a multiplication and a division that would become of significant historical importance in understanding the move of the Holy Spirit throughout the whole twentieth century.

Early in the outpouring, Holiness-Pentecostal writer Frank J. Bartleman expressed deep concern over the health of the revival itself. In *Another Wave of Revival,* Bartleman wrote:

"In the beginning of the Pentecostal work, I became very much exercised in the Spirit that Jesus should not be slighted, 'lost in the temple,' by the exaltation of the Holy Spirit and of the gifts of the Spirit. There seemed to be a great danger of losing sight of the fact that Jesus was 'all, and in all'....The work of Calvary, the atonement, must be the center of our consideration. The Holy Spirit never draws our attention from Christ to Himself, but rather reveals Christ in a fuller way...Many are willing to seek power from every battery they can lay their hands on in order to perform miracles, draw the attention and adoration of the people to themselves, thus robbing Christ of His glory and making a fair showing in the flesh. The greatest religious need of our day would seem to be that of true followers of the meek and lowly Jesus. Religious enthusiasm easily goes to seed. The human spirit so predominates the show-off, religious spirit. But we must stick to our text—Christ. He alone can save. The attention of the people must be first of all, and always, held to Him. A true 'Pentecost' will produce a mighty conviction of sin, a turning to God. False manifestations produce only excitement and wonder...Any work that exalts the Holy Spirit or the gifts above Jesus will finally end up in fanaticism. Whatever causes us to exalt the love of Jesus is well and safe. The reverse will ruin all. The Holy Spirit is a great light, but will always be focused on Jesus for His revealing."[39]

Bartleman's concern would become one to dog the steps of the Pentecostal movement throughout the whole of the twentieth century.

Doctrinal Divisions

Doctrinal divisions began to take place early in the Pentecostal revival. These would increase over the years that followed and determine much of the destiny of twentieth-century Pentecostalism. First of all, there was division within the revival over whether or not speaking in other tongues was *the* singular physical evidence of the "baptism in the Holy Spirit." The gifts of the Holy Spirit, including *glossolalia* (speaking in other tongues) were not new to historical revival movements, especially the Holiness movement. In the early 1900's tongues-speaking had also accompanied outpourings all across the United States and around the world. Many of the early Pentecostals were Holiness people to whom God had come in a fresh way, and to whom tongues-speaking was simply His divine calling card. The insistence, however, that tongues was *the* evidence of the Spirit's

---

39. Frank J. Bartleman, *Another Wave of Revival* (Springdale, PA: Whitaker House, 1962), 94-96. Originally published as *Another Wave Rolls In*.

baptism soon became a divisive issue and caused fragmentation within the movement.

Richard Riss deals at length with A.B. Simpson and the Christian and Missionary Alliance (C.M.A.) as one of the saddest cases in point. As we have already noted, just three months before the Azusa Street revival, there was an unusual outpouring of the Holy Spirit in 1906 at Nyack, the C.M.A. Missionary Training Institute on the Hudson. In 1907, the Holy Spirit also fell among the C.M.A. saints in the Akron-Cleveland area of Ohio. W.A. Cramer, the C.M.A. superintendent in Cleveland, wrote in the *Alliance Weekly* of April 27: "...the power of God fell on me...and the Holy Spirit soon began to speak through me in an utterance I had never learned." Pentecostal revival also broke out that same year in the C.M.A. Gospel Tabernacle in Indianapolis. J. Roswell Flower, who later became the founding secretary of the Assemblies of God, was converted during those meetings.

The Spirit was also similarly poured out in Pennsylvania, New York, and elsewhere. Richard Riss comments at this juncture: "The founder and president of the Christian and Missionary Alliance, A.B. Simpson, struggled a great deal with questions that had arisen as a result of the new Pentecostal revival, especially since so many of the churches in the C.M.A. had been touched by this great outpouring of God's Spirit...According to his biographers, Simpson's diary...recorded a 'sustained, intense searching through prayer and fasting for a deeper, fuller baptism in the Spirit in all His manifestations'; however, [Simpson] never received the gift of tongues. As a result of this, he concluded that, while the gift of tongues was one manifestation of the infilling of the Holy Spirit, it is 'neither necessary nor the sole evidence of such an experience.' "[40] In April of 1910, Simpson crystallized the Alliance position: "We fully recognize all the gifts of the Spirit, including 'diverse kinds of tongues'....But we are opposed to the teaching that this special

---

40. Riss, *op. cit.*, 77-78.

gift is for all or is the evidence of the Baptism of the Holy Ghost. Nor can we receive or use to edification in our work and assemblies those who press these extreme and unscriptural views." Simpson's stand unfortunately fragmented the C.M.A. Richard Riss records: "According to David McDowell, in 1912 A.B. Simpson remarked to him, 'David, I did what I thought was best, but I am afraid that I missed it.' Fifteen years later, Albert E. Funk, foreign secretary of the C.M.A., observed…'the Alliance has missed God!' "[41] Many of those who left the Alliance became part of the early Assemblies of God and its fledgling leadership.

The second issue of doctrinal fragmentation within the Pentecostal movement arose over how many works of grace were involved in the Christian experience. Holiness doctrine by the end of the 1800's held to two works of grace—salvation and sanctification. Heart purity, or sanctification, was held to be a *"second* blessing," or a *"second* work of grace" to salvation. To various of the early Pentecostal leaders (Charles Parham and his disciple William Seymour, in particular), the "baptism in the Holy Spirit" was their *"third* work of grace." Most of the southern Holiness-Pentecostals, as we have already noted, held to both sanctification and the "baptism in the Holy Spirit" as distinct crisis experiences. Churches, which had been formed as "second blessing" holiness churches, simply added the "baptism in the Holy Spirit" (with *glossolalia* as the "initial evidence") as a *"third* blessing." In contrast, William H. Durham of Chicago, in 1910, propounded the "Finished Work" theology, declaring that God's finished work of sanctification takes place *at conversion* and a gradual progressive sanctification takes place thereafter. Frank J. Ewart, one of Durham's successors, commented: "Pastor Durham vigorously opposed the teaching that sanctification was a second, definite, instantaneous work of grace. He said that sanctification was…a growth in the grace and knowledge

41. *Ibid.*, 79.

of our Lord Jesus Christ."[42] Thus, the "Pentecostal Baptism" became Durham's second work of grace (second to salvation, which was itself the "Finished Work"). This vast departure from Parham and Seymour's original Holiness thinking would doctrinally lead to the 1914 formation of the Assemblies of God as an alternative to the existing southern, "three works of grace" Holiness-Pentecostal denominations.

The third severe division within the Pentecostal movement concerned the issue of water baptism. Was baptism a testimony to an already received salvation or an essential part of that salvation? And, was baptism to be in "the name of Jesus" only, or in "the name of the Father, the Son, and the Holy Spirit"? And attached to the latter issue would also be the understanding of the Godhead: Is ours one God in three Persons, or one God in three manifestations?

The first worldwide Pentecostal camp meeting at Arroyo Seco, California, (convened on April 15, 1913) was the catalyst for these weighty issues. Approximately 4,500 people attended the four-week camp meeting, and Maria Woodworth-Etter was the featured evangelist. A word was delivered by another speaker from Jeremiah 31:22 (KJV): "…the Lord hath created *a new thing* in the earth…." To those who had ears to hear and eyes to see, this "new thing" was to be revealed before the camp ended. The "new thing" was introduced by Canadian Pentecostal Evangelist R.E. McAlister—"baptism in the name of Jesus Christ." The next day, early in the morning, a brother, John G. Scheppe, ran through the camp, shouting that the Lord had shown him the truth of "baptism in the name of Jesus Christ." Many of the early Pentecostal leaders accepted the new "revelation" and were baptized accordingly.

Along with the name came the issue of the "oneness of the Godhead" as over against the *Trinitarian* formula and the

---

42. Frank J. Ewart, *The Phenomenon of Pentecost*, 113, as quoted by Tim Peterson, *op. cit.*

Trinitarian concept of the Godhead.[43] This created grave divisions among the Pentecostals as some supported this view and others denounced it as a rank heresy. Frank J. Ewart, the successor in William H. Durham's work in Los Angeles, became one of the early Oneness leaders. Describing his experience at the Arroyo Seco camp meeting, Ewart wrote: "It was at this camp meeting that the truth of the Oneness of the Godhead was openly expounded for the first time. Along with this new revelation went the doctrine of baptism in the Name of Jesus...."[44] Concerning his own fruitfulness in practicing these new understandings, Ewart wrote: "The vast majority of the new converts were filled with the Holy Ghost after coming up out of the water. They would leave the tank speaking in other tongues [and] many were healed when they were baptized...."[45] Vinson Synan, however, comments on Ewart and his co-workers that theirs was a "determined campaign to reconvert and re-baptize the entire Pentecostal movement into their new 'oneness' belief."[46]

Consequently, any number of the early members of the newly organized Assemblies of God (formed in early April of 1914) were baptized in Jesus' name. However, by the fourth General Council of the Assemblies of God, held in St. Louis on October 1-7, 1916, the "New Issue" (as it was then called)

---

43. The term *Oneness* comes from a modalistic understanding of the Godhead. It is of interest to note that Pentecostalism, in its 1900's "Oneness-Trinitarian" controversy, duplicated the same controversy of the declining Church of the fourth century (see Chapter 5). Trinitarian Pentecostals hold to the Wesleyan teaching of the baptism in the Holy Spirit as a "second work of grace" to the new birth, and view water baptism in the name of the Father, the Son, and the Holy Spirit as a testimony to that salvation. Oneness Pentecostals, believing the Spirit of Christ *to be* the Holy Spirit, see the new birth (see Jn. 3:5) *as* the baptism in the Holy Spirit when accompanied by "the evidence" of speaking in other tongues and by water baptism in the name of Jesus, as per Acts 2:38.

44. Ewart, as quoted by Peterson, *op.cit.*

45. *Ibid.*

46. Synan, *op. cit.*, 157.

was confronted under the leadership of J. Roswell Flower. As a result, the Assemblies of God "Statement of Fundamental Truths" made Matthew 28:19 compulsory in all baptismal services and made belief in the Trinity a test of membership. More than one fourth of the ministers affiliated with the Assemblies left, taking a number of congregations with them. "In the long run, the ejection of the 'Jesus Onlies' proved well worth the temporary decline in numbers and prestige. Within a year the Assemblies had all but recovered its losses, and soon became by far the largest Pentecostal denomination."[47]

R.E. McAlister, Frank J. Ewart, and George T. Haywood (a prominent black Oneness Pentecostal leader) organized the Pentecostal Assemblies of the World, which then became the largest black Oneness Pentecostal denomination in the world. Several other Oneness denominations formed were the United Pentecostal Church and the Apostolic Church of Pentecost in Canada. It is also of interest to note that prior to the formation of the Assemblies of God in 1914, many white Pentecostal ministers had accepted ordination at the hands of Bishop C.H. Mason, so that the Church of God in Christ was actually an interracial church from 1907 to 1914. The formation of the "white" Assemblies of God in 1914 then witnessed the exodus of white Pentecostals, and the Church of God in Christ went on to become the largest black Holiness-Pentecostal group in the world, thus ending "a notable experiment in interracial church development."[48]

The Assemblies of God

Indeed one of the largest of the Pentecostal bodies in the world is the General Council of the Assemblies of God (A.G.), with 11,884 churches and 1,407,941 members in the U.S. and an impressive 146,348 churches and 25,362,718 members in

---

47. Edith L. Blumhofer, *The Assemblies of God*, 235.
48. Synan, *op. cit.*, 155.

over 150 nations of the world.[49] When its founding fathers convened in 1914 at Hot Springs, Arkansas, it was not to form a
new denomination, but rather to establish a *fellowship* of
churches. Vinson Synan, however, crisply observes: "Although
the three hundred ministers and laymen disclaimed any desire
to inaugurate a new 'sect' or 'denomination,' the delegates succeeded in doing just that."[50] The Assemblies of God emerges
as the most politically powerful denomination in the Pentecostal movement. Douglas Wead in his biography of C.M.
Ward, Revivaltime[51] preacher, makes this observation:

> "Most of the founders of the *Assemblies of God* were dis
> missed from denominational churches because of their
> experiences. These delegates determined that they would
> never become a denomination, only a fellowship....Today
> *the Assemblies of God* is very much a denomination. With
> in the last fifteen years the influence of its National Head
> quarters has become powerful. Much of what has happened
> to the *Assemblies of God* in recent years has been the work
> of its energetic and skillful General Superintendent Thomas
> F. Zimmerman. Some believe that Zimmerman will be
> remembered in church history as the Bismarck of Pente
> costalism, the man who solidified forty or fifty little Pente
> costal kingdoms and gave them credibility in the eyes of the
> evangelical Christian world."[52]

This pursuit for credibility by which classical Pentecostals[53]
then sought to transform their image from that of the "storefront
across the tracks" to that of a respectable institution within
Evangelicalism has perhaps, more than any other factor, caused

---

49. 1996 Assemblies of God report.

50. Synan, *op. cit.*, 155.

51. The radio voice of the *Assemblies of God*.

52. Douglas Wead, *The C.M. Ward Story* (Harrison, AR: New Leaf Press, 1976).

53. Old-line Pentecostals are called "classical Pentecostals" as opposed to Charismatics or "neo-Pentecostals."

the movement to institutionalize and consequently decline in its effectiveness.

Vinson Synan summarizes the beginning history of the Pentecostal movement thus: "Pentecostalism engendered at least twenty-five separate denominations within fourteen years...by the middle of the century, some Protestant observers were referring to Pentecostalism as the 'Third Force in Christendom'...."[54]

Pentecostalism's Declining Years: 1916–1947

A.C. Valdez, Sr., notes that between 1916 and 1922 there was a marked spiritual decline, but "when the Pentecostal Church needed a standard-bearer, Aimee Semple McPherson burst upon the scene."[55] One observer describes one of her meetings in Los Angeles: "I never, in all my extended ministry, saw so many slain under the mighty power of God...in some instances the Evangelist had only to lift her hands and the power would tumble them over...the Latter Rain is falling, some say even more copiously than the former rain, and we are exceedingly glad to be in the showers." In 1923, this colorful (and controversial) ex-Assemblies of God lady minister founded the International Church of the Foursquare Gospel.

Another anointed evangelist in the 1920's was Dr. Charles S. Price, who was powerfully met by God in Aimee Semple McPherson's meetings in San Jose in 1920. Price then held his first evangelistic meeting in Ashland, Oregon, in 1922. He described the results: "The power fell. Hundreds were saved and hundreds were healed...scores and scores would be prostrated under the power at one time...." Later, in British Columbia, he records: "There were days when from seven hundred to one thousand persons came to the altar, all under the same tremendous conviction of sin."

Woven into the ministry of Charles Price was Kathryn Kuhlman, who received her call to preach in one of Prices' meetings in Albany, Oregon, in 1923. Like Aimee Semple

54. Synan, *op. cit.*, 166.
55. A.C. Valdez, Sr., as quoted by Riss, *op. cit.*, 95.

McPherson before her, Kathryn Kuhlman was both colorful and controversial, and like McPherson, was also overshadowed by the consequences of a divorce. Aimee Semple McPherson died in 1944, a real Deborah in Israel.

The 1930's and 40's saw great revivals around the world, such as in East Africa in the Rwanda Mission among the Anglicans, a revival that continued on for decades—a "Continuous Revival." In 1927, a great awakening had taken place among the praying Baptists in Shantung Province, Northeast China. Converts came to Christ by the thousands. In 1937, Dr. John Sung was powerfully used by God in revival all through China and beyond into Java, Singapore, Malaysia, Burma, and Thailand. God came to Ethiopia between 1937 and 1943. Though the missionaries had been expelled, the church grew from less than 100 to 10,000. (Through the end of the twentieth century Ethiopia has continued to see powerful revivals, bringing multitudes to Christ.) The early 1940's also saw the beginnings of the revival ministry of Bakht Singh in South India.

In America, however, the 1930's and 40's are looked upon as "a time of spiritual decline."[56] Both John T. Nichol and Carl Brumback view these years as a time when the depth of worship and the operation of the gifts of the Spirit that had been well evident in earlier decades became less prominent. "By the end of World War II the American Pentecostal movement needed a renewal."[57] Consequently strong cries were beginning to ascend to Heaven: "O Lord, revive Thy work in the midst of the years, in the midst of the years make it known; in wrath remember mercy."[58]

---

56. Riss, *op. cit.*, 103.

57. Synan, *op. cit.*, 212.

58. Habakkuk 3:2b KJV.

Chapter 12

The Early and Latter Rains of the Twentieth Century

Part II

The Second Half of the Twentieth Century

As we analyze the history of the second half of the twentieth century, it seems as if we can sense a fulfillment of Joel's amazing prophecy concerning the last days: "Be glad then, ye children of Zion, and rejoice in the Lord your God: for He hath given you the former rain moderately, and He will cause to come down for you the rain, the former rain, and the latter rain in the first month. And the floors shall be full of wheat, and the vats shall overflow with wine and oil. And I will restore to you the years that the locust hath eaten...."[1]

As we have previously noted, the powerful events of the second half of the twentieth century had their roots unusually intertwined in the 1948–1950 outpourings of the Holy Spirit

---

1. Joel 2:23-25 KJV.

that took place in northern Canada, Argentina, and the Hebrides, and then all across the United States in the Healing revivals. Through the ongoing impact of these revivals, Spirit-filled believers would grow to become hundreds of millions in number by the end of the 1900's, and one of the most powerful forces for revival and for world evangelism on the face of the earth.

The "Latter Rain Revival" of 1948

In the face of both a spiritual decline within classical Pentecostalism and an increasing splintering and fracturing of the movement, it pleased the Lord to send a visitation from heaven in the very middle of the twentieth century, just after the end of the Second World War. Indeed, "Thou, O God, didst send a plentiful rain, whereby Thou didst confirm Thine inheritance, when it was weary."[2] The year 1947 was one of deep spiritual hunger among Pentecostals. John T. Nichol writes that Pentecostals were especially concerned that "the depth of worship and the operation of the gifts of the Spirit so much in evidence in earlier decades were not so prominent in the thirties and forties."[3]

Thus, George Warnock writes in the preface to the original edition of *The Feast of Tabernacles* that "...in the spring of 1948 God came forth in answer to the prayer and fasting of His children, poured out the gifts of the Holy Spirit, and revealed the fact that now at this time He would bring His Body together, and make His Church one glorious Church without spot or wrinkle."[4]

The scene was North Battleford, Saskatchewan, Canada, and the instruments were George and Ern Hawtin, P.G. Holt, Herrick Hunt, Milford Kirkpatrick, and George Warnock. This

---

2. Psalm 68:9 KJV.

3. John Thomas Nichol, *Pentecostalism* (New York: Harper & Row, 1966), 237.

4. George H. Warnock, *The Feast of Tabernacles* (North Battleford, Saskatchewan: Sharon Publishers, 1951), 3.

mighty and miraculous visitation was called the "Latter Rain," and it quickly spread across Canada, the United States, and around the world, influencing many thousands in its wake. Carl Brumback, in the *History of the Assemblies of God*, observes how initially in this visitation, "a thrill of hope surged through thousands of hearts; a new outpouring of the Spirit was falling upon the dry and barren land!...'"[5] Unfortunately that thrill was short-lived. George Hawtin wrote in the late spring of 1948, "Men who have been praying for twenty years that the gifts would be restored to the church are now afraid to enter in because of the opposition from the organization."[6]

In early 1949, Stanley Frodsham (1882–1969), a leader in the Assemblies of God and long-time editor of the denomination's *Pentecostal Evangel*, wrote concerning his threatened brethren: "It has been so grossly unfair [of them] to link up this new revival which God is so graciously sending, where so many souls are being saved, where so many lives are being transformed, where God is so graciously restoring the gifts of the Spirit with the fanatical movements of the past 40 years... it seems as if the brethren do not want to hear anything that would change them in their prejudices against this gracious new outpouring of God's Spirit." He then further wrote: "I can see that the [Assemblies of God] Council is waging an all out war against the new revival God is sending. They [the leaders of the revival] have made mistakes. But there are frailties in all of God's saints, and I could recite a story of mistakes that have been made by my Council brethren that I have seen during the past 33 years...I have made many mistakes myself."[7]

Unfortunately, Resolution #7 of the 1949 General Council of the Assemblies of God declared of the new move: "We disapprove of those extreme teachings and practices, which being

---

5. Carl Brumback, *Suddenly...From Heaven: A History of the Assemblies of God* (Springfield, MO: Gospel Publishing House, 1961), 331.

6. George R. Hawtin, "Local Church Government," *Sharon Star* (1 May 1948): 4, as quoted by Richard Riss, *A Survey of 20th-Century Revival Movements in North America,* (Peabody, MA: Hendrickson Publishers, 1988), 114.

7. Frodsham, as quoted by Riss, *op. cit.,*119, 121.

unfounded Scripturally, serve only to break fellowship of like precious faith and tend to confusion and division among members of the Body of Christ,[8] and be it hereby known that this 23rd General Council disapproves of the so-called 'New Order of the Latter Rain'...." It appears as if by this stroke of conservatism, the Assemblies of God closed its doors to this fresh Spirit-outpouring, and by so isolating this new movement the Assemblies of God only aided its rapid degeneration toward unbalanced extreme and error, exactly as the institutional Church had done to Montanism in the second century of Church history. This short-lived "Latter Rain" movement then quickly fractured and splintered into various extremes and errors, but not before leaving as a legacy a rich deposit of the truth of God for His Church in the earth. Steve Wilbur, a teacher at Pinecrest Bible Training Center in New York, felt that "the Latter Rain outpouring of the Spirit...came forth with the greatest blaze of prophetic light since the apostolic era...."[9]

Apart from the basic general truths of the Latter Rain movement concerning the restoration of the Body of Christ, which truths have now become the inheritance of the whole Church, a tightly held segment of the Latter Rain continued on with various of the original apostles, headquartered at North Battleford, with their original publication, the *Sharon Star*. These brethren sought to be the end-time restoration of the Church in the earth. Other more balanced inheritors of the "Latter Rain" legacy were Thomas Wyatt and Dick Iverson of Portland, Oregon; Reg Layzell of Vancouver, B.C.; Fred Poole of Philadelphia, Pennsylvania; Mrs. Myrtle Beal of the Bethesda Temple in Detroit, Michigan; I.Q. Spencer of the Elim Fellowship of Lima, New York; J. Mattsson-Boze of Chicago, Illinois; and Ralph Mahoney of the California-based World

---

8. Several of the teachings cited were: "present day apostles and prophets" and "bestowing or confirming gifts by the laying on of hands and prophecy," teachings that would become widespread throughout the Body of Christ by the end of the century.

9. Wilbur, as quoted by Riss, *op. cit.*, 124.

Missionary Assistance Plan. Among others influenced by the Latter Rain visitation, three personalities emerged in the 1970's in the Charismatic movement who sought to lend stability to it: W.J. "Ern" Baxter (who originally labored with William Branham); Bill Britton of Springfield, Missouri; and DeVerne Fromke of Indianapolis, Indiana.

Several other groups have also come down to us as a legacy of the Latter Rain—John Robert Stevens with the churches of the "Walk" and Sam Fife with the "Manchild-Move of God," both veined with exclusivism and some of the "Latter Rain" overdoses of the extremes of the "manifestation of the sons of God."[10] Both of these men, Stevens and Fife, died untimely deaths.

The Holocaust of 1933–1945

The end of World War II brought to light the vast extent of one of the most horrendous tragedies in human history—the systematic annihilation of 6,000,000 Jews and millions of non-Jews in the Nazi gas chambers and burning ovens of central Europe. In defining the purpose of the recently completed United States Holocaust Memorial Museum in Washington, D.C., Museum Director Jeshajahu Weinberg writes: "The museum does not undertake to explain why the Holocaust has happened. This question has yet to be answered by the historians..."[11]— perhaps by both the historians and the prophets.

Jewish author Arthur Katz in *The Holocaust as Judgment* raises the prophetic question:

> "Why was God silent? Nazi soldiers threw our Jewish infants up in the air and caught them on their bayonets. They shot them in the air as target practice. They took our infants out of the arms of their mothers and threw them

---

10. Extremes that tend toward the idea that the sons of God will be physically glorified on the earth before or even without the literal, physical second coming of Jesus Christ.

11. Weinberg, as quoted by Michael Berenbaum, Ph.D., *The World Must Know* (Boston, MA: Little, Brown and Company, 1993), XV.

alive into troughs of burning gasoline. I was left with one of two options: I had to agree with many rabbinical commentators that God is dead or accept the testimony of our Scriptures that God's silences are in direct proportion to our sin. I had to consider the Holocaust as judgment; that it was not an aberration nor an historical accident; that the magnitude of our suffering is directly proportional to the magnitude of our sin. There can be only one meaning for Jewish suffering—the judgments of God on a people who have forsaken the true knowledge of Him and who have not walked in His covenants nor fulfilled their obligation to be His witness people."[12]

In our pursuit of understanding the history of the Church, however, it becomes necessary that, along with Katz' prophetical question, a historical question must also be asked: To what degree was the Holocaust also the result of a New Covenant people (the Church) "who have forsaken the true knowledge of Him and who have not walked in His covenants nor fulfilled their obligation to be His witness people"? We can never forget that many of those who forged the "final solution" were raised as "good" Lutherans and "good" Catholics, and that both the Catholic Church and the Protestant churches in Germany (with precious few exceptions such as Corrie ten Boom, Dietrick Bonhoeffer,[13] and Martin Niemöller) simply turned their heads the other way. "The Roman Catholic Church...did not speak out against the killing of Jews. The Church was in a position to know what was happening...Authoritative information on the killing was sent to the Vatican by its own diplomats in March 1942."[14] By the 1930's and 40's the roots of Church thinking—

---

12. Arthur Katz, *The Holocaust as Judgment* (Pensacola, FL: Chapel Library, 1997), 5.

13. Lutheran pastor Dietrick Bonhoeffer was executed by the SS on April 9, 1945, just before the end of World War II. The Flossenbürg concentration camp doctor who witnessed his execution wrote, "I have hardly ever seen a man die so entirely submissive to the will of God."

14. Berenbaum, *op. cit.*, 156.

both Catholic and Protestant—had long been poisoned by such unholy invective as Chrysostom's, "I hate the Jews...It is the duty of all Christians to hate the Jews" and Martin Luther's vile outburst: "What then shall we Christians do with this dammed, rejected race of Jews?" Thus, we are compelled to ask, if the Holocaust was the stroke of God's judgment against a sinning Judaism, what then shall be the stroke of His judgment against a fallen Church that, by both commission and omission, fueled the fires of that Holocaust?

The Birth of the State of Israel: May, 1948

Serious students of Bible prophecy and Church history see deep significance in the birth of the state of Israel in May of 1948. The British Mandate governing Palestine ended on May 14, 1948, concurrently with the declaration by the Jewish National Council of the independence of the state of Israel. The Israeli-Arab war, a conflict between the new state of Israel and its Arab neighbors that was fought in 1948–1949, left Israel victorious against its enemies and in possession of considerably larger areas of Palestine than had been provided for by the partition created by the United Nations. Many Christians felt that the Lord was restoring Israel as a parallel to His restoration of His Church, thereby making possible a literal fulfillment of the prophetic end-time words of Jesus in Luke 21:20-24 and those of Paul in Romans 11:11-16,22-29.

The Argentine Revival of 1949

Dr. R. Edward Miller describes the humble beginnings of the great revival in Argentina in 1949: "In a little vacant attic room over the garage of the adobe church in Mendoza where I was interim pastor at the time, I began to seek the Lord. I just had to find God's answers for revival and the moving of His Spirit in Argentina—for a divine intervention such as spoken of in the book of Acts...The days slowly passed, lengthening into weeks... months passed...." Dr. Miller then describes the power of the Holy Spirit as He suddenly came to the Mendoza Church: "A rushing wind swept into the room...although we didn't realize it at the time; the Holy Spirit was being out-poured, not only upon us, but upon the whole of Argentina in a new way—an outpouring that would later reach out into the farthest corners of this mighty country...In early June, 1949, that River began to flow out to Argentina in a new and tremen-dous way."[15]

One of the high points of the revival was the miraculous healing of eczema that came to Argentine dictator President Peron in answer to the prayers of American healing evangelist Tommy Hicks and the consequent presidential permission for Hicks to preach in the great Huracan Stadium, the largest sta-dium in Argentina, with its capacity for 180,000 people. Dr. Miller describes the meetings:

> "Night after night the healing virtue of Jesus flowed out to the thousands who released their faith in God. Outstand-ing healings took place, too numerous to recount...The lame were walking, the paralyzed set free. The blind were seeing, stretcher cases healed. Ambulances brought invalid patients and returned empty. Life and health flowed like a river, for God had come to Argentina...Nightly the crowds increased until the stadium could seat no more...a giant waving field of ready-to-be harvested grain...For blocks around the stadium in every direction a great sea of human-ity gathered...Messages reached them through loudspeak-ers...God was visiting Argentina in a sovereign way. He was making a whole nation conscious of His Name, His power and the reality of His gospel. No more could people blindly accept the claims of an oft-times depraved cler-gy...For a time Catholicism remained the state religion, but in name only...Salvation, real and certain, came to many homes. The hearts of thousands were turned from their sins....The blood of Jesus washed people every whit clean and whole. Traditional church people received the

---

15. Dr. R. Edward Miller, *Cry for Me Argentina* (Brentwood, Essex, England: Sharon Publications Ltd., 1988), 22-28.

baptism of the Holy Spirit...A million chains were broken from the minds and hearts of men. The 'strong man' (Matt. 12:28-29) of Argentina was bound...."[16]

This revival would continue in power throughout Argentina during the remainder of the twentieth century, sparking other great moves of God, as we shall shortly see.

The Healing Revivals of the Late 1940's and the 1950's

Closely connected with the Latter Rain anointing, and yet different in emphasis, were the healing revivalists of this mid-twentieth century era. Foremost among these were two different men: William Marrion Branham (1909–1965) and Granville Oral Roberts (b. 1918). Branham, a simple Baptist preacher who was introduced into Pentecostalism through the Oneness Pentecostal stream, rose to prominence in his 1947 massive union meetings in which hundreds of miracles and marvels were reported. He is recognized by many as "the person God used to initiate the Healing Revival of the late forties and early fifties."[17] It was also during Branham's autumn of 1947 meetings in Vancouver, B.C., that pastors and teachers from North Battleford, Saskatchewan, were deeply stirred to seek God for a visitation, thus sparking the Latter Rain outpouring in early 1948. In January 1948, Branham held a large revival in Pensacola, Florida (a city destined for a yet greater move of God in the mid 1990's).

Simplistic and halting, William Branham was an anointed prophet to his generation until his untimely accidental death on Christmas Eve 1965. Unfortunately, the aftermath of Branham's death revealed something of the unhealthy and eerie personality cult that had grown up around him. Some expected him to be resurrected on Easter Day (he was finally buried on April 11, 1966, nearly three and a half months after his death); some of

---

16. *Ibid.*, 43-49.

17. Eddie L. Hyatt, *2000 Years of Charismatic Christianity* (Tulsa: Hyatt International Ministries, 1996), 182.

Floods Upon the Dry Ground

214

his disciples claimed him to be the second Elijah, others believed him to be "God, born of a virgin"; yet others believed him to be "the Lord Jesus Christ," and still others declared him to be "the last-days prophet" whose messages were considered "oral Scripture." It is undoubtedly for these reasons that the Lord removed him.

Different from the more crude William Branham was Holiness Pentecostal preacher Oral Roberts, who was only 29 years old when he began his preaching ministry. Especially in his early years Oral Roberts was the instrument of God for many outstanding healings and miracles. Roberts' talent and organizational skill pushed him to the forefront of the healing-revival scene; he then went on to found a multi-million-dollar ministry complex at Tulsa, Oklahoma: Oral Roberts University.

The hall of fame of the healing-revivalists included others, some of whom we have previously mentioned: missionary-statesman Joseph Mattsson-Boze, O.L. Jaggers, Jack Coe, William Freeman, Thomas Wyatt of Portland, Oregon (publisher of *Wings of Healing*), missionary pioneer T.L. Osborne (publisher of *Faith Digest*),[18] and the beclouded Asa A. (A.A.) Allen, who in his time was an unusually anointed miracle worker. Nevertheless, Allen died alone in June of 1970 in his San Francisco motel room, allegedly of cirrhosis of the liver caused by acute alcoholism. Others of the above have also since gone to be with the Lord.

To the list of healing ministries can also be added Franklin Hall who attained popularity through the *Atomic Power with God Through Prayer and Fasting* concepts (the principles of which influenced many of the other healers), missionary crusader and evangelist Morris Cerullo and the "new anointing," and evangelists W.V. Grant, David Nunn, Rex Humbard,

18. "As they approached their seventies it was said of this husband/wife team [T.L. and Daisy (1924–1995) Osborne] that they had preached the Gospel to more people, face-to-face, than anyone to that point in history" (Hyatt, *op. cit.*, 184).

Jimmy Swaggart, Robert W. Shamback, David Terrell, and Kenneth Hagin. Gordon Lindsay, along with the *Voice of Healing* magazine and *Voice of Healing* conventions, sought to provide cohesion within the healing revivals. In this role, one observer described Lindsay as "the unfortunate conductor of an unruly orchestra."

Through often very imperfect vessels, the power of God was nonetheless displayed. The blind saw, the lame walked, the deaf heard, and the poor had the gospel preached to them.

The decline of institutional Pentecostalism in the 1940's created a vacuum that many eagerly sought to fill. But amidst the miraculous demonstrations and the mighty signs and wonders were often to be found off-color financial and moral practices, power struggles, human egoism and arrogance, independence, rivalry, and dissension. To one of these renowned healing evangelists the Lord allegedly spoke audibly at the very end of his life: "All that you have built is wood, hay, and stubble."[19]

David Edwin Harrell, Jr., comments on this era:

"Gordon Lindsay, who continued to believe that the revival was a great move of God, increasingly denounced the personal ambition and jockeying for position among the evangelists. In 1962, he admitted that many evangelists had adopted questionable methods and he condemned those who continually played on highly sensational themes. Evangelist David Nunn recalled that Lindsay told him privately, 'The day of the evangelist is over.' Many of the ministers had declined, according to Lindsay, 'largely because of a lack of humility and because of a tendency to self-exaltation.' He was sickened by the increasing emphasis on money. The public, Lindsay believed, had every reason to believe that the revival was 'phony'; the unethical conduct of some of the evangelists had become a serious obstacle to the charismatic message. Lindsay later concluded that even at the height of the revival, many of the

---

19. See 1 Corinthians 3:10-15.

evangelists 'hadn't prayed through, they hadn't touched God for their ministry, they just put up their banner.' By the late 1950's he was deeply displeased and discouraged."[20]

By the late 1950's, the healing revivals had largely run their course. One by one, idolized healing personalities were taken off the scene by premature death; others just sank into relative obscurity. Few survived to the end of the twentieth century.

The 1960's were ripe for a fresh work of the Holy Spirit. Eddie L. Hyatt makes this connection: "The Healing Revival provided an important link between the Pentecostal Movement and the Charismatic Renewal which began around 1960. As the Healing Revival waned, the Charismatic Renewal emerged to an even larger and more receptive audience. Several of those who had played prominent roles in the Healing Revival now became instrumental in the successes of the Charismatic Movement."[21]

Other Evangelical Awakenings in the Mid-Twentieth Century

The Hebrides Revival of 1949

In the early hours of a winter morning in 1949, in a little cottage near Barvas village on the windswept Isle of Lewis in the Scottish Hebrides just off of Scotland's western coast, two women were earnestly praying—Peggy Smith, 84 years old and blind, and her sister Christine, two years younger and doubled over with arthritis. They had been in prayer for revival for months, but on this particular morning the Lord gave them a promise: "I will pour water upon him that is thirsty, and floods upon the dry ground...."[22] The devastating effects of World War II had left in its wake a confused and worldly younger

---

20. David Edwin Harrell, Jr., *All Things Are Possible: The Healing & Charismatic Revivals in Modern America* (Bloomington: Indiana University Press, 1975), 139.

21. Hyatt, *op. cit.*, 185.

22. Isaiah 44:3 KJV.

generation, and revival was the only hope for these young people. At the same time God had also spoken to a group of men praying in a barn in Barvas. Kneeling in the straw, they too pled with God for revival. Around 10 p.m., a young deacon stood up and read: "Who shall ascend into the hill of the Lord? or who shall stand in His holy place? He that hath clean hands, and a pure heart...."[23] He then challenged the group: "Are our hands clean? Are our hearts pure?" As these men continued in soul-searching repentance, at four in the morning the awesome presence of God suddenly swept into the barn. Some "fell prostrate on the floor...revival had come and the power that was let loose in that barn shook the whole community of Lewis."

In a vision, the Lord had previously revealed to the blind lady, Peggy Smith, not only that revival was coming, but also the identity of the instrument He had chosen to use: Duncan Campbell. Scotsman Duncan Campbell described the outpouring on a humble cottage prayer meeting: "...We were there on our faces before God. Three o'clock in the morning came and GOD SWEPT IN. About a dozen men and women lay prostrate on the floor, speechless...we knew that the forces of darkness were going to be driven back, and men were going to be delivered. We left the cottage at 3 A.M. to discover men and women seeking God...There was a light in every home, no one seemed to think of sleep."[24]

Later that morning, Campbell went to the church building. It was crowded. Buses came from every part of the island to meetings that God Himself had called. All over the church building men and women were crying out for mercy. Some fell to the floor; many wept. It was 4 a.m. the following morning before Campbell pronounced the benediction (for the second time). The meetings went on for weeks and then they spread to the neighboring parishes. A powerful feature of this revival

---

23. Psalm 24:3-4 KJV.

24. Campbell, as quoted by Colin C. Whittaker, *Great Revivals* (Springfield, MO: Radiant Books, 1984), 183.

was the overwhelming sense of the presence of God. His holy presence was everywhere, and sinners found themselves unable to escape it.

From 1949 to 1952, the move of God spread mightily throughout the Hebrides, and in 1957, God again poured out His Spirit. Typical was the village of Arnol. In the face of strong opposition, the saints were praying. And "before midnight, God came down, the mountains flowed down at His presence, and a wave of revival swept the village...in a matter of minutes...men and women were on their faces in distress of soul."[25]

Of the fruits of the Hebrides revival—whole towns were turned to God. "In homes, barns and loom-sheds, by the roadside, on the peatstack, men could be found calling upon God." Of various bands of converts it was stated: "God is maintaining them all: not one of them has gone back." Many young people heard the call of God and entered the ministry; others answered the call to foreign missions fields. A covenant-keeping God had stepped down from heaven in the middle of the twentieth century, sending shock waves of expectation around the world!

The College Revivals of 1947–1950

Under the sponsorship of Henrietta Mears, director of Christian Education at First Presbyterian Church of Hollywood, California, several conferences were held at Forest Home in the San Bernadino Mountains of Southern California in the spring and summer of 1947. Hundreds of college students from all over the country were present, among them Bill Bright, who had become a Christian only a few months earlier. "They prayed on into the late hours of the night, confessing sin, asking God for guidance, and seeking the reality and power of the Holy Spirit. There was much weeping and crying out to the Lord...Then, the fire fell...God answered their prayer with a vision. They saw before them the college campuses of the world, teeming with unsaved students, who held in their hands the power to change the world.

---

25. *Ibid.*

The college campuses—they were the key to world leadership, to world revival!"[26]

As a direct result, Bill Bright gave up secular business and began preparing for campus work. Billy Graham also had "a powerful experience with the Holy Spirit" during these Forest Home meetings.[27] Others met by God were Jim Rayburn, director of Young Life, and Richard C. Halverson and Louis H. Evans. One of the fruits of this visitation was the forming of the Hollywood Christian Group, which influenced for Christ Colleen Townsend (who became the wife of Louis Evans), Roy Rogers, Dale Evans, and other Hollywood stars. Billy Graham launched his first film crusade employing the talents of this Hollywood Christian Group.

September of 1948 saw the first Pacific Palisades Ministers' Conference near Los Angeles, influenced by Armin Gesswein, a Norwegian Lutheran revivalist through whom an awakening had come in late 1946 at Prairie Bible Institute in Alberta, Canada. The 1949 Conference was described by Norman Grubb, son-in-law of the famous missionary C.T. Studd (and Studd's successor as director of World Evangelism Crusade Mission): "Many were on their faces till 1 A.M. confessing need and failure. Very many had come forward to have hands laid on them for a new experience of the Holy Spirit in themselves and their churches...."[28] Similar visitations came to Minneapolis in 1948 and then in Los Angeles in 1949, in preparation for Billy Graham's campaign there. Similar pastors' Revival Prayer Fellowships sprang up in many other places across North America.

Armin Gesswein, Billy Graham, and others began to meet early in the morning to intercede for revival. Revivals also began to break out in Christian colleges in 1949 and 1950.

---

26. Ethel May Baldwin and David V. Benson, *Henrietta Mears and How She Did It!* (Glendale, CA: Gospel Light Publications, 1966), 232.

27. Winkie Pratney, *Revival—Its Principles and Personalities* (Lafayette, LA: Huntington House, 1994), 155.

28. J. Edwin Orr, *Second Evangelical Awakening in America* (London: Marshall, Morgan & Scott, 1952), 161-162, as quoted by Riss, *op. cit.*, 131.

Bethel College in St. Paul, Minnesota, was touched: "The Holy Spirit has wrought a marvelous work indeed on our campus and we praise Him for it...There was confession of every known sin, and a cleansing of heart and the preparing of vessels to be used of the Lord for His glory."[29]

The flames of revival spread to Wheaton, North Park, Houghton, Asbury, Seattle Pacific, Simpson Bible Institute, the University of Washington, Multnomah School of the Bible, Westmont, John Brown University, Northern Baptist Theological Seminary, California Baptist Seminary, Lee College, Nyack, Baylor University, and Fuller Theological Seminary. National newspapers and *Time* and *Life* carried reports of the revival. The visitation at Asbury was thus described by Dr. W.W. Holland, chairman of the division of philosophy and religion at Asbury: "The floodgates of heaven lifted and God moved into our midst as I have never before witnessed. The Holy Spirit fell... and everything broke lose... the Divine presence was so pronounced...."[30] Dr. V. Raymond Edman, president of Wheaton spoke of the Wheaton awakening as "days of heaven upon earth." J. Stewart Brinsfield, president of Lee College, reported: "The gifts of the Spirit have been manifested among faculty and students alike. To date practically every unsaved person has been brought to Christ...We had no way to count the numbers who received the Holy Ghost...People sought God by the hundreds. This was really a mass revival."

These revivals saw the creation of campus ministries such as Campus Crusade for Christ and the Inter-Varsity Christian Fellowship, and the names of Southern Baptist evangelist Billy Graham, Carl Henry, Harold Ockenga, Robert Cook, Bill Bright, and other evangelical leaders all became intertwined with these revival moves. Other important evangelists of this

---

29. Henry C. Wingblade, president of Bethel College. *The Standard* (Chicago, May 6 & 13, 1949), as quoted by J. Edwin Orr, *Campus Aflame: Dynamic of Student Religious Revelation* (Glendale, CA: Regal Books, 1971), 171.

30. Holland, as quoted by Henry C. James, *God's People Revived: An Account of the Spontaneous Revival at Asbury College in February 1950* (Wilmore, KY: Asbury Theological Seminary, 1957), 7-8.

era were Chuck Templeton, Tom Rees, Bryan Green, Mervin Rosell, Bob Jones, Jr., Hyman Appelman, and Alan Redpath.

Evangelist Billy Graham (b. 1918)

Billy Graham's eight-week, fall of 1949, campaign in Los Angeles, California, was sponsored by *Christ for Greater Los Angeles*, in cooperation with 1,000 churches of all denominations. The gospel was preached to 350,000, and over 3,000 made decisions for Christ. Television star Stuart Hamblen, "under great conviction," awakened Graham from his sleep by telephone and asked him to pray with him. Olympic runner Louis Zamperini and wiretapper Jim Vaus were also converted. Los Angeles was "the spark that set revival fires burning across the nation." Graham had declared: "I believe the greatest need...is that our men and women who profess the name of Jesus Christ be filled with the Spirit...."

The publicity given to the Billy Graham campaign in Los Angeles paved the way for meetings in Boston, Massachusetts; Columbia, South Carolina; and Portland, Oregon. Of the Boston meetings Dr. Harold J. Ockenga reported: "...All of New England is stirred...as a result of the outpouring of the Holy Spirit during the Billy Graham evangelistic campaign in Boston...Hundreds accepted Christ every night."[31] The meetings in Columbia were attended by 40,000 people, including the governor of South Carolina, J. Strom Thurmond. Thousands received Christ. Later in the 1950's the great New York City campaign stirred the city for Christ for months.

Over the years Billy Graham would call "upon more than 100,000,000 people to 'accept Jesus Christ as...personal Savior,' " and 2,874,082 men and women would step forward to do just that.[32] Graham has not been without controversy. Whereas George Bush called him "America's pastor," Harry Truman called him a "counterfeit." Entertainer Pat Boone considered Graham "the greatest person since Jesus," but fundamentalist

---

31. Harold J. Ockenga, article, *Christian Life*, as quoted by Ivan Q. Spencer, "Revival is Breaking," *Elim Pentecostal Herald*, 21:213 (March 1950), 8.

32. *Time* Magazine, November 15, 1993.

Bob Jones II stated that Graham "has done more harm to the cause of Christ than any other living man." But Graham has weathered both applause and derision—"his honor intact." No moral or financial scandal casts its ugly shadow on him; he has lived his own preaching: "You cannot follow Jesus unless you are ready to deny yourself."

Worldwide Revivals

In the mid-twentieth century, God moved mightily, not only in the Western world, but around the globe. Bob Finley, founder of *International Students*, stated, "When Bob Pierce, Gill Dodds and I were invited to Korea we discovered that our Lord had brought us into the midst of a revival that might well have been lifted out of the pages of the book of Acts."

Nicholas Bhengu (called "The Black Billy Graham" by *Time* Magazine) began his first big crusade in Port Elizabeth, South Africa, in 1945. As Bhengu preached, the sick were healed. On one occasion, it was reported that a cripple suddenly jumped up, shouted, and threw away his crutches; he walked, then ran— throwing the crowd into an uproar. In nation after nation, the fire of God was falling afresh.

On January 8, 1956, five missionaries were slain on the Curaray Beach in Auca territory in Ecuador—Jim Elliot, Peter Fleming, Ed McCully, Roger Youderian, and Nate Saint. Their lives would be, as was David Brainerd's life two centuries before them, grains of wheat that would fall into the earth to die, but that would live again in a fresh new wave of missionaries inspired by their commitment to Christ.

Indonesia saw a tremendous revival in the 1960's. In the first three years of the revival, some 200,000 converts were added to the churches. Marion Allen of the C.M.A. noted that almost every type of New Testament miracle was witnessed.

Borneo also saw a tremendous revival in the 1970's, in answer to the fervent prayer of earnest missionaries.

Several Other Momentous Mid-Century Happenings

Several other momentous happenings must be taken into account as shapers of the history of the Church in the mid-1900's and, indirectly, contributors to the ongoing revival and restoration work of the Holy Spirit.

Foremost among these was the birthing of the World Council of Churches at Amsterdam, Holland, in 1948, with some 147 churches from 54 different countries represented. The World Council of Churches defined itself as "a fellowship of Churches which accept our Lord Jesus Christ as God and Saviour." Their original statement was simply that "here at Amsterdam we have committed ourselves afresh to Him, and have covenanted with one another in constituting this *World Council of Churches*. We intend to stay together." The inability of the Council to speak directly to the issues of biblical truth and evangelical experience has caused widespread rejection of the Council by concerned evangelical leaders.

For all its apparent shortcomings, in 1961, in New Delhi, the Third General Assembly of the World Council impressively declared: "We believe that the unity which is God's will and His gift to His Church is being visible as all in each place who are baptized into Jesus Christ and confess Him as Lord and Saviour are brought by the Holy Spirit into one fully committed fellowship." In this spirit, many old-line denominations found themselves wide open for the Charismatic renewal of the 1960's and that true unity created by the bond of the Holy Spirit Himself.

To this end, and no less momentous, was the twenty-first Ecumenical Council of the Roman Catholic Church, Vatican II, the first such council since the notorious Vatican I of 1869–1870. Opened by the well-respected and loved Pope John XXIII on October 11, 1962, the Council continued through 1965 under the direction of Pope Paul VI, who had then been elected supreme pontiff on June 21, 1963. The whole spirit of the Council was in accord with Pope John's historic prayer for "a new Pentecost." It is not surprising, therefore, to read in the twelfth article of *Lumen Gentium*, the Dogmatic Constitution on the Church,

> "It is not only through the sacraments and church ministries that the same Holy Spirit sanctifies and leads the people of God and enriches it with virtues. Allotting His gifts 'to everyone according as he will' (I Corinthians 12:11), He distributes special graces among the faithful of every rank. By these gifts He makes them fit and ready to undertake the various tasks and offices advantageous for the renewal and upbuilding of the Church, according to the words of the Apostle: 'The manifestation of the Spirit is given to everyone for profit' (I Corinthians 12:7). These charismatic gifts, whether they be the most outstanding or the more simple and widely diffused, are to be received with thanksgiving and consolation, for they are exceedingly suitable and useful for the needs of the Church."[33]

Little wonder, with this encouragement, that within just several years after the close of Vatican II, the Roman Catholic Church should have been deeply involved in the Pentecostal movement, as we shall soon note.

The Charismatic Movement (1960–1979): "A New Wave"

As wreckage from the "Latter Rain" revival and the Healing revivals of the 1950's lay strewn on the shoreline of the mid-twentieth century, a new wave began to form in the early 1960's. This was the beginning of the Charismatic movement, destined to become the most widespread and most far-reaching visitation of the Holy Spirit to date. In it was to be found for many an even fuller completion of the promise, "In the last days...I will pour forth of My Spirit upon all mankind..."[34]

This fresh movement of the Holy Spirit had some of its initial beginnings in the ministry of the Full Gospel Businessmen's

---

33. Walter M. Abbott, S.J., ed., *The Documents of Vatican II* (New York: Guild Press, 1966), 30.

34. See Acts 2:17 and Joel 2:28.

Fellowship International, born in Los Angeles in 1951 under the inspiration of wealthy California dairyman Demos Shakarian and Healing evangelist Oral Roberts. Throughout the 1950's and the 1960's the F.G.B.M.F.I. became an instrument in the hands of the Lord to open the hearts of many non-Pentecostal denominational businessmen, and later their ministers, to the Pentecostal experience.

The Charismatic movement also derived much momentum from the life and labors of three denominational ministers in particular: David du Plessis, Dennis Bennett, and Harald Bredesen. David du Plessis, himself baptized in the Holy Spirit in 1918 in South Africa, was a leader in the classical Pentecostal movement and a minister in the Assemblies of God in the United States until 1962, when he was "disfellowshipped" by his brethren for his contacts with the World Council of Churches, whom he had greatly influenced for the neo-Pentecostal cause. Richard Quebedeaux in his book, *The New Charismatics*, commented on David du Plessis: "No single person is more responsible for neo-Pentecostal growth throughout the world than David du Plessis ....Michael Harper calls him 'our Pentecostal father-in-God.' Du Plessis terms himself a Pentecostal 'ecumaniac,' and he is widely known in Charismatic Renewal circles simply as 'Mr. Pentecost.' "[35]

Tireless in his pursuit of Pentecostal "dialogue" with the Vatican and in his pursuit of relationship with the non-Pentecostal ecclesiastical officials of the World Council of Churches, du Plessis had done much "to 'dignify' the Pentecostal experience and message in the minds of an heretofore skeptical and belittling ecclesiastical establishment."[36] David du Plessis rightly takes the place of as a true spiritual father in the Charismatic renewal within institutional Christianity, having influenced

35. Richard Quebedeaux, *The New Charismatics* (New York: Doubleday & Co., 1976), 92.

36. *Ibid.*, 54.

thousands with the dynamic of the Pentecostal message and experience.

Dennis Bennett, an Episcopal Englishman, likewise played a historical role in the unfolding of the Charismatic renewal. It was in his Van Nuys, California, parish, from the fall of 1959 through the spring of 1960, that the Lord began to pour out an unusual measure of His Spirit upon the people. By April 1960, there were some 70 members of St. Mark's Episcopal Church who had received the Pentecostal experience, and by the summer of 1960, both *Time* and *Newsweek* had carried the startling news worldwide. In the heat of the unfavorable notoriety that was generated, Bennett resigned, only to be invited by the bishop of Olympia, Washington, to become vicar of a small, bankrupt mission church of some 200 communicants in Seattle, Washington. Within a year, 85 of its members had received the "baptism in the Holy Spirit," and they became the thriving St. Luke's Episcopal Church of Seattle, attended by thousands every week. This victory served to open doors for Bennett and the Charismatic renewal both in the Episcopal denomination and in other denominational groups as well, especially Lutherans and Presbyterians.

Harald Bredesen, a mild-mannered, mystical man of God, received the "baptism in the Holy Spirit" in the 1950's. He became pastor of the First Reformed Church at Mt. Vernon, New York. In October of 1962 Harald was then instrumental in bringing the Pentecostal message to Yale University; from there it soon spread to Dartmouth, Stanford, and Princeton, giving the Charismatic movement further credibility and influence in the United States and helping to pave the way for the advent of the largely neo-Pentecostal Jesus movement among the youth (1967–1975). Winkie Pratney describes the "Jesus people" phenomenon in these words: "Full of zeal, often with strange ideas and interpretations, not always of unquestionable purity or orthodoxy, they nevertheless exploded across the nation, forcing most of the traditional churches to either re-examine their approaches or react in horror."[37] By the early 1970's it was estimated that there were 300,000 Jesus people.

Through Bredesen's influence many Christians were brought into the Pentecostal experience from a whole cross section of the institutional Church, including entertainer Pat Boone from Church of Christ background. Other neo-Pentecostal leaders who emerged from within the historical Church include Larry Christenson, pastor of Trinity Lutheran Church, San Pedro, California; Robert Frost, then professor of biology at Westmont College, Santa Barbara, California; Graham Pulkingham, former rector of the Episcopal Church of the Redeemer, Houston, Texas; Howard Ervin, American Baptist clergyman; and "Brick" Bradford from the Presbyterian denomination. Within several decades the Charismatic movement spread to all the 150 major Protestant denominations of the world, impacting millions of people.

Other Shapers of the Movement

The Charismatic movement stood as a totally decentralized movement. It spread around the whole world and invaded the ranks of every major denomination. It spiritually enlivened hundreds of millions of people worldwide, and became the theme of countless news reports and magazine articles. It became a movement unlike anything observed to date in the history of the Christian Church. Its leadership sprang from a wide range of backgrounds and emphases, all clustered around the common Pentecostal experience of Acts chapter 2.

We have already noted the names of some of the well-known "in-church" Charismatic movement leaders within various of the established denominations. To this roster can also be added other names of men of a transdenominational character, who also helped to shape the movement into its ongoing form: author Michael Harper, editor of *Renewal* magazine and director of Fountain Trust in Great Britain; Ralph Wilkerson,

---

37. Winkie Pratney, *op. cit.*, 170.

who, in 1960, founded Melodyland Christian Center, across the street from Disneyland in Anaheim, California; Rodman Williams, current professor at Regent University; author Jamie Buckingham from the Tabernacle Church in Melbourne, Florida (now with the Lord); Ken Sumrall formerly of the Liberty Church in Pensacola, Florida; Kenneth Hagin; John Osteen; Dick Benjamin; former A.L.C. evangelist Herbert Mjorud; Gerald Derstine, formerly a Mennonite pastor, who had experienced revival in Northern Minnesota; David Wilkerson, an Assemblies of God minister who founded *Teen Challenge* (presently pastor of Times Square Church, a church experiencing years of revival in New York City); Don Basham and W.J. "Ern" Baxter (both presently with the Lord); Bob Mumford, Derek Prince, Charles Simpson, and John Poole, all formerly connected with the Christian Growth Ministries of Fort Lauderdale, Florida, and contributors to its *New Wine* magazine; and various Jewish Charismatic leaders, such as Arthur Katz, Mike Brown, Mike Evans, Stan Telchin, and Moishe Rosen. *Jews for Jesus* was founded in 1970, and was aggressive in evangelism. "More Jews are being won to Christ in the USA since New Testament times. There are variously estimated to be between 30,000 and 100,000 Messianic Christians; about 15-20,000 have retained their cultural distinctives and meet in Messianic congregations."[38] From Gaithersburg, Maryland, Daniel C. Juster leads in the oversight of a number of these congregations.

The Charismatic outpouring was also furthered by its several widely-viewed television outreaches: C.B.N.'s *700 Club* with Pat Robertson and Jim Bakker's former *PTL Club.*

Various publishing ventures also served to spread the movement like a prairie grassfire and shape its conduct. Among these were Dan Malachuk's Logos International of Plainfield, New Jersey, and Bethany House Publishers of

---

38. Patrick Johnstone, *Operation World* (Grand Rapids, MI: Zondervan, 1993), 567.

Minneapolis, Minnesota. Enough could not be said for the tremendous value of these printed materials, and others like them, in giving direction and impetus to the Charismatic movement. One such early volume was John L. Sherrill's, *They Speak With Other Tongues*. Of benefit to many were also the foundational teachings of Watchman Nee (Ni To-sheng, [1903–1972]), one of China's great apostles in the 1900's. Foremost among these was his *Normal Christian Church Life*. The vision of many within the Charismatic movement for the fuller restoration of the Body of Christ was linked to these printed teachings of Nee.

But unfortunately, out of this very soil sprang up yet another American sect, the Anaheim, California-based Local Church movement of Witness Lee (1905–1997), one-time co-laborer with Watchman Nee in China.

And so the Spirit of God continued to fall throughout the 1960's and the 1970's, and in the wake of this phenomenal revival came a new vision for love and for unity among born-again brothers and sisters, a further plane in the renewal, revival, and restoration of the Church of Jesus Christ.

The Phenomenon of Catholic Pentecostals

As the Charismatic movement began to spill over into all the major Protestant denominations throughout the 1960's, the Spirit of God began to do a new and sovereign work within the Roman Catholic Church in the early part of 1967, beginning with the faculty of Duquesne University in Pittsburgh, Pennsylvania. By February 1967, four among them had received the Pentecostal blessing. Within a month, what had been born in their midst at Pittsburgh had spread both to the University of Notre Dame in South Bend, Indiana, and Michigan State University in East Lansing, Michigan. Among the first to receive at Notre Dame were Kevin (then teacher at St. Mary's College, Notre Dame) and Dorothy Ranaghan. By Easter of 1967, about 30 Catholics in the Notre Dame area had been baptized in the Holy Spirit. From Notre Dame and Michigan State, Catholic Pentecostalism quickly spread to the University of Michigan where the Word of God Community, led by Ralph Martin and Steve Clark, took root and flourished; and from there the fires spread across the whole country from parish to parish within the Catholic Church, particularly through the Life in the Spirit seminars.

By the winter of 1970, there were probably about 10,000 Catholics actively involved in the new Pentecostal movement in the United States, and Catholic prayer groups were springing up in Canada, England, New Zealand, Australia, Latin America, continental Europe, Africa, and the Far East. By June 1974, the Charismatic renewal conference at Notre Dame drew an attendance of 30,000, actually a small percentage of the Catholics involved in the expanding renewal. The *Minneapolis Tribune*, on June 12, 1978, then reported that the Charismatic movement "...has an estimated five million Catholic adherents in the United States..." alone. In 25 years, since its inception, the Charismatic movement has touched the lives of over 70,000,000 Catholics in over 120 nations of the world!

The 1980's: The Third Wave

The 1980's were the best of years and the worst of years. In 1983, C. Peter Wagner, Professor of Church Growth at Fuller Theological Seminary referred to a "third wave" of the Holy Spirit that was already beginning to spill over into evangelical circles. The *first wave*, Wagner said, had been the Pentecostal revival at the turn of the century; the *second wave* had been the Charismatic renewal of the 60's and 70's, which had particularly influenced the more liberal Protestant denominations and the Roman Catholic Church.[37] The *third wave*, Wagner observed, would have a similar impact on the more conservative evangelicals. Along with Wagner, John Wimber (1934–1997) emerged as a recognized spokesman for the *third wave*.[38] Connected with Wimber was the California-based association of

---

37. See Appendix VI for issues of both concern and encouragement regarding the Roman Catholic Church.
38. Hyatt, *op. cit.*

hundreds of Vineyard churches. *Third wave* practices included prophecy, speaking in tongues, being "slain in the Spirit," shaking, "drunkenness," signs and wonders, and other gifts.

Doctrinally, "third wavers," as Evangelicals, defined being baptized in the Holy Spirit as part of the conversion experience,[41] with *all* new believers possessing the potential to exercise any of the spiritual gifts. C. Peter Wagner summed up the "third wave" doctrinal stance in these words: "Doctrinally the third wave takes the position that the baptism in the Holy Spirit occurs at conversion and is not...subsequent to the new birth. Furthermore the third wave does not consider speaking with other tongues as a validation of the believer's having reached some higher spiritual plane."[42] Except for the Association of Vineyard Churches, the third wave did not become an organized movement. Instead it opened "the door for thousands of mainline evangelicals to practice Pentecostal worship and exercise spiritual gifts, even if they felt uncomfortable with classical Pentecostalism."[43]

The Shepherding Controversy

The shepherding controversy of the mid-1970's to the mid-1980's centered around the teaching ministry of five previously mentioned men—Derek Prince, Bob Mumford, Charles Simpson, Don Basham, and Ern Baxter—whose teachings were widely disseminated through *New Wine* magazine, teaching cassettes, books, and conferences. The most famous of these conferences was the 1977 Kansas City Shepherds' Conference with 50,000 in attendance. At the heart of the controversy were charges of heavy-handed shepherding and discipleship. By the mid-70's both the *Full Gospel Business Men* and Pat Robertson's *700 Club* had ostracized the Fort Lauderdale men on the grounds of "controlling the lives of their followers with the

---

41. See Acts 1:5 with First Corinthians 12:13.

42. C.P. Wagner, "Power of the Spirit: The Third Wave," *AD 2000 Together* (1988): 6-7; quoted by Vinson Synan, *The Holiness-Pentecostal Tradition: Charismatic Movements in the Twentieth Century* (Grand Rapids: W.B. Eerdmans, 1997), 272.

43. Synan, *op. cit.*, 272.

overuse of spiritual authority." By 1983, Derek Prince broke rank with the others, disavowing the controversial shepherding teachings and practices. In 1986, *New Wine* magazine ceased publication and the remaining team members disbanded. In 1989, Bob Mumford issued a public apology and a renunciation of the shepherding extremes. In the course of time other ministries also closed down, dogged by similar charges of extreme discipleship and shepherding.[44]

At this time several completely separate groups also met with denunciation and tragedy as a result of authoritarian abuses. For example, David Berg's "Children of God" authoritarian movement was castigated as a cult group, and in 1978, more than 900 members of the People's Temple, an authoritarian cult, followed their leader, Jim Jones, to suicide in Guyana.

The Fall of the Televangelists

The late 1980's also saw the fall of two Assemblies of God preachers—Jimmy Swaggart (of Baton Rouge, Louisiana) and "PTL" televangelist Jim Bakker (of Charlotte, North Carolina). The cover of the February 1997 edition of *Charisma* magazine, however, carried these words: "Ten Years after the Fall—it's been almost 10 years since the PTL scandal tarnished the image of American Christianity. Today Jim Bakker is asking us to forgive him"; and despite charges of financial and moral impropriety and a five-year prison term, many in the Body of Christ were willing, for Jesus' sake, to do exactly that.

On the positive side of the ledger, the late 80's and the early 90's witnessed the emerging of new American Pentecostal evangelists, including Benny Hinn, Kenneth Copeland, and T.D. Jakes, and others.

A Vision for World Harvest

Apart from the third wave, one of the most powerful stirrings to emerge from the 80's was a vision for world evangelism,

---

44. See *Christianity Today*, August 10, 1984, and *Charisma & Christian Life*, March 1990, concerning *Maranatha Campus Ministries*.

which centered around four world evangelization congresses—two held in New Orleans in 1986 and 1987, as well as two held in 1990 in Indianapolis, Indiana, and in Bern, Switzerland. Billy Graham addressed the 1987 New Orleans Congress by video, "congratulating Pentecostals and Charismatics for their record of world evangelization."[45] In 1960, Pentecostals accounted for 14 percent of all evangelicals (11,000,000 strong); by 1990, they had grown to be 93,000,000 strong, and accounted for over 30 percent of all evangelicals (52 percent if denominational Charismatics were added in).

During the 70's and 80's the Lord used Reinhard Bonnke throughout Southern Africa. His 10,000-seat tent became too small to contain the crowds. In 1980, 100,000 people had made decisions for Christ in his crusades. By 1984, Bonnke had dedicated the world's largest tent, seating over 30,000 people and rising to the height of a *seven-story building*. In Lagos, Nigeria, God raised up the largest Christian church in Africa—William Kumuyi's "Deeper Life Bible Church," which, by 1995, was drawing over 200,000 worshipers each week.

The most remarkable Pentecostal-Charismatic growth had taken place in Latin America, where the majority of believers are Spirit-filled and where nearly 40 percent of the members of the world's Pentecostal denominations live.[46] Brazil is an example of the amazing growth of the Pentecostal-Charismatic Body of Christ in South America in the twentieth century. In 1900, there were less than 100,000 evangelical Christians in Brazil. By 1990, there were 26 million evangelical believers, nearly 18 percent of the whole population of Brazil! And many of these were Pentecostal-Charismatic believers.

The momentum of Spirit-filled life helped create a passion for "a church for every people and the gospel for every person by AD 2000."[47] Of special focus has been the "10/40 Window,"

---

45. Synan, *op. cit.*, 269.
46. Johnstone, *op. cit.*, 65.
47. AD 2000 and Beyond.

a swath of geography from West Africa to East Asia, from 10 degrees north to 40 degrees north of the equator, home to the majority of the world's Muslims, Hindus, and Buddhists— billions of lost souls.

Stunning examples of the new missionary explosion has been the conversion to Christ of more Muslims in the concluding several decades of the twentieth century than ever before in world history, accompanied, at times, by miraculous heavenly interventions, such as what happened during the annual Muslim pilgrimage to Mecca in 1991, when a number of Nigerian Muslim mullahs were praying inside the Grand Mosque, the holiest place in all of Islam. Suddenly "Jesus appeared to them and declared that He was God." The Mullahs were converted to Jesus.[48]

Added to these statistics is the growth of the church in Mongolia. In the revival taking place in the capital city of Inner Mongolia, it is reported that "in 13 years the church has grown from two thousand believers to over 150 thousand with no obvious explanation except the move of the Holy Spirit"![49] On top of statistics such as these is the amazing expectation that by the end of the twentieth century the evangelistic "JESUS" film will have been seen by over five billion people!

As the Body of Christ prepares for a new millennium, it faces formidable challenges: 1) the unfinished task of world evangelism; 2) the worldwide holocaust of abortion;[50] 3) the devastation of large segments of the world's population due to the AIDS virus;[51] and 4) the increase in martyrdom, which was prophesied by Jesus as a sure sign of the last days.[52] According

---

48. George Otis, Jr., *Sentinel Group.*

49. *Mission Network News*, February 3, 1998.

50. Abortion has claimed the lives of over 35 million preborn children in the United States alone since the historic 1973 *Roe v. Wade* decision.

51. "More than 30 million people are infected with one of the 10 subtypes of HIV." (*Time* Magazine, February 16, 1998, 64).

52. Matthew 24:9-14.

to *World Missions Digest* nearly 100,000,000 believers have been martyred in the twentieth century, more than in all the previous 19 centuries combined, according to James Hefly.

The 1990's: A Fresh Wind Is Blowing

Vineyard pastor Randy Clark described the seven years from 1987–1993 as a spiritually "dry season."[53] Others shared the same observation. The spring of 1993 witnessed the devastation of a commune at Waco, Texas, in which 86 followers of cult-leader David Koresh were burned to death. Classical Pentecostalism seemed to have somewhat stagnated; the Charismatic movement appeared to have dried up in many places. Even the "third wave," which by 1990 numbered some 33,000,000 believers worldwide, had become merely a ripple on the sea of humanity. A cry was once again beginning to ascend into the heavens: "O Lord, revive Thy work in the midst of the years...."[54]

Two world events greatly and positively impacted the early 1990's: the collapse of Communism (which had caused the death of some 65,000,000 people, among them many millions of true Christians) and the end of the curse of apartheid in South Africa. Both of these events were followed by outpourings of the Holy Spirit in the former Soviet Union and in South Africa, respectively. It is impressive to realize that the collapse of communism came after a seven-year prayer campaign to that end had been launched in 1983.

The Toronto Blessing

On January 20, 1994, a significant revival broke out at Pastor John Arnott's Airport Vineyard Church in Toronto, Canada. All the historically typical signs of revival were present—holy laughter, falling, shaking, healing, spiritual gifts, and even "animal noises."[55] To Vineyard pastor Randy Clark, the instrument

---

53. In a message brought to Immanuel's Church in Silver Spring, Maryland, in September 1997.
54. Habakkuk 3:2b.
55. See page 143 footnote 4.

the Lord used in the initiation of this visitation, the outpouring was as much of a surprise as it was to the assembled saints. To observers, however, it was noted that the Toronto Blessing had been sparked by the "laughing revival" ministry of South African Rodney Howard-Browne, for Clark had just previously attended a Rodney Howard-Browne meeting.

In the first year of the Toronto revival, the aggregate attendance exceeded 200,000 people, from nearly every nation under heaven. By the end of 1995, that figure had risen to 600,000 first-time visitors, and by the end of 1997, the figure was at 1.8 million visitors. Historian Richard Riss believes the "Toronto Blessing" to be "at the very least on a par with what happened at Azusa Street in 1906." By early 1995, over 9,000 first-time conversions had been recorded. The revival, however, came under serious attack by Hank Hanegraff, president of the Christian Research Institute, who declared the Toronto manifestations to be demonic. Andrew Evans, General Superintendent of the Assemblies of God in Australia, however, voiced support for the revival and warned his brethren not to resist a move of God just because it did not originate with them.[56] Unfortunately, by late 1995, it was reported that John Wimber and other of the leadership of the Association of Vineyard Churches had severed ties with the Toronto Airport Vineyard, which became renamed *Toronto Airport Christian Fellowship*. Although the reason for the breach is complicated, it was significantly impacted by the various outward manifestations of the Holy Spirit.

Holy Trinity Anglican Church in Brompton, London, became a center for the "Toronto Blessing" in England, as the revival spread and began to circle the world.

The Philadelphia Revival

October 1994 saw an unusual visitation of the Holy Spirit at the Roman Catholic Presentation Parish in Wynnewood,

---

56. *Charisma* Magazine, November 1995.

Pennsylvania. Monsignor Vincent M. Walsh, of the Archdiocese of Philadelphia, described the events in a booklet, *Experiencing Revival in the Catholic Church*: "The overwhelming presence of God just filled the group. No one moved. No one wanted to move. God had visited us....Word quickly spread and new people began coming." By July 1995 the prayer group had grown to over 200 and by 1997 the parish sanctuary was filled with many hundreds more. Walsh concludes, "In Revival, the special presence of God predominates...we are all just taken up into God's presence...."[57]

The Pensacola Revival

On Father's Day, June 18, 1995, the "River of God" began to flow in the Brownsville Assembly of God Church in Pensacola, Florida. Weary and worn, Pastor John Kilpatrick had invited Evangelist Steve Hill to minister that morning. Steve Hill had experienced revival in Argentina. He had also visited Toronto and had been "touched by the Lord" at Holy Trinity, Brompton, in London. The Spirit of God fell at the end of that Father's Day service, bringing a revival that continues unabated to this day. The nightly calls to repentance have brought over 100,000 seekers to the altar and over 1,600,000 visitors to the church, as nearly 5,000 persons crowd into the facilities for evening meetings.[58] Fortunately, the Pensacola revival gained the approval of the Assemblies of God leadership in Springfield, Missouri, and numerous local Assemblies have since reported revival fire falling in their own midst. Vinson Synan optmistically observed that "the Toronto and Brownsville revivals indicated that, after nearly a century, the spirit of Azusa Street was very much alive among Pentecostals and Charismatics and that such classical Pentecostal denominations as the Assemblies of God had not yet lost their revival zeal and fire."[59]

---

57. Monsignor Vincent M. Walsh, *Experiencing Revival in the Catholic Church* (Wynnewood, PA: Key of David Publications, 1995), 2, 10.
58. Statistics are from Spring 1997.
59. Synan, *op. cit.*, 278.

Unfortunately, Christian Research Institute Hank Hanegraff launched an even more bitter attack against the Pensacola Revival than against the Toronto Blessing, but a miraculous "reconciliation of heart" took place between Hanegraff and the Pensacola leadership in December 1997, for which many praised God. Dr. Michael Brown of the Brownsville Revival School of Ministry was a primary facilitator of this reconciliation.

Other Revivals During the Mid-to-Late 1990's

The April 7, 1995, *Montgomery Journal* carried an article by Terry Mattingly, communications teacher at Milligan College in Tennessee, entitled: "College Students Discover Revivals." Mattingly reported: "Nobody expected spiritual gusts at Coggin Avenue Baptist in Brownwood, Texas, at 8:30 A.M. on January 22. Certainly, nobody expected the start of a revival that would spread nationwide." Mattingly then traced the path of revival through the year 1995 from campus to campus—Howard Payne University, Houston Baptist University, Olivet Nazarene University, Moorehead State University, Murray State University, Louisiana Tech, Criswell College, Sanford University, Southwestern Baptist Theological Seminary, Trinity International University, and Wheaton College where the first service lasted until 6 a.m., and students filled five garbage bags with alcohol, pornography, and other evidence of their sins. Within days, more than half of Wheaton's 2,200 students were taking part. "Confessions of pride, hatred, lust, sexual immorality, cheating, dishonesty, materialism, addictions and self-destructive behavior were heard," chaplain Steve Kellough reported to the Wheaton faculty and staff.

Melbourne, Florida

On New Year's Day of 1995, Randy Clark was invited to speak at the Tabernacle Church in Melbourne, Florida, the church pastored by godly Charismatic author and speaker Jamie Buckingham until his untimely death. The Tabernacle Church meetings were sponsored by five local churches and "an unusual revival broke out immediately, accompanied with holy laughter, falling under the power of the Spirit, and many dramatic physical healings...thousands of people flocked to meetings held six days a week...."[60] By August of 1995, *Charisma* reported "more than 65,000 people now have attended the meetings...Hundreds of people have publicly professed faith in Jesus Christ."

Houston, Texas

October 6, 1996, saw the start of an outpouring of the Holy Spirit on the 3,000-member Christian Tabernacle, a charismatic church on the eastside of Houston. Evangelist Tommy Tenney was the instrument God used. All across the building, people fell under the power of the presence of God. Many decisions for Christ took place. There were also outstanding healings, deliverances, and other manifestations of the Holy Spirit—including clouds of glory and angelic manifestations. The centerpiece for discussion in the Houston visitation was the "split pulpit," which was split into two pieces by an apparent stroke of the power of God. A jagged, lightning-bolt-like edge ran from the top to the bottom of the heavy acrylic pulpit. This visitation went on to affect many churches and communities across Houston.

Baltimore, Maryland

Pastor Bart Pierce of Rock Church reported, "On the 19th day of January, 1997, God showed up in our church in a most powerful way...What started like any other ordinary service turned into a massive outpouring of the Glory of God in our midst...our church has become an oasis for those who are dry and thirsty, for those who are desperate for more of God...There is no agenda...Sometimes the atmosphere is filled with weeping and repentance, sometimes it is perfectly quiet and sometimes there is great joy and laughter and dancing...There are hundreds of testimonies of people whose lives have been touched, healed,

---

60. *National and International Religion Report*, April 3, 1995, 2.

delivered, set free, restored...." In Baltimore and in Washington D.C. there are currently various churches standing together for citywide revival in the Baltimore-D.C. corridor, a happening similar to events in 1997 in Cleveland, Ohio, where deep repentance and reconciliation took place on a citywide level in anticipation of revival on the north coast of the United States.

The year 1997 brought the disturbing suicides of nearly 40 members of the Heaven's Gate Cult in San Diego County, California. Yet 1997 also witnessed an estimated 1,000,000 Promise Keepers assembled in repentance and prayer on Yom Kippur, October 4, on the Washington Mall, in the nation's capitol, beseeching God to again to rend the heavens and come down in revival power in both America and around the world. One of the outstanding features of Coach Bill McCartney's *Promise Keepers* movement has been the long-needed thrust for reconciliation between Jews and Gentiles, as well as between whites and blacks and Native Americans and Hispanics and Asians. On the backdrop of centuries of racial discrimination and hatred, in the latter part of the twentieth century there emerged sincere tears of repentance and the joy of reconciliation as brother embraced brother for Jesus' sake.

The August 24, 1997, *Washington Post* also reported: "Surrounded by a candlelit ocean of young Catholic pilgrims from around the world, Pope John Paul II preached tonight a message of Christian reconciliation marked by an apology for the massacre of thousand of Protestants by French Catholics exactly four and a quarter centuries ago. 'Christians did things which the Gospel condemns', the pope said...He was referring to the slaughter of thousands—and perhaps tens of thousands—in the streets of Paris on St. Bartholomew's Day—August 24, 1572.[61] 'Our common love of Christ pushes us relentlessly to seek the path of unity', the pope said...."

Things marvelous to behold have indeed begun to happen!

---

61. See page 102.

Some Concluding Thoughts

Our study of Church history began with the explosion in the city of Jerusalem at 9 a.m. on a quiet Sunday morning around the year A.D. 30. That was Pentecost Sunday morning, and the explosion was caused by the outpouring of the Holy Spirit Himself. It was a powerful beginning, and a powerful century followed. As initially stated, we were compelled to trace with grief the first 1,000 years of Church history. We observed the the ebbing of that great floodtide of God's presence until it became but a stagnant pool in the Dark Ages, offset only by those sovereign floods of the Holy Spirit that the God of all grace was pleased to pour out from time to time upon the dry and thirsty ground. We have also traced the gradual rise of a fresh tide of God's Holy Spirit in the 600 years of reformation and restoration that followed. We were also able to ride the crest of those great waves of revival and recovery that were so evident in the 1700's, the 1800's, and especially the 1900's—right through to this time of this writing.

Vinson Synan comments, "As the 1990's drew to a close, reports of other astonishing revivals...continued to pour in from all over the world, filling the pages of religious periodicals and Internet websites in the United States and abroad...a new wave of revival that would likely continue through the end of the millennium."[62] And so we have seen how 120 Spirit-filled believers at the beginning of the first century have grown to become nearly one half billion Spirit-filled believers by the end of the twentieth century, the veritable "army of God" and the most powerful force ever seen for the evangelization of the whole world!

We now stop to catch our breath for a moment at the end of this great twentieth century, and we look expectantly to the twenty-first century, looking for the fullness of that final floodtide of God's promised Holy Spirit—an end-time revival

---

62. Synan, *op. cit.*, 278.

destined, in the words of Holy Scripture, to bring about the greatest harvest of souls ever recorded on the pages of human history. And with that revival, we shall see the fuller restoration of the people of God to an expectant virgin simplicity, as the Bride of Christ hails the return of her heavenly Bridegroom to take up His everlasting universal reign. Indeed, it is our cherished hope that we ourselves shall witness in our very own lifetimes that "the kingdom of the world has become the kingdom of our Lord, and of His Christ; and He will reign forever and ever."[63] Amen and amen!

---

63. Revelation 11:15b.

Appendix I

Gnostic Hymn[1]

I was delivered from my bonds,
And am escaped to Thee, my God.
For Thou didst stand by to
(champion my cause; didst)
Redeem me and succour me...
For Thy Person was with me,
And it saved me in Thy grace.

But I received strength and succour from Thee.
Thou didst set lights on my right and my left,
That there might be no darkness about me.
I was bedecked with the covering of Thy Spirit...

I became whole in Thy truth and holy in Thy
righteousness...
I became the Lord's in the Name of the Lord.
I was justified by His lovingkindness
And His peace endureth forever and ever. Amen.

---

1. *Pistis Sophia*, text edited by Carl Schmitt, translation and notes by Violet Macdermot; the Coptic Gnostic Library "Nag Hammadi Studies, V. 9." (Leiden: E.J. Brill, 1978), 301-311. [Information supplied by Freeman Barton, Goddard Library, Gordon-Conwell Theological Seminary, S. Hamilton, MA; Courtesy of Dr. Rik Kline.]

Appendix II

Historian Williston Walker makes the following enlightening comment on the second-century Church's understanding of baptism.

"By the time of Hermas and of Justin the view was general that baptism washed away all previous sins...the great rite of purification, initiation, and rebirth into the eternal life....With the early disciples generally baptism was 'in the name of Jesus Christ'...The Christian leaders of the third century retained the recognition of the earlier form, and in Rome at least, baptism in the name of Christ was deemed valid, if irregular, certainly from the time of Bishop Stephen (254–257).

"Regarding persons baptized, the strong probability is that, till past the middle of the second century, they were those only of years of discretion. The first mention of infant baptism, and an obscure one, was about 185, by Irenaeus....Why infant baptism arose there is no certain evidence. Cyprian...argued in its favor from the doctrine of original sin. Yet the older general opinion seems to have held to the innocency of childhood....Infant baptism did not, however, become universal until the sixth century....

"As to the method of baptism, it is probable that the original form was by immersion, complete or partial. That is implied in Romans 6:4 and Colossians 2:12....Immersion continued as the prevailing practice until the late Middle Ages in the West; in the East it so remains."[1]

John W. Kennedy similarly observes: "Baptismal regeneration was being taught early in the second century, and...of possibly slightly later origin was the baptism of infants...Tertullian, writing in the year 197, condemns the practice along with the practice of baptizing the dead, yet another innovation."[2]

1. Williston Walker, *A History of the Christian Church* (New York: Charles Scribner's Sons, 1959), 87-88.
2. John W. Kennedy, *The Torch of the Testimony* (Gospel Literature Service, 1965; Goleta, CA: Christian Books, reprint), 55.

Appendix III
The Currently Used Text of the "Apostle's Creed"

I believe in God, the Father Almighty,
  Maker of heaven and earth.

And in Jesus Christ, His only Son, our Lord;
  Who was conceived by the Holy Ghost,
  Born of the Virgin Mary;
  Suffered under Pontius Pilate,
  Was crucified, dead, and buried;
  He descended into hell;
  The third day He rose again from the dead;
  He ascended into heaven,
  And sitteth on the right hand of God the Father Almighty;
  From thence He shall come to judge the quick and the dead.

I believe in the Holy Ghost;
  The holy Christian Church,
  The communion of saints;
  The forgiveness of sins;
  The resurrection of the body;
  And the life everlasting. Amen.

Appendix IV

The Nicene Creed

I believe in one God, the Father Almighty, Maker of heaven and earth, and of all things visible and invisible.

And in one Lord Jesus Christ, the only-begotten Son of God, begotten of His Father before all worlds, God of God, Light of Light, Very God of Very God, begotten, not made, being of one substance with the Father; by whom all things were made; who for us men, and for our salvation, came down from heaven, and was incarnate by the Holy Spirit of the Virgin Mary, and was made man; and was crucified also for us under Pontius Pilate. He suffered and was buried; and the third day He rose again, according to the Scriptures; and ascended into heaven, and sits on the right hand of the Father; and He shall come again with glory to judge both the living and the dead; whose kingdom shall have no end.

And I believe in the Holy Spirit, The Lord and Giver of life, who proceeds from the Father (and the Son), who with the Father and the Son together is worshipped and glorified, who spoke by the Prophets. And I believe in one holy Christian and Apostolic Church. I acknowledge one

Baptism for the remission of sins; and I look for the Resurrection of the dead; and the Life of the world to come. Amen.

The Athanasian Creed

Whosoever will be saved, before all things it is necessary that he hold the true Christian faith.

Which faith except every one do keep whole and undefiled, without doubt he shall perish everlastingly.

And the true Christian faith is this: that we worship one God in Trinity, and Trinity in Unity;

Neither confounding the persons, nor dividing the substance.

For there is one person of the Father, another of the Son, and another of the Holy Ghost.

But the Godhead of the Father, of the Son, and of the Holy Ghost, is all one: the glory equal, the majesty coeternal.

Such as the Father is, such is the Son, and such is the Holy Ghost.

The Father uncreated, the Son uncreated, and the Holy Ghost uncreated.

The Father incomprehensible, the Son incomprehensible, and the Holy Ghost incomprehensible.

The Father eternal, the Son eternal, and the Holy Ghost eternal.

And yet they are not three Eternals, but one Eternal.

As also there are not three Uncreated, nor three Incomprehensibles, but one Uncreated, and one Incomprehensible.

So likewise the Father is almighty, the Son almighty, and the Holy Ghost almighty.

And yet they are not three Almighties, but one Almighty.

So the Father is God, the Son is God, and the Holy Ghost is God.

And yet they are not three Gods, but one God.

So likewise the Father is Lord, the Son Lord, and the Holy Ghost Lord.

And yet not three Lords, but one Lord.

For like as we are compelled by the Christian Verity to acknowledge every Person by Himself to be God and Lord;

So are we forbidden by the true Christian religion to say, There be three Gods, or three Lords.

The Father is made of none, neither created, nor begotten.

The Son is of the Father alone, not made, nor created, but begotten.

The Holy Ghost is of the Father, and of the Son; neither made, nor created, nor begotten, but proceeding.

So there is one Father, not three Fathers; one Son, not three Sons; one Holy Ghost, not three Holy Ghosts.

And in this Trinity none is before, or after other; none is greater, or less than another.

But the whole three Persons are coeternal together, and coequal:

So that in all things, as is aforesaid, the Unity in Trinity, and the Trinity in Unity, is to be worshipped.

He therefore that will be saved must thus think of the Trinity.

Furthermore, it is necessary to everlasting salvation that he also believe rightly the incarnation of our Lord Jesus Christ.

For the right faith is that we believe and confess that our Lord Jesus Christ, the Son of God, is God and Man;

God, of the substance of the Father, begotten before the worlds; and Man, of the substance of His mother, born in the world;

Perfect God, and perfect Man, of a reasonable soul and human flesh subsisting.

Equal to the Father, as touching His Godhead; and inferior to the Father, as touching His Manhood.

Who, although He be God and Man, yet He is not two, but one Christ;

One; not by conversion of the Godhead into flesh, but by taking the Manhood into God;

One altogether; not by confusion of substance, but by unity of person.

For as the reasonable soul and flesh is one man, so God and Man is one Christ;

Who suffered for our salvation, descended into hell, rose again the third day from the dead.

He ascended into heaven; He sitteth on the right hand of the Father, God Almighty; from whence He shall come to judge the quick and the dead.

At whose coming all men shall rise again with their bodies, and shall give account for their own works.

And they that have done good shall go into life everlasting; and they that have done evil, into everlasting fire.

This is the true Christian faith, which, except a man believe faithfully, he cannot be saved.

Appendix V

The Story of Darwin's Final Recantation

Lady Hope, who visited Charles Darwin during his last days on earth, has the following to say regarding his views on evolution toward the end of his life:

"It was on a glorious Autumn afternoon when I was asked to go and sit with Charles Darwin. He was almost bedridden for some months before he died. Propped up with pillows, his features seemed to be lit up with pleasure as I entered the room. He waved his hand towards the window as he pointed out the beautiful sunset seen beyond, while in the other he held an open Bible which he was always studying.

" 'What are you reading now?' I asked.

" 'Hebrews,' he answered, 'still Hebrews. The Royal Book, I call it….' Then he placed his fingers on certain passages and commented upon them. I made some allusions to the strong opinions expressed by many unbelievers on the history of the creation and then their treatment of the earlier chapters of the book of Genesis. He seemed distressed, his fingers twitched nervously and a look of agony came across his face as he said—'I was a young

man with unformed ideas. I threw out queries, sugges-
tions, wondering all the time over everything. And to my
astonishment the ideas took like wildfire. People made a
religion of them.' Then he paused and after a few more
sentences on the holiness of God and the grandeur of this
Book, looking at the Bible which he was holding tenderly
at the time, he said: 'I have a summer house in the garden
which holds about thirty people. It is over there (pointing
through the open window). I want you very much to speak
here. I know you read the Bible in the villages. Tomorrow
afternoon I should like the servants on the place, some ten-
ants and a few neighbors to gather there. Will you speak to
them?'

" 'What shall I speak about?' I asked. 'Christ Jesus,' he
replied in a clear emphatic voice, adding in a lower tone,
'and His salvation. Is not that the best theme? And then I
want you to sing some hymns with them. You lead on your
small instrument, do you not?'

"The look of brightness on his face I shall never forget,
for he added, 'If you take the meeting at 3 o'clock this window will be opened and you will know that I am joining
with the singing.' "[1]

---

1. Quoted from the *Bombay Guardian*, March 25, 1916, by Prof. H. Enoch in
"Evolution or Creation" (Union of Evangelical Students of India, P.O. Box
486, Madras 7, India, 1966), 165-167.

Appendix VI

The Different Faces of the Roman Catholic Church at the End of the Twentieth-Century

Three distinctly different reports surfaced in 1997 from within the Roman Catholic Church. They represent different faces of the Roman Catholic Church at the end of the twentieth century. And they are both encouraging and alarming.

First of all, a "Joint Declaration on the Doctrine of Justification" was finalized between the Roman Catholic Church and the Lutheran Churches in 1997. We quote, in part, from this amazing document:

> "The Lutheran Churches and the Roman Catholic Church have together listened to the good news proclaimed in Holy Scripture...We confess together that all persons depend completely on the saving grace of God for their salvation...We confess together that God forgives sin by grace and at the same time frees human beings from sin's enslaving power and imparts the gift of new life in Christ...We confess together that sinners are justified by faith in the saving action of God in Christ...We confess together that persons are justified by faith in the Gospel 'apart from works prescribed by the law'...We confess

together that good works—a Christian life lived in faith, hope and love—follow justification and are its fruits...We give thanks to the Lord for this decisive step forward on the way to overcoming the division of the Church. We ask the Holy Spirit to lead us further toward that visible unity which is Christ's will."[1]

However, on August 25, 1997, *Newsweek* Magazine carried an article of a different nature entitled "Hail Mary." The article discussed "a new dogma of the Roman Catholic faith: that the Virgin Mary is 'Co-Redemptrix, Meadtrix of all graces and advocate for the people of God."

Newsweek reported: "Such a move would elevate Mary's status dramatically beyond what most Christians profess...." *Newsweek* envisioned the results of such a move: "Catholics would be obliged as a matter of faith to accept three extraordinary doctrines: that Mary participates in the redemption achieved by her son, that all graces that flow from the suffering and death of Jesus Christ are granted only through Mary's intercession with her son, and that all prayers and petitions from the faithful on earth must likewise flow through Mary, who then brings them to the attention of Jesus."

Newsweek also commented that this "seems to contradict the basic New Testament belief that 'there is one God and one mediator between God and man, Christ Jesus' (I Timothy 2:5)," and then tersely observed: "In the place of the Holy Trinity, it would appear, there would be a kind of Holy Quartet, with Mary playing the multiple roles of daughter of the Father, mother of the Son and spouse of the Holy Spirit...."

---

1. In a parallel document, "The Gift of Salvation," released on November 17, 1997, and signed by 20 Evangelicals (Dr. Bill Bright and Dr. Charles Colson among them) and 15 Roman Catholic educators (with Father Richard John Neuhaus in the lead), it was co-jointly stated: "We agree that justification is not earned by any good works or merits of our own; it is entirely God's gift, conferred through the Father's sheer graciousness, out of the love that He bears us in His Son, who suffered on our behalf and rose from the dead for our justification....In justification, God, on the basis of Christ's righteousness alone, declares us to be no longer His rebellious enemies, but His forgiven friends...." (*Prison Fellowship Ministries*, newsletter).

French Catholic theologian René Laurentin, an internationally known specialist on Mary, strongly opposed the proposed dogma as "un-Scriptural and an affront to the uniqueness of Christ's redemptive death...." In the wake of the *Newsweek* article, other voices of caution from within the Catholic Church were heard, calling this thinking "theologically inadequate, historically a mistake, pastorally imprudent and ecumenically unacceptable."[2] At the same time, the pope himself sought to calm the waters by stating in a papal audience: "In acknowledging the exceptional gifts which God conferred upon Mary in his love for all mankind, the Christian faithful in no way make her equal to God."[3] Any decision on the part of the Vatican to so elevate Mary could create such a hailstorm of opposition from both evangelical Catholics and Protestants, that the objections of 1517 could pale in comparison.

In August of 1997, and in contrast to the above, Ralph Martin, a Catholic charismatic leader, reported the following in a newsletter concerning his then recent ministry in India: "I was invited to speak at the 25th anniversary celebration of the Catholic charismatic renewal in India, held in Bombay...During the conference, thousands responded to the call to commit their lives to Jesus or come back to Jesus...I met one young Catholic layman who has been led to preach the gospel among tribes in a northern Indian state. He has been instrumental in 25,000 of these tribes-people coming to Jesus and being baptized in the Catholic Church over the past several years. Great signs and wonders are being done through this man including four resurrections from the dead...[At a] retreat center in Southern India...More than a hundred thousand Hindus have come to faith in Jesus through this ministry...."

In the United States, a 1997 Barna Research survey[4] commented on "the rapid expansion of born-again Christians within

---

2. Mariologist Father Salvatore Perrella in the *Catholic Standard* (Catholic News Service, October 1997).

3. October 22, 1997, General Audience.

4. From a Focus on the Family newsletter.

the Catholic Church," noting that almost one-third of all Catholic adults "fit the classification of being born-again." In 1997, that was 16 percent of the total American adult born-again population, one in every six born-again Christians!

At this juncture it is fitting to quote from the Epilogue of the original version of this work, *Root Out of a Dry Ground*. In view of the doctrinal divisions that yet exist among Christians, such as the issues regarding Mary raised earlier, these words encourage us:

"When we look at what actually exists at present...we see a Church that has come a long way in recovery since the Dark Ages. But we see a Church that is still very immature and very much divided (if not in love, then surely in faith). That which is yet on the horizon for this generation is clearly that final forward push towards 'the measure of the stature of the fullness of Christ,' that we may '*all* attain to the unity of the faith, and of the knowledge of the Son of God, to a mature man....' Thus the fervent prophetic prayer of our Lord Jesus in His final hours for the oneness of His church will be answered visibly upon the earth—'that they may *all* be one; even as Thou, Father, art in Me, and I in Thee, that they also may be in Us; that the world may believe that Thou didst send Me.'...The most important thing for us in this generation is that we simply walk very tenderly and softly before the Lord, so as not to second-guess how exactly He shall consummate all things in His church and bring in everlasting righteousness...In every generation He has wrought a brand-new thing. And we are truly on the threshold of a further brand-new working of God that is destined to bring *all* true believers together...that all the world might know and see that He has sent His Son, Jesus, to be the Savior of the world! Hallelujah!"

Appendix VII
Mormon Doctrinal Error

On the following page you will find a reproduction of a page from the Mormon newspaper, the *Millennial Star* (Vol. XV, No. 48 [November 26, 1853], 769). In this particular article, "Adam, Our Father and God," Brigham Young declares that Adam is his God. This is just one example of the doctrinal error that the Mormons initially embraced.

You can find other examples and similar reproductions in "Where Does It Say That?", which is an exposé of Mormonism compiled by Bob Witte. It is available from Gospel Truths, P.O. Box 1015, Grand Rapids, MI 49501.

The Latter=Day Saints'

MILLENNIAL STAR.

HE THAT HATH AN EAR, LET HIM HEAR WHAT THE SPIRIT SAITH
UNTO THE CHURCHES.—*Rev.* ii. 7.

No. 48.—Vol. XV.   Saturday, November 26, 1853.   Price One Penny.

ADAM, OUR FATHER AND GOD.

(From the Journal of Discourses.)

My next sermon will be to both Saint and sinner. One thing has remained a mystery in this kingdom up to this day. It is in regard to the character of the well beloved Son of God; upon which subject the Elders of Israel have conflicting views. Our God and Father in heaven, is a being of tabernacle, or in other words, He has a body, with parts the same as you and I have; and is capable of showing forth His works to organized beings, as, for instance, in the world in which we live, it is the result of the knowledge and infinite wisdom that dwell in His organized body. His son, Jesus Christ has become a personage of tabernacle, and has a body like his father. The Holy Ghost is the Spirit of the Lord, and issues forth from Himself, and may properly be called God's minister to execute His will in immensity; being called to govern by His influence and power; but *He* is not a person of tabernacle as we are, and as our Father in Heaven and Jesus Christ are. The question has been, and is often, asked, who it was that begat the Son of the Virgin Mary. The infidel world have concluded that if what the Apostles wrote about his father and mother be true, and the present marriage discipline acknowledged by Christendom be correct, then Christians must believe that God is the father of an illegitimate son, in the person of Jesus Christ! The infidel fraternity teach *that*, to their disciples. I will tell you how it is. Our Father in Heaven begat all the spirits that ever were or ever will be upon this earth; and they were born spirits in the eternal world. Then the Lord by His power and wisdom organized the mortal tabernacle of man. We were made first spiritual and afterwards temporal.

Now hear it, O inhabitants of the earth, Jew and Gentile, Saint and sinner! When our father Adam came into the garden of Eden, he came into it with *a celestial body*, and brought Eve, *one of his wives*, with him. He helped to make and organize this world. He is MICHAEL, *the Archangel*, the ANCIENT OF DAYS! about whom holy men have written and spoken—HE *is* our FATHER *and our* GOD, *and the only God with whom WE have to do*. Every man upon the earth, professing Christians or non-professing, must hear it, and *will know it sooner or later*. They came here, organized the raw material, and arranged in their order the herbs of the field, the trees, the apple, the peach, the plum, the pear, and every other fruit that is desirable and good for man; the seed was brought from another sphere, and planted in this earth. The thistle, the thorn, the brier, and the obnoxious weed did *not* appear until after the earth was cursed. When Adam and Eve had eaten of the forbidden fruit, their bodies became mortal from *its effects*, and therefore their offspring were mortal. When the virgin Mary conceived the child Jesus, the Father had begotten him

An Updated History of the Church Is Only Possible by Ongoing Updating!

—A Personal Commitment From the Author —

One major drawback with all history books, no less the ones dealing with Church history, is simply this: *What has happened since the last chapter was written?* History books quickly become outdated unless they are updated. In an attempt to address this dilemma, it is my intent, with the help of other historians, to write a yearly historical update to *Floods Upon the Dry Ground,* which will cover all the relevant events of each year. I will then make that update available by March of the following year. These updates will be accessible on our Immanuel's Church homepage on the Internet. Our Internet address is http://www.immanuels.org. The first of these historical updates will be for the year 1998 and will be available by March of 1999, *Deo volente* (Jas. 4:15).

Charles P. Schmitt

Bibliography

Abbot, Walter M., ed. *The Documents of Vatican II*. New York: Guild Press, 1966.

Allen, William E. *History of Revivals and Worldwide Revival Movements*. Antrim, N. Ireland: Revival Publishing Company, 1951.

___. *The History of Revivals of Religion*. Antrim, N. Ireland: Revival Publishing Company, 1951.

Baldwin, Ethel May & David V. Benson. *Henrietta Mears and How She Did It!* Glendale, CA: Gospel Light Publications, 1966.

Berenbaum, Michael, Ph.D. *The World Must Know*. Boston: Little, Brown and Company, 1993.

Bettenson, Henry, ed. *Documents of the Christian Church*. London: Oxford University Press, 1943.

Boles, James B. *The Great Revival, 1787–1805*. Lexington: University of Kentucky Press, 1972.

Brumback, Carl. *Suddenly...From Heaven: A History of the Assemblies of God*. Springfield, MO: Gospel Publishing House, 1961.

Bullinger, E.W. *Companion Bible*. Grand Rapids, MI: Kregel Publications, 1993.

Buswell, J. Oliver. *A Systematic Theology of the Christian Relgion*, Vol. 1. Grand Rapids, MI: Zondervan, 1962.

Catholic Encyclopedia PLACE?: Encyclopedia Press, 1913.

Chappell, Paul G. *The Divine Healing Movement in America.* Ph.D. dissertation, Drew University, 1983.

Chevreau, Guy. *Catch the Fire.* London: Marshall Pickering, 1994.

Christenson, Larry. *A Message to the Charismatic Movement.* Minneapolis: Bethany Fellowship, Inc., 1972.

Coulter, E. Merton. *College Life in the Old South.* New York: Macmillan, 1928.

Douglas, Major. *George Fox—The Red Hot Quaker.* Cincinnati: God's Bible Book Store, n.d.

Edwards, Brian H. *Revival! A People Saturated With God.* Durham, England: Evangelical Press, 1990.

Enoch, H. "Evolution or Creation." *Bombay Guardian.* 25 March 1916.

Ewart, Frank J. *The Phenomenon of Pentecost.* St. Louis, MO: Pentecostal Publishing House, 1947.

Finney, Charles G. *Short Life of Charles G. Finney.* Belfast, N. Ireland: Revival Publishing Company, 1948.

Freeman, Joel & Don B. Griffin. *Return to Glory.* Woodbury, NJ: Renaissance Productions, Inc., 1997.

Fritts, Roger. "An Open Letter to Coach Bill McCartney, Founder and CEO of the Promise Keepers." 28 September 1997.

Fuller, Barney. *The Burning of Strange Fire.* Lafayette, LA: Huntington House, 1994.

Glover, Robert Hall. *The Progress of Worldwide Missions.* New York: Harper, 1960.

Gordon, A.J. *The Ministry of Healing.* Harrisburg, PA: Christian Publishers, 1961.

Greenfield, John. *When the Spirit Came.* Minneapolis, MN: Bethany House, 1967.

Harrell, David Edwin, Jr. *All Things Are Possible: The Healing & Charismatic Revivals in Modern America.* Bloomington: Indiana University Press, 1975.

Hazard, David. *You Set My Spirit Free*. Minneapolis, MN: Bethany House, 1994.

Hudson, Winthrop S. *Religion in America*, 2nd. ed. New York: Charles Scribner's Sons, 1973.

Hurlburt, J.L. *Story of the Christian Church*. Grand Rapids: MI: Zondervan, 1967.

Hyatt, Eddie L. *2000 Years of Charismatic Christianity*. Tulsa: Hyatt International Ministries, Inc., 1996.

Katz, Arthur. *The Holocaust as Judgment*. Pensacola, FL: Chapel Library, 1997.

Kennedy, John W. *The Torch of the Testimony*. Gospel Literature Service, 1965; Galeta, CA: Christian Books, reprint.

Lake, John G. *Spiritual Hunger/The God-Men*. Dallas: Christ for the Nations, 1980.

Letters of J.N. Darby (1840–1880). New York: Loizeaux Bros. Inc.

Miller, Dr. R. Edward. *Cry for Me Agentina*. Brentwood, Essex, England: Sharon Publications, Ltd., 1988.

Neander, Augustus. *General History of the Christian Church*. Boston: Crocker Brewster, 1853.

Newel, Linda King & Valeen Tippetts Avery. *Mormon Enigma: Emma Hale Smith*. Chicago: University of Illinois Press, 1994.

Nichol, John Thomas. *Pentecostalism*. New York: Harper & Row, 1966.

Orr, Edwin J. *Evangelical Awakenings in Southern Asia*. Minneapolis, MN: Bethany House, 1975.

Parham, Sarah. *The Life of Charles F. Parham*. Baxter Springs, KS: Apostolic Faith Bible College, 1930.

Peterson, Tim. *The History of the Pentecostal Movement*. Owatonna, MN: Christian Family Church and World Outreach Center.

Pratney, Winkie. *Revival—Its Principles and Personalities*. Lafayette, LA: Huntington House, 1994.

Qualben, Lars P. *A History of the Christian Church*. New York: Thomas Nelson & Sons, 1933.

Quebedeaux, Richard. *The New Charismatics*. New York: Doubleday & Company, 1976.

Raboteau, Albert J. *Slave Religion*. New York: Oxford University Press, Inc., 1978.

Renwick, A.M. *The Story of the Church*. London: InterVarsity Fellowship, 1958.

Riss, Richard. *A Survey of 20th-Century Revival Movements in North America*. Peabody, MA: Hendrickson Publishers, 1988.

Roberts, Alexander & James Donaldson, eds. *The Ante-Nicene Christian Fathers*. Vols. 1, 3, 5. Peabody, MA: Hendrickson Publishers, Inc., 1994.

Schaff, Philip. *History of the Christian Church*. Vols. 1, 5. New York: Charles Scribner's Sons, 1882.

___. *Medieval Christianity*, Vol. 1. Grand Rapids, MI: William B. Eerdmans, 1960.

Schaff, Philip & Henry Wace. *Nicene and Post-Nicene Fathers of the Christian Church*, Vol. 10, 2nd series. Grand Rapids, MI: William B. Eerdmans, 1978.

Schmitt, Charles P. *New Wine in New Wineskins*. Grand Rapids, MI: Fellowship of Believers, 1965.

Stead, W.T. *The Story of the Welsh Revival*, New York: Fleming H. Revell, 1905.

Suenens, Cardinal Leon Joseph. *A New Pentecost?* New York: Seabury, 1975.

Sullivan, F. *Charism and Charismatic Renewal: A Biblical and Theological Study*. Dublin: Gill and Macmillan, 1982.

Synan, Vinson. *The Holiness-Pentecostal Tradition: Charismatic Movements in the Twentieth Century*. Grand Rapids, MI: W.B. Eerdmans, 1997.

Walker, Williston. *A History of the Christian Church*. New York: Charles Scribner's Sons, 1959.

Wallis, Arthur. *In the Day of Thy Power*. London: Christian Literature Crusade, 1956.

Walsh, Michael, ed. *Butler's Lives of the Saints*. San Francisco: Harper, 1991.

Walsh, Monsignor Vincent M. *Experiencing Revival in the Catholic Church*. Wynnewood, PA: Key of David Publications, 1995.

Warnock, George H. *The Feast of Tabernacles*. North Battleford, B.C.: Sharon Publishers, 1951.

Watchtower. "1992 Service Year Report of Jehovah's Witnesses Worldwide."

Wead, Douglas. *The C.M. Ward Story*. Harrison, AR: New Leaf Press, 1976.

Whittaker, Colin C. *Great Revivals*. Springfield, MO: Radiant Books, 1984.

Witte, Bob. *Where Does It Say That?* Grand Rapids, MI: Gospel Truths, n.d.

Other
exciting titles
by the Schmitts

A HEART FOR GOD
by Charles P. Schmitt.
This powerful book will send you on a 31-day journey with David from brokenness to wholeness. Few men come to God with as many millstones around their necks as David did. Nevertheless, David pressed beyond adversity, sin, and failure into the very forgiveness and deliverance of God. The life of David will bring hope to those bound by generational curses, those born in sin, and those raised in shame. David's life will inspire faith in the hearts of the dysfunctional, the failure-ridden, and the fallen!
ISBN 1-56043-157-1

THE DELIGHT OF BEING HIS DAUGHTER
by Dotty Schmitt.
Discover the delight and joy that only being a daughter of God can bring! Dotty Schmitt's humorous and honest anecdotes of her own life and struggles in finding intimacy with God will encourage you in your own personal walk. Now in the pastoral and teaching ministry with her husband Charles at Immanuel's Church in the Washington, D.C. area, Dotty continues to experience and express the joy of following her Father.
ISBN 0-7684-2023-7

Available at your local Christian bookstore.
Internet: http://www.reapernet.com

Other
Destiny Image titles
you will enjoy reading

THE GOD CHASERS (Best-selling **Destiny Image** book)
by Tommy Tenney.
Are you dissatisfied with "church"? Are you looking for more? Do you yearn to touch God? You may be a *God chaser*! The passion of Tommy Tenney, evangelist and third-generation Pentecostal minister, is to "catch" God and find himself in God's manifest presence. For too long God's children have been content with crumbs. The Father is looking for those who will seek His face. This book will enflame your own desire to seek God with your whole heart and being—and to find Him.
ISBN 0-7684-2016-4

WOMEN ON THE FRONT LINES
by Michal Ann Goll.
History is filled with ordinary women who have changed the course of their generation. Here Michal Ann Goll, co-founder of Ministry to the Nations with her husband Jim, shares how her own life was transformed and highlights nine women whose lives will impact yours! Every generation faces the same choices and issues; learn how you, too, can heed the call to courage and impact a generation.
ISBN 0-7684-2020-2

ENCOUNTERING THE PRESENCE
by Colin Urquhart.
What is it about Jesus that, when we encounter Him, we are changed? When we encounter the Presence, we encounter the Truth, because Jesus is the Truth. Here Colin Urquhart, best-selling author and pastor in Sussex, England, explains how the Truth changes facts. Do you desire to become more like Jesus? The Truth will set you free!
ISBN 0-7684-2018-0

THE POWER OF BROKENNESS
by Don Nori.
Accepting Brokenness is a must for becoming a true vessel of the Lord, and is a stepping-stone to revival in our hearts, our homes, and our churches. Brokenness alone brings us to the wonderful revelation of how deep and great our Lord's mercy really is. Join this companion who leads us through the darkest of nights. Discover the *Power of Brokenness*.
ISBN 1-56043-178-4

AUDIENCE OF ONE
by Jeremy and Connie Sinnott.
More than just a book about worship, *Audience of One* will lead you into experiencing intimacy and love for the only One who matters—your heavenly Father. Worship leaders and associate pastors themselves, Jeremy and Connie Sinnott have been on a journey of discovering true spiritual worship for years. Then they found a whole new dimension to worship—its passion, intimacy, and love for the Father, your *audience of One*.
ISBN 0-7684-2014-8

Available at your local Christian bookstore.

nternet: http://www.reapernet.com

Other
Destiny Image titles
you will enjoy reading

Other
Destiny Image titles
you will enjoy reading

CORPORATE ANOINTING
by Kelley Varner.
Just as a united front is more powerful in battle, so is the anointing when Christians come together in unity! In this classic book, senior pastor Kelley Varner of Praise Tabernacle in Richlands, North Carolina, presents a powerful teaching and revelation that will change your life! Learn how God longs to reveal the fullness of Christ in the fullness of His Body in power and glory.
ISBN 0-7684-2011-3

SECRETS OF THE MOST HOLY PLACE
by Don Nori.
Here is a prophetic parable you will read again and again. The winds of God are blowing, drawing you to His Life within the Veil of the Most Holy Place. There you begin to see as you experience a depth of relationship your heart has yearned for. This book is a living, dynamic experience with God!
ISBN 1-56043-076-1

THE LOST ART OF INTERCESSION
by Jim W. Goll.
The founder of Ministry to the Nations, Jim Goll has traveled the world in a teaching and prophetic ministry. All over the globe God is moving—He is responding to the prayers of His people. Here Jim Goll teaches the lessons learned by the Moravians during their 100-year prayer Watch. They sent up prayers; God sent down His power. Through Scripture, the Moravian example, and his own prayer life, Jim Goll proves that "what goes up must come down."
ISBN 1-56043-697-2

WORSHIP: THE PATTERN OF THINGS IN HEAVEN
by Joseph L. Garlington.
Worship and praise play a crucial role in the local church. Whether you are a pastor, worship leader, musician, or lay person, you'll find rich and anointed teaching from the Scriptures about worship! Joseph L. Garlington, Sr., a pastor, worship leader, and recording artist in his own right, shows how *worship is the pattern of things in Heaven!*
ISBN 1-56043-195-4

Available at your local Christian bookstore.
nternet: http://www.reapernet.com

4:23

Other
Destiny Image titles
you will enjoy reading

WOMAN: HER PURPOSE, POSITION, AND POWER
by Mary Jean Pidgeon.
When the enemy slipped into the garden, he robbed Eve and all her daughters of their original purpose, position, and power. But today God is bringing these truths back to women. He is setting His daughters free and showing them their value in His Kingdom. Let Mary Jean Pidgeon, a wife, mother, and the Associate Pastor with her husband Pastor Jack Pidgeon in Houston, explain a woman's *purpose*, *position*, and *power*.
ISBN 1-56043-330-2

NON-RELIGIOUS CHRISTIANITY
by Gerald Coates.
If Jesus Christ returned today, how much of "church" would He condone or condemn? In this book, Gerald Coates contends that "religion" is the greatest hindrance to making Jesus attractive to our family, neighbors, and co-workers. Humorous yet confrontational, this popular British speaker and church leader will surprise you with his conclusions. This book could change your life forever!
ISBN 1-56043-694-8

THE COSTLY ANOINTING
by Lori Wilke.
In this book, teacher and prophetic songwriter Lori Wilke boldly reveals God's requirements for being entrusted with an awesome power and authority. She speaks directly from God's heart to your heart concerning the most costly anointing. This is a word that will change your life!
ISBN 1-56043-051-6

PERCEIVING THE WHEEL OF GOD
by Dr. Mark Hanby.
On the potter's wheel, a lump of clay yields to a necessary process of careful pressure and constant twisting. Similarly, the form of true faith is shaped by a trusting response to the hand of God in a suffering situation. This book offers essential understanding for victory through the struggles of life.
ISBN 1-56043-109-1

Available at your local Christian bookstore.

nternet: http://www.reapernet.com

Other

Destiny Image titles
you will enjoy reading

FROM THE FATHER'S HEART
by Charles Slagle.
This is a beautiful look at the true heart of your heavenly Father. Through these sensitive selections that include short love notes, letters, and prophetic words from God to His children, you will develop the kind of closeness and intimacy with the loving Father that you have always longed for. From words of encouragement and inspiration to words of gentle correction, each letter addresses times that we all experience. For those who diligently seek God, you will recognize Him in these pages.
ISBN 0-914903-82-9

THE ASCENDED LIFE
by Bernita J. Conway.
A believer does not need to wait until Heaven to experience an intimate relationship with the Lord. When you are born again, your life becomes His, and He pours His life into yours. Here Bernita Conway explains from personal study and experience the truth of "abiding in the Vine," the Lord Jesus Christ. When you grasp this understanding and begin to walk in it, it will change your whole life and relationship with your heavenly Father!
ISBN 1-56043-337-X

ENCOUNTERS WITH A SUPERNATURAL GOD
by Jim and Michal Ann Goll.
The Golls know that angels are real. They have firsthand experience with supernatural angelic encounters. In this book you'll read and learn about angels and supernatural manifestations of God's Presence—and the real encounters that both Jim and Michal Ann have had! As the founders of Ministry to the Nations and speakers and teachers, they share that God wants to be intimate friends with His people. Go on an adventure with the Golls and find out if God has a supernatural encounter for you!
ISBN 1-56043-199-7

Available at your local Christian bookstore.

Internet: http://www.reapernet.com